VIA

Ethics and Architecture

Editors

John Capelli
Paul Naprstek
Bruce Prescott

No. 10

The Graduate School of Fine Arts
University of Pennsylvania
1990

VIA is the journal of the Graduate School of
Fine Arts of the University of Pennsylvania. It
is edited, designed and produced by students
in the Department of Architecture.

VIA 10 was composed in Garamond No. 3 by
G & S Typesetters, Austin, Texas, and printed
on Lustro Dull Stock. Two thousand copies
were printed and bound by Cypher Press, Ben-
salem, Pennsylvania.

Send editorial correspondence to:
VIA
Room 102, Meyerson Hall
University of Pennsylvania
Philadelphia, PA   19104-6311

Distributed by:
Rizzoli International Publications, Inc.
300 Park Avenue South
New York, NY   10010

ISBN: 0.8478.5510.4
ISSN: 0506.8347

Copy Editor: Mary Schoenung

The editors of VIA 10 wish
to thank the following
individuals:

Margaret Irish

The editors of VIA 9 and VIA 11.

Harry Eaby of Cypher Press

Bill Grosskopf of G & S Typesetters

Daniel Garofalo

Frances Hegeler

The Office of Adèle Naudé Santos

Samuel Crothers Associates

Several contributing authors used different
means to avoid using the masculine term for
the third person singular pronoun. In the absence of consensus in this matter, the editors
have resorted to the established use of masculine terms, for clarity and editorial
consistency.

COVER: *Daniel H. Burnham and
Edward H. Bennett, American,
partnership 1903-1912, View of the
proposed development of the City
Center, Chicago, plate 137 from the
Plan of Chicago, 1909, delineated
by Jules Guérin (American, 1866-
1946), tempera and pencil on toned
paper, 1907, 84.7 x 122 cm,
RX17016/29.*

CONTENTS

Lucian Krukowski

ART AND ETHICS IN KANT, HEGEL, AND SCHOPENHAUER

1

The major reference sources for this paper are as follows: Immanuel Kant, *Critique of Judgment* (1790); *Metaphysics of Morals* (1785); G. W. F. Hegel, *Aesthetics* (Knox, tr.) (1835); *Phenomenology* (Baillie, tr.) 1807; *Reason in History* (1837); A. Schopenhauer, *World as Will and Representation* (Payne, tr.) (1819).

Fig. 1. *Paul Cezanne*, Houses in Provence, *c. 1880. Cezanne's formal preoccupation with landscape affirms the philosophical role Kant assigns the perception of nature.*

For modern readers, the aesthetic theories found in eighteenth and nineteenth century philosophy often sound grandiose and unsustainable. There are many reasons for this. One perhaps is the impact of analytic philosophy with its general rejection of speculative theorizing and, particularly, its rejection of metaphorical language in philosophical discourse. Another reason, of a very different kind, may be our present unwillingness to assign to art the task of fulfilling such lofty ideals as these earlier philosophies demand. Despite such cautions, however, it is also not surprising that the period and theories in question increasingly come to demand our attention. Indeed, one of the inducements they give for our returning to them *is* the centrality, there, of the role of aesthetics in the general concerns of philosophy. Our fascination with this philosophical stance is heightened when we contrast it with the peripheral role that is generally accorded aesthetics today. But nostalgia is neither my taste nor my aim here, for I believe that such comparisons as we make between then and now are useful for our present difficulties in theorizing about art. Some of these difficulties, as we know, come out of having assigned our immediate past ("modernism") to a historical past, a period we no longer consider ourselves to be part of. Where we are now is often called "postmodernism," but this unhappy word only identifies our uncertainties

about where it is we are. I do not have an alternative term or theory to propose here; my more modest purpose is to see how we can profit from a better understanding of the "linkages" between philosophy and art in early modernism. Such an understanding could help us find out what we now no longer believe, and this in turn may show us the reasons why modernism is now—suddenly but inexorably—historical. The beliefs I have in mind are about what art requires us—artists and audience—to be like in order for it, art, to function as we want it to. Another way of putting this is to ask what effects creating and appreciating, properly done, have on those involved and, by extension, on the greater society.

My way of showing what "requires" and "properly done" come to is to look at the relation between aesthetic theory and ethical theory in Kant, Hegel, and and Schopenhauer.[1] Through this comparison, I attempt to show how each philosopher identifies the nature of the work of art: what he wants such works to be like, what is required for their creation, and what is proper to their appreciation. In this regard, I also ask how each philosopher relates the concept of moral agency to his aesthetic theory; specifically, whether the criteria that determine what it is to be an ethical person have any place in the requirements for the making and appreciating of art.

For purposes of discussion, I divide aesthetic activity into two parts: appreciation and creation, the first personified by the spectator or audience, and the second by the artist or creator. My first question, then, is what the ideal for each of these roles would be like, respectively, in the aesthetic theories of Kant, Hegel, and Schopenhauer. My second question is how these aesthetic exemplars compare with the ideal of a moral agent as found in the ethical theories of each philosopher. My third question is whether this mix of aesthetic and ethical considerations tells us anything about specific artworks. Here, I identify some artworks that I believe are particularly clear pictorial analogues of each theory and give some reasons for my beliefs. This reference to pictorial material is not a major part of my paper but, as such attempts have a history of misunderstandings, I interrupt the exposition of my main theme with a brief discussion on what I mean by a "pictorial analogue to a theory."

In a general sense, the relation between artwork and theory that I have in mind is one of equivalence: neither is considered as a substitute for the other. I do not believe that works "illustrate" theories nor that theories "explain" works, for these are functions that subordinate theories or works to one another, and the erroneous presumption is made that either can be reduced to the other. Of course, philosophical theories are explanatory in nature, but their explanations are not so much directed at the world as to how we think about the world. Much the same holds true for artworks. Few would argue that art shows us how the world actually is, but certainly, through art, we come to know how we view the world. The histories of both art and philosophy provide us with the monuments that result from these efforts, and these monuments are alike in that we expect them to be superceded in time but not, on that account, devalued. Yet, the correspondence between work and theory is difficult to propose, and even more difficult to justify. I can claim, as I do below, that paintings of Cezanne are a good analogue to Kant's aesthetic theories, but I cannot "prove" this. Nevertheless, it seems evident that Cezanne is a better choice here than, say, Rubens. In defense of this choice, I could point to various structural and thematic similarities, and attempt to show what makes them similar. But I would also have to indicate why certain similarities are more important than others.

Actually, claims of this type are made all the time, by critics and historians, as well as philosophers. But we distinguish between them more on the basis of their evocativeness than their truth. The better claims, like potent metaphors, make the world seem richer and less slack; the poorer ones are invariably dull. Whether such claims are to be taken seriously—whether they in fact constitute "knowledge"—is a deep and vexed problem. But I feel that to abandon the effort to make and justify such analogies, or to substitute the psychologisms of "personal preference," is to philosophically abandon much of the world. So I offer my analogues between artworks and aesthetic theories as good ones of their kind, and I give my reasons below. I anticipate—and this would be a vindication of my position—that the reader will look for better choices and better reasons.

II

Now I return to my main theme: the role of ethics in the aesthetic theories of Kant, Hegel, and Schopenhauer. Simply to compare the aesthetic theories would seem problem enough without bringing ethics into it. But there also is a problem with keeping ethics out. Each of these historical figures was a systematic, and "system-making" philosopher, not merely an "aesthetician" in today's academic sense; the mandate of philosophy in those heady times was to be holistic and integrative. Thus, questions about art, beauty, creativity, became unavoidably linked to other philosophical concerns, and were regarded as particular approaches to the other questions—about the nature of knowledge, the world, and moral action—which needed answering for the completeness of the philosophical enterprise. Indeed, for each of the philosophers at issue here, the understanding of art and beauty provides them with cogent answers, not otherwise attainable, to these other questions.

I begin my discussion with a brief overview of the three theories and then examine each in greater detail. Kant views the experience of beauty as erecting a bridge between the separate contents of his first and second critiques, one that offers the possibility of a synthesis between empirical knowledge and moral law— between the realms of "nature" and "freedom." Thus, he considers art to be at its best when it appears most like nature; but the appearance he wants is one of formal harmony between elements—not the picturesque ingratiations of illusion. Nature need not be represented by artworks but it must be exemplified in them. In the Kantian system, it is the appearance of harmony and order in the beauties of nature, and in artistic structures derived from nature, that suggests a rational "ground" for nature. This gives us reason to hope, although not to know, that the experience of beauty is evidence of an actual order *in* nature— evidence, perhaps, of a divine intelligence responsible for that order.

Hope is not knowledge however because, for Kant, sensory information cannot assure us that the world is as we perceive it to be. Thus, despite the suggestiveness of aesthetic experience, Kant's system remains dualistic, divided between the "phenomenal" world of our perceptions and the "noumenal" world of things as they actually are. Hegel rejects this duality and the limitation it places on knowledge. He particularly rejects Kant's posit of the noumenon, or "thing in itself"—existence outside of any perception—which we cannot know or, at best, can know only indirectly. In developing his own philosophical position, Hegel begins with the opposing thesis that thought and being are unified—that there is no world outside of, or inaccessible to, our knowing. Arguing against the "static" architectonics of the Kantian categories, Hegel locates this unity in process, in the temporal dynamics which determine the experiences of an individual life as well as the collective historical experiences of cultures. Such process is viewed as not simply ongoing, but as cumulative, with each stage an improvement on the inadequacies—the incompleteness—of its predecessor. This cumulative development is shown to exhibit a "dialectic" structure: the successive stages, designated as thesis, antithesis, synthesis, superceding each other in the search for completeness. Hegel personifies this principle of process through the provocative term, *Geist*, or "spirit." This is a difficult notion which weds the concepts of temporal change and historical progress, and proposes that spirit is made manifest—"reified"—through specific cultural symbols. In our context of discussion, the history of fine art provides us with the symbolic evidence of spirit's progress. In opposition to Kant, Hegel places art above nature, for he considers artistic beauty to evidence a higher stage than does natural beauty of the world's

evolution through time. Art serves not only as a manifestation of spirit's workings, it is also assigned the role of symbolizing the stages of development and thereby of showing their *telos*: the rationale behind their development. Thus, in Hegel's system, the history of art is a history of progress, insofar as art is regarded as a symbol of culture.

Schopenhauer, although he admired Kant and despised Hegel, regarded both concepts— that of a synthesis between nature and reason, and that of progress in the history of culture— as illusions. According to his philosophy, what we can know of the world is merely our idea of it: the representations we make through our symbol systems. What remains—Schopenhauer's analogue to Kant's "thing in itself"—is "will," which he identifies as a ceaseless, irrational, insatiable appetite manifest in all the gradations of nature, from inorganic matter to human society. For Schopenhauer, there is no reconciliation between realms, between representation and will, such as the one Kant wanted between nature and freedom. Additionally, will, although it is the principle of change for Schopenhauer, has no *telos*—no goal or development—and thus, there is no progress, no "reason in history," of the sort Hegel posits for spirit. Schopenhauer assigns art the task of showing us the world "as it really is," independently both of the demands of our appetites (the "ravages of will") and the representations that pass for scientific knowledge. Art offers us a different kind of knowledge, an access to will-less essences drawn on the model of Plato's "forms." This is a knowledge, however, that is gained at the expense of action, for it is useless in the conduct of our lives. Nevertheless, such knowledge does facilitate what Schopenhauer considers to be the primary virtue of withdrawal from all demands made by willed ambition, and the only reward for such virtue is the peace that comes with this withdrawal. It follows that the practice of art here, both in the creating and the appreciating, is based on passivity and resignation, an approximation of the contemplative practices found in Eastern religions.

III

With this overview in place, I now turn to my more specific concern with the relationship between creating and appreciating, between artist and spectator, in each philosophy. In the

"Analytic of the Beautiful," Kant gives four categorical conditions for the appreciation of beauty: his ideal spectator must (1) have an attitude of "disinterestedness" toward the subject, which in turn permits (2) the perception of a formal "purposiveness" within that subject. (3) Such perception can lay claim to the logical properties of "necessity" and (4) "universality," although these latter properties remain subjective and thus are to be interpreted as recommendations rather than as formal rules. To put all this another way: aesthetic appreciation, for Kant, requires an indifference to both the physical description and the material value of the subject—even to its actual existence. What is wanted, only, is the perception of an order, a harmony of parts: a perception that, while it is subjective, serves as an exemplar for the perception of others. Under this theory, we cannot prove that something is beautiful, but we nevertheless expect that others view it as we do. But why do we expect this? And what "others" do we have in mind?

An extreme answer to this question (one which I nevertheless propose) is that Kant's "ideal spectator" is also his "moral agent." The claim is that one cannot appreciate beauty unless one approaches its subject as one approaches the subject of one's moral obligations: I attempt to fulfill my moral obligations because they are right—not because of the benefits that will accrue to me or to others, or because my chances for success are good. Of course, I do have an interest in doing the right thing, but it is an interest based on a concept of duty to which I freely subscribe, and which all rational individuals should follow. My stance as regards my own (prudential) interests, however, is to consider them secondary to my moral obligations. Indeed, the less these other interests are involved, or the less I take heed of them, the better is my chance for making a purely moral judgment. But it is such "disinterestedness" that *also permits me to judge that something is beautiful,* and supports my claim that others should agree with me.

It is evident that Kant wants us all to be moral. It is less evident that he would want us all to experience beauty, but I think he does. We must remember that he construes beauty to be a sensible signpost of rationality in nature, a suggestion of a divine order. As such, it provides one answer to the question why we should be moral, namely, because that is the way things essentially are—are designed to be.

We know that beauty offers us no proof of this, but it does offer hope, which encourages us to act "as if" nature were compatible with our actions: as if morality had a sensuous face.

Kant cared more for nature than for art, probably because what he needed philosophically could be most directly found in nature, and possibly out of distaste for all the "interest" in which connoisseurship, professionalism, and patronage in art are steeped. At any rate, he does discuss the artist at length, but he does so in the "Analytic of the Sublime," where he identifies sublimity with experiences which defy perceptual containment: experiences of boundlessness, infinite magnitude, and power.[2] In this transition, his thesis moves from the perception of beauty as evidence of an ordered nature, to the actions of the artist who, in creating beauty, serves as "a force of nature" through which the "nature" of nature is made manifest. This concept has echoes in Plato's *Symposium* where inspiration is the vehicle for the message of a god who uses the ecstatic sybil as a voice.

But it is a commonplace that the possessed and ecstatic are not responsible for what they say or do. And if what they bring about proves to be of benefit, then strictly speaking, they should not be given credit for it. The question that, above, I ask about the spectator now reappears: must Kant's artist—*qua* artist—also be a moral agent? The answer would appear to be "no," for morality, in any acceptable sense of the term, implies that one can decide about one's responsibilities. However, the only artist of Kant's concern is the "genius," through whom are produced the authentic images of beauty; and genius is a "gift" which one cannot decide to attain since it is not susceptible to effort. But it is also evident that, for Kant, immorality—decisions that favor perverse interests—is prohibitive to creativity as well as to appreciation, for the refusal to universalize one's actions on the moral plane could only encourage pandering to popular success on the aesthetic. The morality of Kant's genius, then, seems to be "built in" to this status. The creative capacity seems to be inseparable from an "innocence," a pre-reflective incapacity to trivialize or misdirect the gift of genius. So the artist gives evidence, through his activity, of a "natural morality" much as the experience of beauty gives evidence of rationality in nature. Perhaps, in this conjecture, we can also find a trace of Kant's admiration for Rousseau and his concept of the "noble savage".[3]

2
Second book of the first part of the *Critique of Judgment*, particularly the "dynamical sublime."

3
Jean-Jacques Rousseau, *Emile* (1762).

Fig. 2. *Kasimir Malevich,* Suprematist Composition: Red Square and Black Square, *1914 or 1915. Hegel requires that the metaphysical striving for the absolute must prevail, even if poetry is at some point left with nothing further to say.*

As exemplar for Kant's aesthetic theories, I nominate the works and person of Cezanne. Cezanne's formal preoccupation with landscape affirms the philosophical role Kant assigns the perception of nature. While Cezanne accepted the "direct observation" dictum of the Impressionists, he criticized them for being content with "surface" and "ephemerals." His own program transformed direct observation into the presentation of geometric structures that he *knew* underlay the immediate givens of natural appearances.[4] I believe that a fruitful comparison could be made here between this program and the relation Kant makes between sense data and the categories of the understanding, for in both cases sensory input is viewed as inchoate unless organized (given form) by an active cognition.[5] As to Cezanne himself: His impatience with gabfests in the artists' cafes, his inability to sustain a career in Paris, and his generally "curmudgeonly" exterior can be interpreted not as a lack of social graces, but as a need to avoid relativism. In his self-isolation, Cezanne did not risk the vitiation that comes with exposure to the clamor of alternative possibilities—in style, objectives, procedures, hopes. Not that Cezanne had a worked-out social critique, he just could not stand those places, those people, and all that talk—which is, perhaps, a requirement for the Kantian "genius."

IV

Hegel is often called a "philosopher of culture," a phrase that carries connotations of a tension between "culture" and "nature." However, nature, in Hegel's philosophy, is not the all-encompassing principle under which everything else is subsumed. It is more limited, a nature that is the both the residue of past achievements, and the inert barrier to new ones. It plays the role of the material hindrance to spirit's development. For Hegel, history is a kind of morality play, with the triumph of "spirit" over "matter" as its theme. There is no doubt that he considers this process end-directed and, despite all setbacks, inevitable. What this "triumph" actually comes to, however, is more perplexing. As we know, Hegel left a considerable theoretical legacy as well as much disagreement over its content. The *telos*, or end, of spirit's development has been variously interpreted: Theologically, it can be seen as the reunion of God and the world; politically, as the achievement of a society that is

classless and, thus, fully just; ethically, as the emergence of a holistic "humanism" out of the partiality of competing and restrictive dogmas; formally, as the union of particularistic spheres of knowledge (art, science, religion) within the "absolute" knowledge of philosophy; aesthetically, as art forms evolving from a sensuous to a conceptual mode of self-presentation.

In the Hegelian aesthetic, art symbolizes the stages of cultural development by exemplifying them in sensuous form. "Progress," then, as it is a mark of culture, can be predicated of art as well. Indeed, up to a point, we can best understand cultural progress through the succession of its art forms, for each epoch shows forth its ascendancy—and limitations—in the particular mix of "matter" and "spirit" that characterizes its architecture, sculpture, painting, music, and literature. Progress is understood here as the dematerialization of the artistic vehicle within the course of history. The sequence of the above listing, then, is not casual. Rather, it corresponds to Hegel's own hierarchy of the arts in which architecture is given the lowest position and literature the highest. The specifics of this hierarchy are too complex to be pursued here, but some comments can be made.[6] Both the efficacy and the limitations of art as a symbol of "progress in history" are located in its sensuous nature. The premise here is that art, although a symbol, is also an actual synthesis between matter and spirit, and the "truths" it shows can best—perhaps only—be shown through this synthesis. As a consequence, there are truths that art cannot show, for they concern realms where sensuality becomes a hindrance to knowledge. Hegel, in a gesture toward artistic autonomy, does locate the ideal of a perfect synthesis, of a "perfect art," in classical Greek sculpture. But in the broad historical span spirit prevails, although this is at the expense of the balance required for artistic perfection. So, here, progress conflicts with perfection, and art is doomed, as it were, to transcend itself: its progress includes an awareness of its own eventual irrelevance. Hegel identifies poetry as the highest of the arts inasmuch as it is discursive: its medium is language. But language is also the medium of philosophy and, as Hegel requires that the metaphysical striving for the absolute must prevail, even poetry at some point is left with nothing further to say.

When we ask about the relationship between moral sense and creativity in Hegel's theory—between spectator and artist—we see

4
Paul Cezanne, Letter to Emil Bernard, 1904.

5
Immanuel Kant, *Critique of Pure Reason* (1781), especially the "Transcendental Analytic."

6
See Chapter I of my book, *Art and Concept: A Philosophical Study* (Amherst: University of Massachusetts Press, 1987).

7
Larrisa Zhadova, *Malevich* (New York: Thames & Hudson, 1982).

that the differences are far smaller than they are for Kant. Actually, "spectator" is a poor term for Hegel's construal of appreciation. Its implications of detachment and passive receptivity are not what Hegel has in mind. He sees the process as one of interaction, where the work and our perception of it are mutually formed, one by the other. Equally, we do not find Kant's strong contrast between the rational, universalizing, moral agent and the unique, gifted "conduit of nature's voice." Rather, for Hegel, the moral individual is one who is sufficiently free of the inertia of the present to intuit the future and then act on it. The creative individual is different only in that artistic insight results in a revelatory symbol rather than in direct social action. Both spectator and artist—the best of each—are, using Hegel's term, "world-historical individuals." Notwithstanding the personal risks they face, they give form to the future by correctly interpreting the dialectics of present social inadequacies. For art to be an effective cultural symbol, it must have a critical function; artworks must symbolically present the potential of the future as well the hindrances to that future. Proper appreciation in this context entails, at least, understanding such symbols and, better, acting on them. The impact of this theory has been profound. In the early twentieth century, for example, one has only to consider the "isms" that make up modernism—and to read the many manifestos—to realize the power of "historical correctness" as a criterion for style. Correspondingly, in the programs of the many collective social movements of that time, Socialism, Marxism, etc., the need for a "historical justification" of political action is central.

Hegel provides us with many examples of artists and works in the course of his *Aesthetics*. These, however, are mostly examples prior to his own time which were chosen to demonstrate his categorization of the historical past. It is tempting, here, to offer a work by an artist contemporary with Hegel, one central to the drama of Romanticism and Napoleon; Delacroix would be a good choice. But, instead, I offer a later example, one that shows the impact of Hegel's theories on twentieth century art: Kazimir Malevich. The primary reason for this choice is that Malevich, more than other pioneering abstract or non-objective artist, placed almost total weight on the theoretical evocativeness of his works. He did so by reducing their formal complexity to a minimum.

These works, the so-called "Suprematist" compositions, are of an iconic simplicity, and offer little gratification in matters of painterly virtues. In fact, the historical challenge of these works is located precisely in the claim that they are art of great consequence *because* they have abandoned such virtues. These works project a sense of finality, of having brought artistic sensibility to the edge of "pure idea," to the "end of art." However, for Malevich, reaching this edge did not portend nihilism but rather signaled a welcome transformation in both art and society: the end was also a beginning. At that time, abstract art was in its early ascendancy. It was supported by the critical view that representational concerns were a thing of the past. The only question that then seemed relevant was whether the transformation of mimetic concerns into purely formal ones would be gradual, as is found in Cubism, or whether the demise would be abrupt and dramatic, as heralded by the abstract turn of Malevich and such other artists as Mondrian and Kandinsky. But this is much the same question that was then being asked about the process of social transformation. We remember that that these works, by Malevich, Lizzitsky, and others of that group, were done in the period during the First World War and the Russian revolution, that is, about 1914 to 1924. This activity was brought to an end by Stalin's purge of Trotsky.[7] However, during this brief period, avant-garde art, primarily abstractionism, became the officially accepted style in the Soviet Union. Its emancipation from the older aesthetic forms gave it credibility as a collective enterprise and as a symbol of the new social order. The destruction of this ideal, and the consequent history of radical movements in Europe, needs no retelling here.

V

Compared with Kant and Hegel, Schopenhauer is not a philosopher of the first rank. For me, his importance lies not in his attempts at systematic work, but in his introduction of the notion of irrationality into philosophy, a move which profoundly influenced such later figures as Nietzsche and Freud. His identification of "will" as the primal force underlying reality is justified, not by reference to external events, but rather to internal ones, the affective life of "feelings." We know that will exists because it is evidenced in our drives, hungers, ambitions; and we know it is inexorable through our in-

Fig. 3. *Max Ernst*, The Temptation of St. Anthony, *1945. Schopenhauer gives art the dominant role perhaps because of the relief it affords us from the aridness of pure thought.*

8
Sigmund Freud, 'The Relation of the Poet to Daydreaming' (1908).

ability to ever be satisfied. All representations we make of the world, whether scientific theories, social and moral institutions, or ideals, are actually in the service of the will; they are so many attempts to control the world and satisfy our needs. And as all such attempts are futile, the knowledge on which, purportedly, they are all based is illusory: "maya."

In a less-than-convincing set of extrapolations, Schopenhauer moves from the introspective evidence of will's manifestation in us to its primacy in all natural processes, organic and inorganic. The formation of crystals, nest building, and the struggles for empire are gradations of the selfsame will manifested in particular events. But such "gradations" are not a sign of increasing value, or "progress." Here Schopenhauer expresses his dislike of Hegel by rejecting a basic tenet of Hegel's thought, namely, he denies that process, whether natural or historical, has any rationality or goal.

It would not do, however, for Schopenhauer to give will total dominion over reality. After all, he has to protect his own writings from its distortions. To avoid such consequences, Schopenhauer introduces a third realm into his dualistic system, a realm through which things can be seen "as they really are," as essences or pure ideas. Such essences do not manifest the various gradations of will, nor are they the practical representations of ordinary empirical knowledge. Unlike Kant's "thing in itself," they can be known, although the course of such knowledge entails a "journey" by the aspirant to knowledge: a progressive emancipation from the demands of will. These essences constitute a realm in Schopenhauer's philosophy that is constructed much on the model of the Platonic realm of "forms," and the essential knowledge of reality that this realm provides is instantiated through works of art. We might agree that whatever havoc this concept of ideas plays with the symmetry of Schopenhauer's general theory, it does attest to his philosophical interest in art. Indeed, the role he gives to art exceeds the place accorded it by either Kant or Hegel. For, here, it is only artworks that *show* us how the world really is—although we may also know this reality through the introspection that leads to the moral life. Schopenhauer's interest in Indian philosophies lies not only in their suggestiveness for his view of the world, but in their proposals for what one ought to do, given that the world is as it is. For him, the moral individual is the one who, through contemplation and renunciation of de-

sire, manages to stand outside the will. Equilibrium and knowledge are achieved at the expense of ambition, and together they bring peace. Such peace, however, is not a positive pleasure, but simply the absence of pain. The role of art here is revelatory: it provides a "will-less" subject for contemplation; and thus the ethical and the aesthetic are joined.

Peculiarly, of the three theories we are considering, it is in Schopenhauer's that the artist fares most poorly. The insights attained are at the expense of the ability to cope, and thus emerges the image of artist as "neurotic." To see the world "innocently," to put aside praxis for essence, to go past things to their "forms," is a rare gift; in this Schopenhauer follows Kant. But the optimism of the Enlightenment is gone, and here the gift has a price. Success in the world requires obedience to the dictates of will. But success, as later couched in Freud's triad of "power, money, and love," is a delusion which the artist must see through in order to create anything of value.[8] However, unlike the moral individual who adopts the philosophical posture of withdrawal, the artist is caught between the two realms. To make art requires action, and the work when completed wants to be projected. Thus, artistic activity depends on the very processes that artworks reject in their contents, and the resulting ambivalence is corrosive to the artist's well-being. Unlike some later theorists, Schopenhauer does not regard this traumatic state as a pathology for which a cure must be sought. Rather, he thinks of it as a sacrifice of sorts, an unavoidable consequence of the effort to create truthful representations of the world. It is not clear from his writings what metaphysical needs such representations satisfy, for he does not consider them the sole paths to such truth. As we know, Hegel sees the sensuous vividness of art as ultimately a limitation on what art can express, the higher realms being reserved for philosophy and religion. Schopenhauer, not accepting this ascent of categories, gives art the dominant role perhaps because of the relief it affords us from the aridness of pure thought. Perhaps, too, in anticipation of romanticism's later infatuation with irrationality, he had come to suspect the truths that thought provides.

Schopenhauer's views on the particular arts are marked by the exalted place he gives to music. While the other arts provide representations of the will's "objectifications"—its various manifestations in the furniture of the world—music alone is a direct analogue of the will. Music is a temporal abstract art, and thus structurally resembles the dynamics of emotional life.[9] If I were to pick a musical work as exemplar here, I would choose one by, say, Wagner (who admired Schopenhauer) or Berlioz. Finding an appropriate painting, which I do attempt, is harder. One approach might be to choose an expressionist whose works are marked by strong pictorial rhythm and singularity of viewpoint; Van Gogh or Soutine would be good candidates. I take another approach, however, which attempts to place Schopenhauer's thesis of the Platonic "forms" into the context of subconscious imagery, the context of surrealistic art. I do this because the sources of surrealist imagery (dreams, fantasies, hallucinations) have been considered as pathways to a reality which is more basic than the one of "ordinary" consciousness. The surrealist attack on traditional art was not to deny, as the abstract movements did, that picturing phenomenal reality was of no further consequence for art. Rather, Surrealist theory identified a new reality whose picturing requires a new artistic regimen of skills and attitudes.[10] Access to the subconscious is sought through techniques of free association and projection, through automatic writing, collage and frottage, all designed to discover the methods of spatial and temporal representation adequate to this subjective world. Here it must be emphasized that the value of surrealist art was not presumed to rest merely on the facilitation of individual access to a repressed psyche. If this were all, the value would remain personal and therapeutic. Rather, the claim is that the subconscious, in its important sense, is collective, and that private images are manifestations of the "universal archetypes" of myth, ritual, and religion.[11] Interpretations of these archetypes produce an explanatory power that rivals science, for these interpretations are of forces that underlay the ones identified by "respectable" explanations of culture and nature. Schopenhauer's thesis of the primacy of will over representation can thus be seen as central to Surrealism.

In addition to automatic techniques, Surrealist artists used other methods to find and project this material. One such involves a return to traditional skills by adapting certain "old master" techniques to the representation of surrealist imagery. In this approach, picturing a dream world is based on a logic which permits the distortions and reversals—but not

elimination—of the spatial cues and canons of proportion found in academic art. While the surrealist painting does not mirror the world of ordinary perception, it does remain convincing as a "window" into that other world it does mirror: it remains convincing as an illusion.

Surrealism was a rich source for many major artists of the twentieth century, notably Picasso and Miro, who adapted its methods for other artistic ends. But for my exemplar, I choose an artist whose preoccupations with Surrealist theories remained relatively constant and undiluted: Max Ernst. In the course of his career, Ernst employed many different techniques in developing his images. These variations mark his fluctation between the socially directed or "Dada" aspects of Surrealism, and the more private (and literary) concerns with fantasy and myth. Among these latter are some that use the traditional methods I refer to above, and that show the influence on Ernst of the fantasy art of the German and Flemish Renaissance.[12]

Schopenhauer's contention that artists are "punished" for their ability to bypass the will in penetrating the surface of things, applies to Ernst in a particular way. He did not suffer from the psychological incapacities that Schopenhauer stresses. But he was among those artists singled out by the Nazi cultural ministry as "decadent," and he barely escaped with his life while losing members of his family. Schopenhauer identifies the will as "a-moral," but if we entertain that concept at all, we must at least presume that the will's social objectifications are subject to moral judgment. The question, then, of the "artist as neurotic" takes on a normative character when we ask how neurosis, the inability to cope, is understood within the context of an immoral society. This conception of the avant-garde artist as a victim of society, and of the artwork as a testimonial to and, perhaps, a vindication of that sorry state, are recurring themes in modern art and are a legacy of Schopenhauer's.

VI

I have tried, here, to show how three major philosophers view the creation and appreciation of art, and how they assess the importance of art for the philosophical issues of knowing, and acting in, the world. Each philosophy treats this relationship differently: Kant looks for the ideal in a reconciliation of the sensible and the rational; Hegel begins by assuming

9

An interesting discussion of this can be found in Suzanne Langer's *Feeling and Form* (New York: Charles Scribner's Sons, 1953).

10

See Andre Breton, "What is Surrealism?" (1934).

11

The reference here is to theories of the "collective unconscious" as espoused by Carl Jung and others.

12

The richness of fantasy and technique in such artists as Bosch, Breugel, Gruenewald, etc., has had more of an influence on surrealism than is usually noted.

this union and then plots its evolution through the course of history; Schopenhauer sees neither reconciliation nor progress and settles for a passive wisdom. If my location of these theories in the later concerns of modern art is at all plausible, then their formative role for that art seems undeniable. But this role changes when we become satiated with the ways we know that art under these theories, and we want to see it in other ways. This desire is not simply tied to the need for improving our historical narratives, it stems from the inadequacies of these theories in providing either good reasons for making art these days, or criteria for judging the art that is now being made.

Kant offers us the harmonies of nature as an exemplar for our art. But environmental depredation, not harmony, is the present reality, and our physical world stands not as a counter to our excesses but, rather, as their victim. Cezanne's purity of gaze is now masked by self-obsession, and there are no more innocent objects. Today's artistic images do not serve as documents of reality, but rather provide us with an abundance of alternatives and substitutes. We handle competing extremes in form and subject with equanimity, and have a high tolerance for irrelevancy. What would an "untrammeled gaze" be like today, toward what would it be directed, and how would it present itself in artistic form?

The inward retreat of Schopenhauer fares no better. The subconscious never did achieve a physiological location in the brain; psychoanalysis is embarrassingly tied to wealth and privilege; drug therapy has become the staple of psychiatry. More importantly, dreams and fantasies are now demystified: although they may give evidence of fecund individual sensibilities, they do not constitute an alternative to science in providing ways we can know the world. "Self-expression," once the radical cry for artistic freedom, has become a methodological staple in our art schools, and we have come to realize that we all, in fact, do express ourselves—all the time. What, then, is the special agency or obsession in us that could translate our present experiences, and their expressions, into art of value?

I have saved the Hegelian thesis for the last because, in one sense, it is the most difficult—and painful—to relinquish. A basic tenet of modernism is that art progresses. This is a Hegelian legacy. One may split the criteria, as Hegel did, and deny that the progress is in

purely *aesthetic* terms, but yet assert that there is an irrevocable pattern of formal and stylistic change in the history of art—a "dematerialization"—that corresponds to progress in culture itself. We now find it hard to believe this in political terms, harder to apply it to present art. Major signposts of the avant-garde (pictorial abstraction, dodecaphonic music, novel syntax in literature, perhaps the "International Style" in architecture) are no longer seen as harbingers of the future. Instead, they have been rejoined with many other, recently obscure, stylistic contenders in an essentially "Mannerist" situation. Because these artistic contraries now so peacefully coexist, questions as to what role our present art does play in and for its culture become more difficult to ask. The very attempt seems so dated—even crotchety—but I will make it nonetheless.

This essay concludes, then, with, a series of questions. Put in more general terms than the ones presented above, they are: How, in retrospect, do we assess these earlier theories of Kant, Hegel, and Schopenhauer? What in them do we continue to believe or find useful, and what have we discarded—sometimes without knowing it? What do we want our art now to be, and what do we now expect appreciation to do for us? Does—should—can—art have a function, these days, that extends the aesthetic into other concerns? Such questions, of course, will generate others, and the answers might prove illuminating. For example, those holding a formalist view will argue that, throughout the history of art, the only good art is about art, and that these days, as ever, the truth will out. A contrasting position would be that we've made too much fuss about this "art" thing, and that we should let market forces have their way. There are some that might take the new infatuation with old art to signify a return to academic verities, and seek to establish programs that reduce and professionalize the class of artists. Others, those nostalgic for the early avant-garde, will hope that things become unsettled enough for art to again include social agendas with its aesthetic concerns, thereby generating manifestos and protest exhibitions. Still others will insist that making art is just a nice thing to do. As with my questions, such answers should generate others. I hope that some one or more of them might be good enough to show us a way of getting from our present "post" period into one that has its own name.

A philosopher and painter, **Lucian Krukowski** has been teaching since 1955. He is currently a professor of philosophy at Washington University, where he has also served as dean of the School of Fine Arts and chairman of the Department of Philosophy. His paintings have been featured in individual and group shows in New York and St. Louis. He is the author of numerous articles and papers on art and philosophy, including *Art and Concept: A Philosophical Study*, published in 1987.

Interior courtyard of the Ecole des Beaux Arts, Paris.

David Bell

INMEDIASRES

All deep, earnest thinking is but the intrepid effort of
the soul to keep the open independence of her sea;
while the wildest winds of heaven and earth conspire
to cast her on the treacherous, slavish shore.
—Herman Melville, *Moby Dick*

1
Hans-Georg Gadamer, "The Universality of the Problem," in *Philosophical Hermeneutics* trans. and ed. by David E. Linge (Berkeley: University of California Press 1977, 5.

2
Ibid., 5.

The French *philosophe* Denis Diderot between the years 1761 and 1774 wrote a curious literary work entitled *Rameau's Nephew* which in a very real way reveals the plight that we find in much contemporary architectural theory, production, and education. In a dialogue between an "I" (who we presume is Diderot) and an eponymous "He" (a fictitious artist and nephew of the famous composer Jean-Philippe Rameau), Diderot presents us with a fascinating discussion on life, art, society, and morality. These two conversants represent two very different ways of perceiving the world. The significance of their dialogue lies in its implicit recognition that the world inhabited by its two protagonists was undergoing profound transformations. The characters of "I" and "He" manifest many of these changes which would come to affect the way one understands oneself, others, and the relationships among all in a world becoming ever stranger.

The "I" in this dialogue presumes himself to be possessed with intellectual and psychological integrity, an individual certain of his identity even in the increasingly relativistic sociopolitical reality of this changing world. This "I" is the personification of the historical consciousness which allows one to hold oneself "at a critical distance in dealing with witnesses to past life" and have an interpretive authority when examining works of art from any period or culture. As Hans-Georg Gadamer points out in his essay, "The Universality of the Problem" this is a self-deceptive form of alienation.[1]

The "He" is a different creature. He has no center to orient to and assumes whatever role society expects of him. He is an opportunistic *Zelig*, a chameleon-like personality, a disintegrated self who is acutely aware of, even accepts his alienation. In fact he has abandoned his self and all absolutes (moral or otherwise) as a matter of survival. "Nothing is less like him than himself" Diderot proclaims. And "He" himself states: "All I know is that I would like to be somebody else." "He" has no true self, only self-consciousness. For him art has lost its "original and unquestioned authority . . ." and become a mere object of aesthetic judgment alienated from the "authentic experience that confronts us in the form of art itself."[2] Rameau's nephew is an artist divorced from his own historical being. "He" is, again using Gadamer's terminology, alienated into aesthetic consciousness.

In the post-war period of the twentieth century and particularly within the last twenty years there has appeared a proliferation of architectural theories. In many quarters, including many architecture schools, this numbing pullulation seems to have fostered a belief that we have finally reached the horizon of history. Through culture's tidal action, a plurality of theories is cast on the shores of the present. But each of these theories is presumed to be equivalent in value to all the others. Different, yet equal, they stand ready to be appropriated and employed in design. Because of their profusion and intellectual seductiveness, insidious illusions both of great personal self-validation and freedom-of-choice are attached to this array as a whole as well as its specific parts. This plurality pretends to reconcile the alienations of both the "I" and the "He." Amidst it, one operates by seeking that theory (and one *will* find it) which corresponds most closely to the way one thinks, feels, feels one thinks or thinks one feels; then a certain degree of psychological comfort is achieved because one knows to which group, which theoretical position, one belongs. Yet, while all these theories are putatively available for scrutiny, the conceptual framework for their arrangement and presentation for selection is often completely overlooked, or if acknowledged this framework remains nevertheless unexamined. Usually the only indication of its presence is given by the exhortation that one can apply any theory or combination of theories to a situation as long as the result is "good"— "Do whatever you like as long as it's good."

This statement of utilitarian teleology presumes that the end of protracted thoughtful actions, that is, the making of the best possible state of affairs, is established or can be established, in one's mind at the outset of that effort. Yet the real question of "*What is* good?" is left unasked. This injunction of the "good" suggests a need for an ethical thinking in relating theory and architectural design. However, ethical thought is so overshadowed by the relativity of values which is often taken as implicit in the plurality of available theories, that such thought is truncated with respect to the lives and situations with which the architect's efforts intervene. The presumption of relativism as a way to explain and give basis to a discussion of the plurality of values constitutes a presupposition, a metaphysical guarantee, that these values are all fundamentally equivalent, possibly incommensurable and substantially complete; in other words each is good in its own way and must be accepted on those terms.[3] Throughout the course of this essay I shall try to amplify and clarify certain of these terms and in doing so contend that this relativistic basis, when put forward as a theoretical position, ideology or ultimate legitimation, neither explains the pluralistic situation in which we find ourselves nor justifies any of our actions in it. It is instead a plausible construction, a representation, an "appearance," within the plurality it seeks to describe. We should always be wary of allowing such "appearances" to be construed as a manifestation of a more "real" and hence "true" (even if relativistic) world behind these appearances, a world provided for us by a hidden cause. As Nietzsche so astutely pointed out, "[t]he 'apparent' world is the only one: The 'real' world has only been *lyingly added*." His important point here and throughout the chapter of *Twilight of the Idols* from which this quotation comes is that ours is not a world given to us but one (the only one) which we are incessantly making, unmaking, and remaking through our thoughts and actions.[4] It is a point which informs many of the arguments made in the present discussion.

3
The terms incommensurable, equivalence, pluralism, and relativism are derived from various sources. In addition to Gadamer's *Philosophical Hermeneutics* and his *Truth and Method*, trans. and ed. by Garrett Barden and John Cumming (New York: Crossroad, 1985), I include Richard J. Bernstein, *Beyond Objectivism and Relativism* (Philadelphia: University of Pennsylvania Press, 1983) and Richard Rorty, *Philosophy and the Mirror of Nature* (Princeton: Princeton University Press 1979). The relationships of pluralism to equivalence have been addressed by Hal Foster, "Against Pluralism," in *Recodings* (Seattle: Bay Press, 1985), 12–32; and David Bell, "Reflection," *Journal of Architectural Education* 40, no. 3 (Spring 1987):1. In the present essay I have used the word relativism to describe a polemical or ideological attitude toward pluralism. Relativism thus suggests a values orientation to plurality, whereas pluralism is a recognition of the fact of plurality. I realize, especially given the discussions of this essay, that this particular distinction in terms of value and fact is too simplistic. It is due both to my limitation of space and philosophical breadth.

4
Friedrich Nietzsche, *Twilight of the Idols*, trans. R. J. Hollingdale (Harmondsworth: Penguin Books 1975), 36. The chapter from which this quotation comes, entitled " 'Reason' in Philosophy," is an elaboration of this quotation within the context of Nietzsche's conception of the significance of the body to thought and value formation. He closes this chapter with an important but disturbing observation (p. 41):

6. *We have abolished the real world: what world is left? The apparent world perhaps? . . . But no!* With the real world we have also abolished the apparent world!

(Mid-day: moment of the shortest shadow; end of the longest error; zenith of mankind; INCIPIT ZARATHUSTRA.)

In effect he upends some of the assertions with which he begins his discussion and positions the reader, as he always does, between things, never allowing one to grasp an anchor within the writing.

5

For some, including Nietzsche (see his *The Gay Science*) this is an awful event. For a political discussion see Michael Harrington, *The Politics at God's Funeral* (New York:Penguin Books, 1983), especially pp. 84–107; and for a theological discussion see Mark C. Taylor, *Erring* (Chicago: University of Chicago Press, 1984), especially pp. 19–33 and pp. 97–120. It is valuable to recognize a difference which I think exists between Nietzsche's atheism and (dare I say it?) popular atheism. The latter dismisses the existence of God altogether, i.e., never did, does not now, never will exist. Nietzsche phrases God's existence in historical terms, i.e., "God is dead," which means that God was once with us and is now departed, the only vestige being that God is the "object" of faith. For Nietzsche there is unquestionably a confrontation with nothingness and a desire to make one's way in the face of this disturbing fact.

6

This is quoted by Calvin Tomkins, *The Bride and the Bachelors* (New York: Viking, 1965), 2. Edward Said, in the essay "Conclusion: Religious Criticism," in *The World, The Text and the Critic* (Cambridge: Harvard University Press, 1983), 291, notes with some alarm the theologization of the secular which is at work in contemporary criticism:

Questions of theory are generally questions about the acceptance or rejection of certain values. Yet the relativistic attitude toward theory effectively neutralizes the idea of value as a substantive part of life. Nevertheless, the problem of value in relativism is different from the "value-freedom" of positivism. This latter directly denies the effectiveness of values in the construction of a useful description and explanation of the phenomena of the world and prefers only to accept empirically authenticatable facts. We confront in relativism a much more confusing construction which operates not on the rejection of this plurality of values but on its virtually uncritical acceptance.

As architects, educators, and more importantly as individuals who live daily in a very complex world, where do we turn? Certainly we can never go back to the resolute "I" of Diderot. Despite whatever we might wish, our world does not revolve around an authoritarian center from which emanates a comprehensive morality, that is, prescriptions which govern all human action and production—even art. The Judeo-Christian God is dead or dying. Yet the fact that not all atheists are cheering God's demise, but consider it with some horror, should provide stimulus to reflect on the consequences of this event.[5] The plurality of God's surrogates, which since the nineteenth century would include science, sociology and anthropology, history, language, culture, art (in the guise of *l'art pour l'art*), and architecture (conceived as an autonomous practice), have had even less staying power and positive significance for humanity. It was an atheistic Marcel Duchamp who, scoffing at the art establishment, declared "Art as religion,—it's not even as good as God."[6]

What now seems to be the only alternative is the depressing cynicism of Diderot's "He": a world predicated on the complete relativity of values and immediate gratification of the senses. Art in this sense cannot be much more than a relentless search for novelty wherein cleverness becomes humanity's greatest virtue. In a relativistic architecture, as will be demonstrated later in this essay, one finds evidence of

a perpetual polar oscillation, a dialectic of frustration, between the two alienated consciousnesses of the "I" and the "He"—the historical consciousness and the aesthetic consciousness.

Although we may accept the assessment that much of the contemporary, relativistic consciousness can be characterized by the alienation of the "He" and the "I," it is another thing altogether to suppose that these seeming ruptures of the human spirit with the world can be treated and cured; that a definitive answer can be given to our question "to where do we turn?" These conditions are not personality problems which can be resolved by psychology or sociology, definitely not by architecture. This alienation, which we all experience, comes about through our fears in facing the possibility that there is nothingness at the center of human existence: no God, no final answers to any of our questions, no fixed point of reference, no foundation (not even reason) for knowledge or understanding in the pursuit of any creative venture, no stability even in our own individual consciousnesses. We are left with the dread of not knowing what to do or think at the beginning of any situation.

As Diderot's dialogue suggests there is a crisis not only of authority but of authenticity as well. A look at the courtyard of the Ecole des Beaux-Arts as it existed in the nineteenth century can help give some dimension to this crisis. This courtyard mixes together and confuses the authentic with the simulation. The Doric column is hardly authentic but stands alongside authentic fragments as an equal. Yet if we understood the authenticity of an artifact as connected to "the location of its original use value" we might at least pause to consider that maybe this column is the only authentic thing present because, though a replica, it is a replica made for this place whereas the fragments no longer are connected to the situations which produced them.[7] Or perhaps the Doric column and the "authentic" fragments both, but in different terms, can be called reproductions. Even further one might want to question this whole enterprise of trying to assess authenticity if such an assessment must be made by examining a simulation—the photograph. This crisis has direct bearing on the issues this essay investigates. Like those issues it is diffuse, circular, and requires the elaboration of contingent concerns.

The quotation in the paragraph immediately above comes from Walter Benjamin's seminal essay entitled "The Work of Art in the Age of Mechanical Reproduction" where subsequent to making this remark he both defines concisely the terrain of this crisis and provides an opening for exploring its complexities:

But the instant the criterion of authenticity ceases to be applicable to artistic production, the total function of art is reversed. Instead of being based on ritual, it begins to be based on another practice—politics.[8]

The word "politics" here suggests the ceaseless, daily give-and-take between each of us and the world of which we are *a part* (not apart) in order to realize our desires. Politics consists of those fluctuating and difficult relationships between ourselves, our institutions, and the insinuations of each within the other. More specifically, Benjamin's statement contends that the politics involved in the production of art makes art *not* a subjective act of personal expression directed to a passive audience of receivers who will, if they are sensitive enough, be edified by its evident truths. Political processes in art recognize no privileged interpretation or absolute meaning of an artifact and see any interpretation as perenially subject both to change and involvement with theory. Meaning neither resides in the object nor exclusively in its creator's consciousness, but with all who experience it at any particular moment of its history. There is a kind of necessary exchange between interpreter and object which defines, that is, makes, each of them, their relationship together, and the world.

The relativistic basis for pluralism very much begs questions of the relationship between theory, production, and politics. But what advocates of this relativism often forget or fail to realize is that the selection or choice of theories is itself not a neutral act. It changes the nature of the theory selected and hence anyone's "good" reasons for selecting a theory or subscribing to certain values are not independent of or inert with respect to that theory or those values.

Through the uncritical acceptance of this plurality one might conclude that relativism simulates political processes in the design and making of artifacts just as a computer simulates highly complex mathematical operations by carrying out a vast number of simple addition operations at high speeds. It is almost as if relativism in the guise of epistemology is a last-ditch attempt to hold still an unstable world while playing a polemical role as advocate of a world of variability and flux. Relativism's uncritical acceptance of the plurality of values, its tendency to treat them as equivalent in merit but incommensurable, as if they somehow constituted an intellectual amusement park, seems almost to be a strategy to depoliticize at its outset any kind of discussion about these values. Their differences are trivialized through their isolation.[9] They come to be regarded as "special interests." It is partly through this paradoxical connection of equivalence and incommensurability that relativism works constantly to explain away, to level out conflicts and even the appearance of conflicts. But it is precisely in the *search for* rapprochement of incommensurables that politics exist.[10]

The "search for," carried out as it must be with the knowledge that there may be nothingness at the center of human existence and charged therefore with the need to remain open to the improbable, leads one to a very old question: "How does one live one's life well?" It is a question which can never be answered straightforwardly, but only by living one's life. As Aristotle points out in his *Nicomachean Ethics* this is a political question, but it is a special kind of political question having to do with ethics. As suggested above a significant and continuing problem within contemporary life upon the death of God is a consumptive need among people for some kind of anchorage within the world, for an orientation, an establishment of normative patterns of conduct.

What one discerns today is religion as the result of exhaustion, consolation, disappointment: its forms in both the theory and practice of criticism are varieties of unthinkability, undecidability, and paradox together with a remarkable consistency of appeals to magic, divine ordinance, or sacred texts.

7
Walter Benjamin, "The Work of Art in the Age of Mechanical Reproduction," in *Illuminations*, trans. by Harry Zohn, ed. by Hannah Arendt (New York: Schocken Books 1978), 224.

8
Ibid., 224.

9
We see this particularly in the ideas of two individuals who, though their influence seems now to be on the wane, very much set the tone for architectural theory and production during the period of the last 10–15 years. They are Charles Jencks and Peter Eisenman. Jencks essentially advocated an anything-goes approach within design before withdrawing to a stylistic Classicism. Eisenman, making no truth claims, asserted that his work was an investigation into architecture's autonomous aspects and was completely disconnected from the world. He proposed that architecture can be conceived wholly independent from experience and accountability. (See also note 34 below.) Eisenman's views have somewhat modified to the point where, if I interpret correctly a recent series of his lectures, he now seems to be an advocate of what I can only think to call deconstructive stylistics.

10

"*Search for*" gets emphasis as the important part of this statement because we must accept the strong likelihood that rapprochement may never be achieved. Despite this latter fact it is nevertheless a significant aspect of our existence as historical creatures that we maintain an openness to the improbable.

It is within these terms that Gadamer in *Truth and Method*, p. 271, and Bernstein in *Beyond Objectivism and Relativism*, p. 167, accept the validity of the thesis of incommensurability. They reject an incommensurability which contends that differing horizons and forms of life have ultimately no way of communicating. They accept an incommensurability which admits of one's both being open to the possibility of communicating while recognizing that it is our own prejudices which prohibit or make difficult this understanding. The former proceeds from an a priori knowledge while the latter proceeds from an acceptance of not-knowing. (See also Note 28 below.)

11

Bernstein, *Beyond Objectivism and Relativism*, 39, especially his extended quotation from Gadamer's "Hermeneutics and Social Science," in Gadamer's *Philosophical Hermeneutics*.

12

Bernard Williams, *Ethics and the Limits of Philosophy* (Cambridge: Harvard University Press, 1985), 6–8.

These longings tend to exaggerate the authority of experts with the expectation that they, having mastered the technical complexities of one or more disciplines, are likewise in a preferred position to provide us with ethical and political guidance.[11] However, although we really must be suspicious of the moral authority of experts we cannot deny that ethics, art, technology, science, interpretation, and history become conflated in our processes for making things. Recognizing the unavoidable confusion of fact and value in human thought and action is a critical point in ethics. Ethics considers the manifold consequences of the realization of our thoughts in the world, as does morality. Having said this, even in light of the immediately preceding statements, it is valuable to distinguish between morality and ethics.[12]

Both of these words, morality and ethics, etymologically suggest a connection to custom or the accepted ways of behavior in society. However, morality tends to emphasize certain aspects of ethics which can be formalized or phrased as obligations or duties. In examining the nature of moral thinking Immanuel Kant proposed a much stronger notion of morality than one based on social obligation. He argued that there exists in each of us, independently of the rest of the world, a moral imperative, a legislator of our behavior, which is an a priori foundation of our being. It is this imperative which provokes us to act ultimately with the most genuine morality, even if such behavior contravenes social or legal obligations.

Whereas morality, no matter what its level of consideration, tends to establish explicit boundaries, a priori foundations or standards for human behavior, the notion of what is ethical at any moment is vague and not often explicit. Ethical experience through one's thoughts and actions also is not consciously directed toward the reification of categories of virtue such as courage, justness, generosity, etc.[13] Contrary to Kantian moral philosophy, it does not have to proceed from a priori moral principles. Yet this does not condemn ethics to hedonism; it simply means that it is not systematic. Ethics' lack of formality and system does not preclude the possibility of content. But its content cannot be given directly by an external agency, it is coeval with the immediacy and contingency of one's involvement in specific situations. This situational aspect of ethics is dependent on one's application of reflective thinking over introspection, that is, the consideration of the mutuality of the individual, the situation, and the unknowns which exist between these over a subjective self-examination.[14]

Aristotle, in his *Nicomachean Ethics*, sought to limit Platonic intellectualism in examining questions of what is good and hence founded ethics as a discipline independent of metaphysics. He emphasized the contingent nature of ethics in questions regarding the "good" over Plato's extreme mathematical exactness which considered the "good" as an external unchanging ideal, an object of contemplation removed from this world. "There cannot be a Form common to the good-as-such and the good as a relation", Aristotle argues.[15] One's dealings with the Platonic (metaphysical) "good" are predicated on comprehensive analyses through which universal principles are revealed. The good is manifested in the world by imitating these principles and being vigilant in their application to the living of life. Through rational thought, competing considerations can be weighed against each other using some common terms of comparison and all decisions can "be based on ground that can be discursively explained."[16]

Aristotle approached this question of the "good" in another way entirely. He saw that the situations of our lives are profoundly different each from every other one and that it is our own actions which give each situation its fundamentally inimitable quality. In his ethics the realization of the good comes about as a kind of ongoing critique of the concrete actions of people in specific situations. Thus we might say that ethics arises out of one's recognition that there is in every situation a complex reciprocal relationship between the situation and those who act within it and constitute it. (My use of discursive language here may give the mistaken impression that the situation is somehow independent of those who act within it.) One's actions do not determine the situation nor vice versa. However, just because there can be found no universal foundation common to every situation which will structure our actions, this does not necessarily mean that the decision of what is right, good, or true in any situation is a relativistic matter, that is, it is not an arbitrary decision of the will which allows one to do as one pleases. There is, as Gadamer points out throughout his work, always the matter of our historicity, our intimate but problematic and vague connection to any situation which automatically contravenes the antinomianism of subjective morality. In fact one's presence within a situation is never full presence in that no one can ever be fully present, only historically present. Presence therefore is perhaps more a matter of intervention. Once in the situation one cannot effectively be divorced from it or its history. One's presence by intervention changes the situation immediately, and one's continued action within the situation precipitates further changes. I think it is significant that in illustrating his ethics Aristotle chooses the artist and the athlete as his exemplars, for they must think with material, body and intellect.[17]

The connections between ethical thought and action *and* the human experience of one's own historicity are profound because as Gadamer has demonstrated we are always in the process of overcoming (Nietzsche's revaluation of all values) or opening up our horizons specifically through the recognition of our own finitude or by challenging the incommensurables.[18] Some discussion of this has already occurred; further elaboration will be made later in this essay. Reductive thinking or the distillation of fixed ideas and values from experience, no matter how sophisticated the mental processes or the propositions, has no real justification in the ethical enterprise. Ethical thought then is subject to the problematic conditions of Nietzsche's world of appearances, where things do not have permanence, where

13
It is valuable to distinguish between behavior and experience. Behavior deals with what is being observed, it is the outward manifestation of experience. Experience is much more inclusive but it cannot be fully observed. It has to do with the uniqueness and hiddeness of our thoughts and feelings in any situation. Its nature is such that we must recognize that even in our conscious state our own behavior may seem mysterious, i.e., not transparent, to ourselves.

14
Taylor, *Erring*, pp. 39–40, discusses three kinds of relationships between Subject and Object: Cognition, Reflection and Reflexion. Although my terminology differs I think his discussion would be helpful to the interested reader if read critically.

15
Aristotle *Nicomachean Ethics*, trans. Martin Ostwald (Indianapolis: Bobbs-Merrill, 1962) p. 11 (I., vi., i.). Similar assertions can be found also in I., vii. and II., ii.

16
Williams, *Ethics and the Limits of Philosophy*, 18.

17
In *Truth and Method*, p. 38, Gadamer makes a brief but revealing discussion of ethics in light of Kant's moral philosophy which attempted to separate ethics from aesthetics:

. . . *such a thesis sounds strange to our ears* [that Aristotle's ethics is profoundly and comprehensively an ethics of good taste]. *For one reason, because we generally fail to recognize the ideal normative element in the concept of taste and are still affected by the relativistic-sceptical argument about differences of taste. But above all we are influenced by Kant's achievement in moral philosophy,*

which purified ethics from all aesthetics and feeling.

18
Gadamer, *Truth and Method*, 310–325.

19
Ibid., 284.

20
Authors whom I have found valuable in considering Aristotle's ethics in order to articulate my own views in the present essay also find points of disagreement with him. These authors are Gadamer, of course, in *Truth and Method*, p. 316, where he differs with Aristotle on the nature of experience, saying "[w]hat concerns Aristotle about experience is merely its contribution to the formation of concepts"; Williams, *Ethics and the Limits of Philosophy*, where on p. 9 he disagrees with Aristotle on the power of right judgment, then on pp. 43–44 he undertakes a critique of Aristotelian teleology; and Michael Novak, *The Experience of Nothingness* (Hagerstown: Harper, 1977), p. 77, differs with Aristotle on the importance of the ethics of the mean (*mesotes*).

21
Aristotle, *Nicomachean Ethics*, p. 153 (VI., v., v.). The use of the word "good" here seems question-begging when taken out of context in this quotation. The paragraph from which it comes is:

What remains, then, is that it is a truthful characteristic of acting rationally in matters good and bad for man. For production has an end other than itself, but action does not: good action is itself an end. That is why we think that Pericles and men like him have practical wisdom. They have the capacity of seeing what is good for themselves and for mankind, and these are, we believe, the qualities of men capable of managing households and states.

22

I cite here for example Donald Schön, *The Reflective Practitioner* (New York: Basic Books, 1983).

23

Phronēsis in Aristotle's terms was dependent on the existence of *nomoi* (funded laws), i.e., community standards, which existed within the *polis*. We have to accept today the possibility, despite documents which guarantee fundamental rights and laws, that such *nomoi* do not exist or are constantly being circumvented. Such *nomoi* certainly are not clear as regards architecture beyond what is codified in building and zoning regulations. Such a notion of *nomoi* and the crisis their contemporary absence causes for *phronēsis* is what Bernstein suggests in *Beyond Objectivism and Relativism*, pp. 157–159. However, a somewhat different attitude toward the relationship of *nomoi* and *polis* can be found in Gilles Deleuze, and Felix Guattari, *A Thousand Plateaus* (Minneapolis: University of Minnesota Press, 1987), 353ff. Here I interpret them as arguing that the force of the *polis* is an institutionalizing force which works to polarize the world. On one hand it presents itself as the center of order, a complexly hierarchical and extensive State which is in opposition to but evangelistic (or imperialistic) toward everything which is not structured in terms of its governance. This other realm is that which this State organism (with its politics, science, culture and education) sees as lacking even *nomoi*. Deleuze and Guattari contend that beyond this Same/Other (Order/Disorder) opposition there lies the *nomos*, which seeks not the processes of coding and decoding implicit in the operations of the State machine but a perpetual process of territorializing and deterritorializing. It is non-linear, non-hierarchical, non-objective, and not given to centering either space or thought in terms of Same and

persistence is the most one can expect. Thus ethical experience as with our own presence, *intervention*, in a situation cannot appear completely all at once or all at one. Laws independent of the actions which they are supposed to govern are and can be only partial, since they cannot contain the practical reality which emerges from the action itself.[19] There is an essential aspect of otherness to ethical experience, but it is of a worldly strangeness, not a transcendental nature.

Ethics deals with means, ends, and their relationships. However, one must ultimately recognize that in our world of situational appearances and events as opposed to a transcendent world of a priori categories of space and time, in our world without authoritative center, any end is subject to becoming a means to another end and that ends themselves, when seen as limits, have a peculiar ephemerality or instability. My own differences with Aristotle have to do with what I perceive as his too-clear distinction between action and production based on this question of ends.[20] Aristotle contends that "production has an end other than itself, but action does not: good action is itself an end."[21] I would not dispute that this difference in the nature of their ends is problematic, especially for us living in our pluralistic, decentered world. Such a contention, which he develops from a belief that art is a matter of production and not action, leads him to propose that practical wisdom, or what he calls *phronēsis*, and which we might also call thought-in-action, is not related to production but to action. This assertion is perhaps due both to Aristotle's penchant for categorization and his dialectical style of argumentation. These latter two are metaphysical foundations for his writing and thinking which should not be taken at face value. It is important therefore to consider that the ambiguous relationship between production, action and the good in terms of their ends for making architecture in the contemporary situation acquires ethical density within the context of *phronēsis*.[22]

The notion of *phronēsis*, thought-in-action, a kind of perpetual reciprocity between theory and practice, has operative value for a world which is a stream of contingencies.[23] For as Aristotle himself argues, ethical action in concrete situations is neither given by the world, inherent in it, nor even in our hearts. *Phronēsis*, he proposes, is "concerned with human affairs and with matters about which deliberation is possible."[24] It arises from the application of one's judgment, the judgment of the *phronimos*, the wise individual, within a specific situation.[25] Evident here in these notions of *phronēsis* and *phronimos* is a perplexing circularity which may have to do with both the limitations of language and our tendency to want to see prescriptions emerge from text and distill concepts from experience (an Aristotelian tenet, see note 20) which can become paragons for future action. Judgment, however, is an act of discernment which resists prescriptions, fixities, distillations, and generalizations. The action and production (even the existence) of *phronēsis* and the *phronimos* are not things which already exist but are always becoming, that is, are in the process of being made. They are dependent on one's powers of discernment, one's drive to understand no matter what the obstacles are, to interpret and to realize that one's own presence, one's intervention, in a situation means simultaneously that one's prejudices, values, assumptions, rationalizations, habituations of thought have automatically come into play there in the midst of the situation as an inseparable part of it. All understanding and interpretation one makes will have to account for these and accept that there can never be clear beginnings or ends for the making of judgments; no origin and no finality.

The ethical question arises in architecture because the production of architecture is thought-in-action taking place in the world. It is always within history, no matter how it is expressed or its purposes directed. Even the most recondite of architectural production or theorizing intervenes in our lives. In putting forward this nucleus of issues regarding ethics, *phronēsis*, production, thought and action, I am deliberately trying to raise some questions about the state of theory in contemporary architecture, especially in architectural education, where there is a marked increase of interest in theory, and in architectural practice, where there seems to be a marked decrease of interest in theory. What is valuable in bringing forth these issues and questions is not the authority which any of these claims might have about how we should live, make, think about, or teach architecture but their capacity to allow an entrance into the discussion of values and problems of contemporary life. In this capacity these serve as both critical tools and critical challenges to the establishment of horizons for our understanding (this latter is what Aristotle calls *synesis*) in the ethical making of architecture.[26]

Understanding is an event moving in history. Its passage is intimately connected to our thoughts and actions. It defies categorizations regarding the past which would create and sustain the dialectic of an "I," the transcendental subject of grammar, against a "them," objects for interpretation. We can never remove history from the circumstances of our present because the past always defines the interpreter's ground when he is concerned with understanding. The interpreter should acknowledge both his own historicity and especially prejudices, along with the historical characteristics or properties of what he is interpreting, and affirm the possibility of understanding.[27] In the daily workings of architectural education I have often experienced and observed, both in myself and students, the grip of a kind of aphasia when having to examine critically works of architecture—my own, their own or someone else's. When this happens it seems that there is an assumption that one's own history has nothing to do with, is irrelevant to, the architectural work under question and further (perhaps concomitantly) that there is some secret message contained in and projected by this work that one is incapable of perceiving. The impression is strong that the work possesses an intrinsic strangeness and presents an insurmountable obstacle to easy understanding, that these can only lead to the discomfort of misun-

derstanding which would therefore be better to avoid altogether. But perhaps such a misunderstanding, especially when addressing the multitude of issues in one's own design, should not be viewed as an obstacle but as a productive difference, an otherness of potentially great value. It may be "that every misunderstanding presupposes 'a deep common accord.'"[28]

This is easy advice to give but it can be difficult for anyone—teacher, student, practitioner—to put into action. It is not advice which solves problems or provides a method. It allows movement but only if one can suspend, and moreover question, one's own agendas, the rules which normally guide one's conduct and obligations, and plunge oneself into the uncertainties which necessarily accompany any misunderstanding. In education this might mean the relaxation (*not* renunciation) of the demand for an objective end to a project, a particularly difficult proposition for architecture design professors, myself included, to accept. This stretching beyond our boundaries, of confronting rather than avoiding or placating misunderstanding is a constituent part of ethical thinking. And once these differences appear, they become not just part of what one might call one's ethical life, but of one's *life*. They can therefore neither be simply rejected as wrong nor acknowledged but ignored. The first is the outright arrogance of Diderot's "I," the second the cynical relativism of the "He."

One commonly-held theoretical tenet of contemporary architecture maintains that architectural form should be capable of being read at multiple levels and therefore be accessible to any audience. This implies that interpretation should either always be easy or just be whatever anyone wants it to be. Misunderstandings, which, while they can provoke unsettling questions and might also reveal "a deep common accord," should be or can be avoided or dismissed. Thus the elite, the cognescenti, may have their interpretations and the populists are likewise allowed theirs. Everyone can invent his own reality, his own history, his own world. This is a notion of interpretation which distances one from the

Other. It is a background of situationally based practices, a "distribution . . . without division into shares . . . without borders or enclosures" (p. 380). It is by nature vague, vagabond, nomadic. In Deleuze's and Guattari's terminology I would construe *phronēsis* to be nomadic thought.

24
Aristotle, *Nicomachean Ethics*, 157 (IV, vii).

25
Jean-François Lyotard and Jean-Loup Thébaud, *Just Gaming*, trans. Wlad Godzich (Manchester: Manchester University Press, 1985), 48–49. In this dialogue Lyotard ruminates on the nature of judgment and has put forward the idea that judgment is not something which exists independently of situations. He further relates judgment to desire saying " . . . the compulsion to judge proceeds simply from desire or from the faculty of pleasure and pain."

26
Attempts to use metaphysical justification to manufacture distinctions between architecture and building are both symptomatic and productive of the further polarization between theory and practice. An exemplary case of this can be found in Peter Eisenman, "Aspects of Modernism: Maison Dom-ino and the Self-Referential Sign," *OPPOSITIONS* 15/16 (Winter/Spring 1979): 118–128.

27
Gadamer, "Aesthetics and Hermeneutics," in *Philosophical Hermeneutics*, 95–104.

28
Gadamer, "The Universality of the Problem," in *Philosophical Hermeneutics*," 7. There is a tantalizing knot of arguments which surrounds this very pregnant statement by Gadamer. The arguments are exemplified in a debate between

Gadamer and Jacques Derrida which took place at the Goethe Institute in Paris in 1981. An interpretive summary of the debate appears in Richard A. Palmer, "Improbable Encounter: Gadamer and Derrida," *Artpapers* 10 (January/February 1986), pp. 36–39. This debate, of course, is one of hermeneutics vs. post-structuralism and addresses the issue of incommensurability, the question as to whether one's encounter with a work of art opens up a world (Gadamer) or if that work resists such opening (Derrida). The present article, though it relies on much in Gadamer, is actually situated in the interstice of his debate with Derrida.

29

Foster, "Against Pluralism," in *Recodings*, 25–26.

30

Michel de Certeau, *Heterologies: Discourse on the Other*, trans. Brian Massumi (Minneapolis: University of Minnesota Press, 1986). Throughout this book de Certeau addresses the nature of discourse as situational and distinct from language, which he considers to be an object and construct of philosophers.

architectural situation being interpreted and places the individual in a world parallel to, but motionless and predetermined with respect to, that situation. The result is a vision of architecture which allows—and indeed relishes—differences, but trivializes them to the extent that only immediate and superficial appearances can be considered (differences in detail, historical reference, formal organization of the object, identifiable meaning). It is a world of private knowledge. It tends toward the hermeticism of pure self-knowledge where difference becomes an end in itself and fuses with the consciousness which imagines it. It is no longer also a means, a being in the middle of a sustained, perpetually ramifying discourse. Differences of real significance which challenge the assumptions implicit in the just-mentioned trivial differences are suppressed. They are differences which would engage us to reflect on the kind of life an architectural intervention in a particular situation might lead to, they provoke our thoughts and feelings on what we are and why we are in such a situation. These kinds of differences of critical reciprocity, because they demand sustained attention rather than provide immediate gratification, because they do not incessantly reaffirm what we already know, and because they work from misunderstandings, are ever more today discounted by the majority culture which can find no way to subsume, hence mollify, them.[29]

It is criticism which mediates this misunderstanding. But it is a particular kind of criticism, one which is neither evaluative nor corrective. It is discourse. It meanders and takes shape with the situation of which it is part and in the process takes account of its own historicity.[30] It is a kind of discussion, a conversation which occurs between the critic and the work being examined or made, where various questions regarding their mutual historicity are sought out. Criticism in these terms is neither a scientific observation or analysis where objective information is extracted from a passive source by an authoritative observer, nor is it the simple subjective asking of "What does this work mean to me?" (at least not without asking what "me" is). Both of these positions avoid completely the possibility of the misunderstanding which attends any critical intervention. Both presume a finite end or conclusion to any critical engagement. Yet something tangible, something unforeseen and "other," always emerges, perhaps even gives articulation to the space between conversants in a discussion. It is their shared life in language, in the construction of discourse without end, and in perpetual flux. It is their search for understanding.

If we look etymologically at the word criticism we see that an important root meaning is "separation." From this we may infer that it has something to do with the circumstances related to the rupture of a limit, the sudden awareness of an uncertainty, the disappearance of stability, the discovery of a difference or discontinuity which defies reconciliation with or deflects explanation by an existing system of knowledge or understanding. Criticism invites crisis to threaten those comfortable realities manufactured by custom and theory. The experience of a loss, that is, the combination of a desire to be whole with an awareness that such is not, cannot, be the case, is significant to the production of critique.

When, as it is bound to happen in contemporary life, questions arise which put into crisis the nature of the ends of a particular action, similarly are questions about the nature of beginnings provoked. From where, for example, does one start in the deliberative action of making something? This is a complex set of issues which Edward Said has examined brilliantly with respect to literary production in his book *Beginnings*. He puts forth a notion of beginning which distinguishes it as a more general condition than the idea of origin. This latter, which he calls a transitive beginning, is the idea that a source, an authoritative center, exists and can be revealed for any undertaking and that this origin for any activity anticipates the nature of its end. For this reason Said suggests that any thinking predicated on the search for origins is metaphysical. On the other hand, intransitive beginning is worldly and secular. It cannot anticipate its end or even presume that one exists without contingency. The intransitive beginning is directed toward open exploration and the "animation of knowledge" as much as it is the making of something.[31] It is perhaps my own delusive intuition, but it seems that questions about beginnings have a strong aesthetic coloration, even though there are ethical implications to them. Alternatively, concerns about ends, while certainly subject to aesthetic considerations, are very strongly ethical ones. Moreover, both aesthetic and ethical issues seem to address how one shouldn't begin or end as much as how one should. Gadamer suggests that this negativity is a powerfully important aspect of our understanding and interpreting experience. In *Truth and Method* he says "the negativity of experience has a curiously productive meaning" and "Every experience worthy of the name runs counter to our expectation."[32] Gadamer also states that "every beginning is an end and every end is a beginning."[33] The lack of absoluteness about the world, about how we live, extends to questions of beginnings and ends. These two are never clear cut and every day we find ourselves asymptotic to these perpetually shifting limits, always between, in the middle of things, *in medias res*.

In order to assess more concretely the implications of the nucleus of concerns discussed above it is valuable to examine and critique several influential architectural theories, positions, and theoretical tendencies. These are by no means the most current ones.[34] However, I believe they are the most prevalent. They are usually employed eclectically rather than synthetically. While my examination of them is far from comprehensive, the criticisms I make are an attempt to understand their place within the contexts of their and our own histories. Although neither advocacy nor indictment of these theories is intended, I am critically suspect of them all due to their strong, unreflected-upon prejudices toward architecture as a formal object. These are prejudices which virtually exclude consideration of the nature of experience in architecture. It is im-

portant here not to misconstrue the word "experience" (see note 13), especially not in terms of behaviorism, regionalism, or any nostalgias of rootedness or "homecoming." Experience is situational, highly complex, and resists a priori formulations. The limitations of this examination will certainly throw into relief my own prejudices, preoccupations, and ignorances. The positions and theories addressed are significant contributions to architectural thought and practice. However, each of them, in the sense that they are theories, are flawed.

By theory I mean something similar to Aristotle's *theoria* where a mental activity is engaged in a search for truth, but different in the sense that once this truth is believed to have been discovered it is applied to practical situations, the quotidian realm of the vagaries of ethics and politics. Further as stated immediately above, I would include also as theory tendencies of thought as well as ideological positions, even though these may differ from a pure definition of theory. The consequence of the necessary flaws which accompany any theory, as I have been arguing and will continue to argue, is the recognition that every theory contains a risk, a danger—one which is essential to the very idea of theory, a danger which is bifacial: every theory from the most muddled to the most articulate makes and delineates limitations on how one should think, act and make; the theorist will of necessity fail to recognize completely these limitations. These limitations are essentially prejudices and their discovery through the reflective experience of *phronēsis* may be what is truly valuable about theory as opposed to the intentionality, specifity, prescriptiveness, and apriority of theory's constructs and propositions. We could never know or fully uncover all our prejudices in any given situation or even over a long period of time. This is due to both the intimacy of our connection to the events of any situation and our embeddedness in history and language. Thus not knowing, that is, not having conscious knowledge of a stable of simple or complex facts, is of major importance. It is a

31
Edward Said, *Beginnings* (New York: Basic Books, 1975), 76–77, 372–373, 380.

32
Gadamer, *Truth and Method*, 317–319.

33
Ibid., 429. I don't believe this should be construed to be a statement of equivalence of beginnings and ends. If so, it would collapse into the relational relativism which Gadamer's project has specifically tried to overcome. It is more a statement of productive ambiguity which suggests the bifacial character of beginnings and ends. It is a statement of their simultaneity, not their equivalence.

34
It is obviously an impossible and perhaps unwise task to be comprehensive in the examination of contemporary theory. Those on which this essay focuses for the most part profess a direct reliance on history and historical form. Those which take other directions and in fact stand in some ways as a critique of more historically-preoccupied work can only be dealt with here by inference. For, despite important differences, they seem in many cases to share a faith in relativistic pluralism (OMA) or hyperrationality (Tschumi and Eisenman) with others which are discussed here. It is significant as well that all have been exceptionally active in relation to the media, either being pursued by or pursuing them. It may be worth noting as well a persistent preoccupation by all with form as the bedrock of architecture. Mark Wigley's introductory essay to the recent MoMA exhibition entitled "Deconstructivist Architecture" gives an overview of the work of several contemporary architects. Repeatedly he attaches his commentary to this formalist bedrock, suggesting that this work is an interrogation of pure form. He does

not question at all the priority of form itself in our conception of architecture and in several places makes the determinist presumption that architectural form which appears unstable will induce in the viewer "a sense of unease." This is an unabashed application of the pathetic fallacy. See Mark Wigley, "Deconstructivist Architecture," in *Deconstructivist Architecture* (New York: Museum of Modern Art, 1988), 10–20, but especially 19.

35
Friedrich Hölderlin, "Patmos," in Richard Unger, *Hölderlin's Major Poetry* (Bloomington: Indiana University Press, 1975), 181. In German this is

Wo aber Gefahr ist, wachst
Das Rettende auch.

36
See Joseph Rykwert, *The First Moderns* (Cambridge: MIT Press, 1983), 8–10, and also his *On Adam's House in Paradise* (New York: Museum of Modern Art, 1972), 123ff, for an enlightening discussion of Juan Bautista Villalpanda's early seventeenth century efforts to align "Vitruvian rules and the revealed specifications [for Solomon's Temple] found in Scripture."

slipping out of positive knowledge, a disquieting confrontation with our own prejudices; prejudices which just our presence, *our intervention*, in a situation brings. Their recognition opens us to understanding. As the German poet Hölderlin so eloquently puts it:[35]

Where danger is, grows
The saving power also.

Contemporary architectural thought and production have come to be significantly dominated by a powerful ideology, a ruling metaphysics, alluded to throughout the foregoing commentary. I do not believe, however, that the various tendencies which constitute these thoughts and actions together necessarily add up to a monolithic master theory. Their content and direction may be traceable to a variety of architectural treatises and writings published during the approximately one-hundred-year period of the Enlightenment. Two of these treatises, *Entwürff einer Historischen Architektur* (1721) and *Précis des leçons d'architecture données a l'école Royale Polytechnique* (1802–1805), are of special interest here because both are pragmatically oriented and are not primarily concerned with the discursive nature of the theory they advance. They rely as much or more on the images they include. At the times of their respective formulations the positions they represented posed striking new attitudes toward history and its relationship to the making of architecture.

In 1721 Johann Bernhard Fischer von Erlach published an extraordinary architectural treatise entitled *Entwürff einer Historischen Architektur*, a project which demanded his effort for more than sixteen years. In this book we find, perhaps for the first time in history, an architectural polemic grounded in a general history of architectural form. Instead of citing the traditional column orders as the absolute authority for architecture (the obligatory introductory discussion of these is dispensed with completely), there are illustrated as exemplars architectures of the Near East and antiquity. With this approach to architecture Fischer von

Erlach simultaneously established an incipient typology of historical form and proposed an idea that architectural meaning does not necessarily emerge from its indigenous circumstances, but can be imported from distant and culturally disconnected sources. Although it is unlikely that Fischer von Erlach could have imagined such a system without the pioneering approaches of many of the architects of the Italian, English, and French seventeenth centuries, there was a significant difference. They too advocated a historical architecture, a rhetorical, narrative as well as mimetic architecture. The dramatic increase of interest in Vitruvius and the architecture of Roman antiquity beginning in the fifteenth century is well known. With this burgeoning of interest came exegeses of sacred and other texts. These were intended to demonstrate the operative presence of the Judeo-Christian God even in the architecture of classical antiquity.[36] Thus architecture could be understood as rooted in a continuous authoritative progression from pagan Rome and the Church's use of classicism justified. It was a time when religion and politics were effectively fused. But Fischer von Erlach greatly extended the repertoire of forms from the ancient and contemporary worlds to invent a fully cosmopolitan pluralist architecture. This portended a crisis in accepted notions of the progressive evolution of architectural form from a God-sanctioned classical origin. It also suggested the potential for irreparable fissures in the edifice of the obligatory connection of religion to politics. The tendency in his thought was to presume that architecture could be assembled incrementally from this increased pool of cultural and historical sources. He in fact states in the Preface to the *Entwürff*:

The Author's Intention has been more to furnish Admirers of the Art with Designs in sundry Species of Architecture, and to lay down plans for those, who make Profession of the Art, to raise new Inventions upon, not to instruct the Learned.

These "sundry Species of Architecture" from history were not necessarily considered important as bearers of intrinsic principles of order like the column orders, but instead for their presumed intrinsic meanings. They could be conscripted from history and conflated with new purposes to suggest completely new associations (not necessarily new interpretations) of these old (and intrinsic) meanings. Here began to emerge a pluralistic and representational architecture, a relativistically based architecture, where the image of a thing, that is, its simulation, its counterfeit, is regarded as having equivalence to the thing itself. These conscripted fragments no longer have an obligatory relationship to their source nor is their production limited. They are signs which, in the words of Jean Baudrillard, are in "free production." The assumption that these signs, these conceptual fragments, can transport meaning with little distortion from distant sources to a new site suggests that the obligatory connection these have or might have had to the native conditions of their making ("the location . . . of original use value") have, in these processes of translation and equivalence, become ambiguous. (Are Fischer von Erlach's Karlskirche and the conditions which bring it into existence really equivalent to the Temple of Jupiter and Peace because their porticoes have similar forms?) The process of relocation is mediated with the sign/fragment by the systematic abstractions of reason, which presume to state emphatically, authoritatively, and clearly the purpose for this employment.[37]

In Fischer von Erlach's work we find a strong sense of authoritarian political justification. Through the employment of these signs and fragments there emerges a new obligatory connection between architectural form and the principles of authority it intends to establish for society. With some caution one might say that this work of Fischer von Erlach prefigures the later idea of architecture as a science, that is, science in its eighteenth century definition as positive knowledge. Even if one cannot incontrovertibly state this, one can still say that Fischer von Erlach's masterpiece, the aforementioned Karlskirche, testifies both to the growth of the idea of architecture as a weaving together of historical references and the capacity that this had to consolidate and give legitimacy to power.[38]

In the early nineteenth century Jean-Nicolas-Louis Durand's *Précis des leçons d'architecture données à l'école Royale Polytechnique* (1802–1805) proposed a somewhat different approach to both the development and uses of architectural form. He examined the significant buildings of history, categorized them by functional type, that is, temple, theater, market, etc., and sought to distill from them their underlying formal principles, adjusting always for regularity and strict symmetry. From this he posited the existence of architectural types independent of history. To understand this operation one has only to see the idealized reconstruction drawing of the Acropolitan Propylaea (after a drawing made by Julien-David LeRoy) which Durand chose as one of the illustrations to the frontispiece of his *Recueil et parallèle des édifices de tout genres anciens et modernes* (1800) and read in his Foreword:

> . . . *Far from having wished to correct* [the works of the great masters], *I have tried to show in a clearer way the spirit that reigns in their magnificant productions.*

For Durand all architecture could be developed systematically from various tables of types presented primarily as plan and elevation. He considered architecture to be independent not only of history but of myth as well, and he exposed the traditional architectural orders (after the ideas of Perrault in the seventeenth century) as items of customary usage containing no intrinsic significance. He argued that the orders should be proportioned in accordance with material and structural necessities and stripped of their role as guarantor of the comprehensive formal order of a work of architecture. The hierarchical implications of the orders vis-à-vis the organization of the building were replaced by the essentially non-hierarchical strategies of the Cartesian grid. Ultimately all parts of the architectural work were referred to this grid. Despite the inherent

37
Jean Baudrillard, *Simulations* Semiotext(e), (New York: Columbia University, 1985).

38
The specifics of the development of the Karlskirche as a way to give social, historical, political, and religious legitimacy to the reign of Charles VI (i.e., the employment of architectural references from Solomon's Temple, the Temple of Jupiter and Peace, St. Peter's, the Hagia Sophia, etc.) are discussed in Rykwert, *The First Moderns*, 70–75.

contradiction between the non-hierarchical im-plications of the grid and the clear hierarchy of symmetry both were important to Durand for their powers of regulation.

Durand's concerns reveal a tendency in his thought: his sublime conceptual detachment of architecture from any historical or mythical ground and its subsequent atomization into independent, disconnected components. Al-though Durand's specific advocacy was for function and economics, his work seems to be most concerned with the reduction of architec-ture to a precise system of graphic representa-tion. The application of this system bypassed or at least abridged the act of design by offering the possibility of a quasi-infinite variety of ar-chitectural configurations which could be made by selecting and joining together the nor-mative forms presented in his tables of types. In his preemption of the actual force of history, Durand not only flattened architecture into ex-ercises in graphic reasoning carried out on spatially independent gridded planes but also created a system which supplied for all intents and purposes, an artificial history for each indi-vidual building. He advanced the ideas that typological systems are the necessary and suffi-cient fount of architectural knowledge; that action and design must indeed by preceded by some positive knowledge, graphically con-veyed. Durand's system was the architectural apotheosis of the Enlightenment's *esprit sys-tematique*. His aspirations to render architecture as a utilitarian service to the state enforced on it a new conception: as science, as applied knowledge, as technique. However the legacy of this theory has been not to eliminate myth from architectural production. Instead it pro-posed a new myth, a curious and ambiguous master-narrative, which asserts that architec-ture-as-building was finally liberated from the forces of myth and myth-making.

Many of the ideals which underlay the ten-dencies in the works of Fischer von Erlach and Durand were developed, articulated, and elab-orated continuously throughout the eighteenth century by the *philosophes*. This group, to which Diderot himself belonged, was neither completely monolithic in its beliefs nor con-fined by national boundaries, but the typical *philosophe* can perhaps be concisely described as anyone of the eighteenth century who per-petually submitted the worlds of tradition and myth to criticism. Their aims in this were to remove all prejudices and preconceptions about the world from the conduct of human affairs and to establish a hegemony of objective knowledge guided by reason. But theirs was not solely an epistemological movement; it had sociopolitical roots as well. The *philosophes* were the propagandists of the ideology of knowl-edge, which stressed the importance of positive intellectual knowledge as humanity's instru-ment for acquiring power over its own destiny rather than leaving this and other issues up to the superstitions of religion or the Machiavel-lian operations of the state. Their questioning of authority was a quest for a rightful authority based, not on myth and heredity, but on the possession of superior knowledge. The essence of the *philosophes'* thinking provided an impor-tant bearing point for the critical thought of Immanuel Kant and the system of G.W. F. Hegel. Kant finds the actual content of the world (which could be called "reality") to be ultimately unknowable with absolute cer-tainty. This does not at all mean that we cannot know anything; rather it implies that there are limits to our knowledge, that knowledge oc-curs entirely within the framework of our humanity. In a sense then the world (which can only be seen in human terms) becomes con-verted into the object of this knowledge and the conscious human subject is at its center. Kant's proposition is that our world is not given to us by God or any other external agency, but is created by the conjunction of the data provided by our senses with certain invariant and a priori structures of cognition in the human mind. This simulation of "reality" by a system of human specific knowledge presupposes that knowledge cannot emerge sit-uationally but is ultimately governed by intel-lectual givens and categories which constitute our being. The knower and what is known, Kant holds, are intimately connected; and human reason, governed by a prioris, is an instrument synchronous with the workings of a natural, phenomenal universe which is the limit of what can be known.

Hegel, following the thought of Kant, elaborated in depth a system which explained the process of humanity's rapprochement through history with this natural, phenomenal, and knowable world. This system not only explained why nature, though knowable, resists the advances of the knower but suggested as well that this dialectical engagement of human consciousness with nature was directed toward the end (i.e., goal or *telos*) of absolute knowledge. He held that with humanity's eventual arrival at this point of the fusion of human consciousness and its objects, with this attainment of absolute knowledge or even an awareness that such is possible and imminent, the validity and the necessity of experience is effectively overcome.[39]

It is the nature of reflective thought to destroy knowledge and challenge the imperative to know. This is especially the case of ethical reflection (which differs from technical reflection) when it is put into action as *phronēsis* in the production of architecture. Such reflection, because it is experientially based, tends to gnaw away at the beliefs and theories that one holds. These latter two are usually predicated on specific knowledge. Ethical reflection always makes one stop to question what one is doing; it introduces some discomfort because it may mean the complete reassessment of one's goals and values. Ethical reflection always introduces noise into a well-ordered system. It is a kind of parasite in that it becomes attached to the practice it considers and modifies it. "Noise is a joker."[40]

Many contemporary architectural theories, despite surface differences, are direct heirs of the ideology of knowledge which propagated through the *philosophes* to culminate in the thought of Kant and Hegel. Aspects of this ideology are abundantly evident in the work of Fischer von Erlach and Durand although both, obviously, were either isolated from or peripheral to the philosophical mainstream. This ideology forces our perceptions and understandings of architecture to oscillate between the poles of historical constant and aesthetic technique. Several theories which operate today are similar to Fischer von Erlach's in supposing that architectural production proceeds from a comprehensive knowledge of historical forms and their meanings. There is a contemporary presumption that architecture necessarily partakes of, is filial to, a grand historical narrative. This is evidenced in two ways: either as a historicist contextualism which calls for the manipulation of simulacra of past architectures in order to extend, replicate, and/or evoke the existing physical context or as a suprahistorical exploration, a conceptual archeology, into the mythopoeic potential of evocative archetypes such as the labyrinth, the tower, the bridge.

However, an insurmountable gulf separates contemporary work from that of Fischer von Erlach. In our own day architectural meaning can find no firm ground on which to rest. It cannot even pretend to the kind of cultural and social stability that seems to have provided a firm conceptual foundation for architecture in the eighteenth century. Today, such meaning is all relative. This is the contemporary pluralist epiphany and concomitant with it architecture has somehow lost (not been liberated from) its potential for political content and surrendered itself to the extremities of historical objectivism and aesthetic subjectivism.

Like Durand, many contemporary rationalists propose that there is a kind of encyclopaedic "history" which stands behind each architectural work. This "history," defined as tables of types, embodies eternally valid principles of form which came into being as the resolution of timeless problems. These types or formal "kits of parts" exist uncorroded and precede any circumstances involved in the real action of history. These tables of types, of architectural abstractions, act as a reservoir not unlike the contemporary historicist's profusion of meaningful forms.

An important distinction should be made between Durand's pluralist conception of type and the monistic conception put forth by

39
Although it is unwise to quote out of context with the seeming end of epitomizing an individual's full philosophical position, especially that of Hegel, it may nevertheless be instructive to do so in this case. The following comes from the third part entitled "Ethical Life" of G.W.F. Hegel, *Philosophy of Right*, trans. T.M. Knox, (London: Oxford University Press, 1976), 109:

. . . when his character is ethical, he recognizes as the end which moves him to act the universal which is itself unmoved but is disclosed in its specific determinations as rationality actualized. He knows that his own dignity and the whole stability of his particular ends are grounded in this same universal, and it is therein that he actually attains these.

40
See Williams, *Ethics and the Limits of Philosophy*, pp. 167–169, for a critique of the notion of "ethical knowledge." The quotation here comes from Michel Serres, *The Parasite* (London: Johns Hopkins University Press 1982), 67. Noise both is a destroyer and constructor, it is forever between means, *in medias res*.

41
See David Bell, "NOMADS," *Midgård* (Minneapolis: University of Minnesota School of Architecture, forthcoming) for an extended discussion and critique of Quatremère de Quincy's notion of type, its influence and relationship to contemporary typological theory.

42
See Robert Adam, *Works of Robert and James Adam, Esquires*, vol. 1 (1773), 4:

. . . *the rising and falling, advancing and receding, with the convexity and concavity, and other forms of the great parts, have the same effect in architecture, that hill and dale, foreground and distance, swelling and sinking have in landscape: That is, they serve to produce an agreeable and diversified contour, that groups and contrasts like a picture . . .*

Quatremère de Quincy. De Quincy defines type as a kind of regulative architectural *principle* enmeshed in the *vague* circumstances of everyday life. Although it is a dualistic definition, these two are dialectically engaged in such a way that a meaningful architectural ideal, represented by the type, is always conserved in the architectural transaction. Quatremère de Quincy's notion of type was not tabular and thus he did not provide as part of his theoretical arguments tables of classified forms.[41]

For most contemporary rationalists the type embodies a universal and irreducible truth which is mediated by form. The locus of type, they hold, is not only in individual buildings but also in the city. They conclude that type is a formal, theoretical construct which allows us to structure our knowledge of the city. They use terms of street and square, fabric and monument, or other (often dialectically paired) morphologies *and* the various ordering characteristics which are implicit in any specific type. Their intention, which comes about very legitimately as a critique of the effect on the post-war city of the conjoined forces of twentieth century technological disruption and nineteenth century bourgeois institutional values, is to resurrect the form of the pre-industrial city. History as a flow of events in which all of us are involved both politically and ethically is denied, but it is affirmed as an object which can be held and viewed at a critical distance. All too often in the works of typologists (I cite here those whose work is a technical appendix to Camillo Sitte—the Kriers together, despite their manifest differences, GRAU, and others) it is never clear why any one type or typological configuration, when proposed, is preferable to another beyond aesthetic considerations, that is, these decisions seem to be alienated within aesthetic consciousness. Again, as with those strands of thought descending from Fischer von Erlach, we find a peculiar polar oscillation of theory between the establishment of historical absolutes and aesthetic subjectivism. There is in these pluralistic practices (whether historicized or rationalized) a suspension of ethics as a practice situated within the complexities of life as it is lived and an imposition of a morality predicated on the unquestioned acceptance of select architectural and urban traditions in concert with an aesthetic relativism.

The Contextualists cannot be understood as a monolithic group any more than Historicists or Rationalists can; perhaps even less so because many whom we call Historicists or Rationalists can be regarded as having Contextualist sympathies. In essence the Contextualists accept both the ahistorical typological ideals of the Rationalists and the more circumstantially oriented contextual/historical determinism of Historicists. They have given the status of theoretical foundation to the perpetual dialectic of constancy versus change (type versus context). Like the Rationalists they cite the city as the necessary theater of architectural activity and construe it within somewhat strict formal categories. Again like the Rationalists, the Contextualists are engaged incessantly in a series of dialectical operations, however, they perceive these through the fundamental screen of the two-dimensional figure/ground representation and resolve them once and for all by an authoritarian act of the designer. This is similar to a schematization of the design task made by Robert Adam in the eighteenth century and which helped to establish some of the principles of the Picturesque movement. Adam advocated that design be considered as dependent upon the interaction of various dialectical pairs to produce an architecture that made a complete scene like those of landscape painting.[42] In this light it should be remembered that Colin Rowe's contextualism derives in part from his simultaneous observations on modernist painting and traditional landscape garden planning. The result is his conclusion that the latter bears a number of formalistic resemblances to modernist compositional strategies of the collage.

There is an irony in the development of this approach. It was originally conceived both as a critique of the narrow technological preoccupations and simplistic global planning programs of many of the moderns and as an attempt to redeem the spatial order of the traditional city. Yet one may have to conclude that at the scale of the city, the milieu to which contextualism is expressly directed, the presumption of the architect as the authoritative explainer and interpreter of culture through space and form, substitutes a cultural/aesthetic technology for a mechanistic/behaviorist one.

Rowe closes *Collage City* with the proposition that we extend to the present in modified form the nineteenth century Napoleonic idea that the city should be a museum:

[The museum] came into existence in order to protect and display a plurality of physical manifestations representing a plurality of states of mind—all assumed to be in some degree valuable; and, if its evident functions and pretentions were liberal, if the concept of museum therefore implied some kind of ethical ballast, hard to specify but inherent in the institution itself (again the emancipation of society through self-knowledge?), if, to repeat, it was a mediating concept, then it is in terms analogous to the museum that one might postulate a possible solution for the more eminent problems of the contemporary city.[43]

The museum arose as a public institution out of a very complex web of events in the late eighteenth century (along with prisons, schools, and hospitals). Each of these institutions in its own way differed from its forerunners in serving as a site for the observation, correction, and improvement of its occupants. In the case of art and the museum this latter, the museum, was to provide a place for the determination of both the authenticity and interpretive accuracy of the artifactual objects that it contained. It was to act as a stimulus for the general cultural improvement of the public. These institutions of the eighteenth and nineteenth centuries were conceived as instruments of that ideology of knowledge epitomized by Kant and Hegel. There is a latent moral imperative to them[44] which Rowe rightly, though parenthetically, recognizes. The museum presumed to speak with authority

for the art object's creator; it did not, however, elucidate the author's original intentions (which may not be so important to us compared to what the artifactual object is), but the museum's own interpretation of those intentions. In other words, the museum acted to force works of art out of their disquieting silence, their mythopoeic potential, and compelled them to speak, but only within the terms of a representation which the museum sanctions. The museum, however, does not simply give legitimacy to art; it makes it. The museum dislocates the artifact and inserts it in a heterogeneous context foreign to the artifact's original situation; it arrests the trajectory of the artifact's being and provokes the rhetorical question which Gadamer asks in his essay, "Aesthetics and Hermeneutics":

Is it really the case that a work of art, which comes out of a past or alien life-world and is transferred into our historically educated world, becomes a mere object of aesthetic-historical enjoyment and says nothing more of what it originally had to say?[45]

The courtyard of the Ecole des Beaux-Arts in the nineteenth century, cited earlier in this essay, is a potent graphic illustration of the museum's power as an institution to provoke uncritical pluralism.

André Malraux, in his concept of the "Museum Without Walls," suggested that through photography art in all its forms, from all times and all places, can be ubiquitously manifest in the present.[46] One might even suppose from this assertion that photography is the instrument *par excellence* for realizing Hegelian absolute knowledge. Colin Rowe, as has already been discussed, can be construed to be suggesting something akin to this in projecting the development of architecture and the city as monumental forces of cultural recapitulation. The pluralistic, heterogeneous collecting action of the collage is seen as a kind of designer's analogue to the museum. Both the formulations of Rowe and Malraux recognize clearly the plurality and relativism of contemporary perceptions yet seem to ground them-

43
Colin Rowe and Fred Koetter, *Collage City* (Cambridge: MIT Press, 1978), 136.

44
Michel Foucault, *Discipline and Punish*, trans. Alan Sheridan, (New York: Vintage, 1979) and *Power/Knowledge*, trans. C. Gordon, L. Marshall, J. Mepham, and K. Soper (New York: Pantheon, 1980), especially "Body/Power" and "The Eye of Power."

45
Gadamer, "Aesthetics and Hermeneutics," in *Philosophical Hermeneutics*, p. 97, asks this question as a way to force the issue certainly not of the importance of original meaning but rather as a way to argue that a work of art is not bound by its historical horizon; that it always comes forth as a challenge to interpretation and understanding. He argues that a work of art therefore "occupies a timeless present" (p. 96 and p. 104) and I would agree further, but in less absolute terms, that it is persistent intervention. It is valuable to contrast this with André Malraux, *The Voices of Silence*, trans. Stuart Gilbert (Princeton: Princeton University Press: 1978), 14, 15:

The effect of the museum was . . . to divest works of art of their functions. It . . . ruled out associations of sanctity, qualities of adornment and possession, of likeness and imagination. Each exhibit is a representation of something, differing from the thing itself, this specific difference being its raison d'etre *. . . The art museum invites criticism of each of the expressions of the world it brings together; and a query as to what they have in common.*

46
Malraux, *Voices of Silence*, 17–46.

47
Baudrillard, *Simulations*, 146.

48
Jean Baudrillard, "The Ecstasy of Communication," in *The Anti-Aesthetic*, ed. Hal Foster (Port Townsend, Wash.: Bay Press 1983), 126–133.

selves in a faith that there is something to be authenticated by these formulations. Taken alone, the choice of illustrations for their respective books, with their preponderences of high culture, works already authenticated by the museum machine, may give some indications of their intentions. It is clear too that both see the museum as a kind of machine of reproduction. For both Rowe and Malraux it seems that art, architecture, and the city at their foundations are governed by form, that their form is what constitutes their authenticity and this form can legitimately be reproduced and extended everywhere because it is this form which in its presence educates, instructs, and informs us about the enduring essence of humanity expressed in its art. The historicity of a work of art; its situationality; its existence as difficult intervention in our lives, rather than either amiable fellow citizen or evangelist; its quality as a specific action in relation to a specific material, subject to interpretation and reinterpretation—in short its intersection with our experience—has less relevance than the power of its form to invoke the presence of the pluralistic, relativistic culture which produced it. The power of simulation, of infinite reproduction, seems for both Rowe and Malraux an essential property for the world-become-museum.

The impulse of the museum strongly colors many of current architecture's theoretical positions. Architecture seen within historicist, rationalist and contextualist discourses as the concatenation of various historical fragments and/or constructed upon a foundation of architectural a prioris with the intent of cultural-aesthetic edification is virtually the apotheosis of the museum. The museum is a powerful institution of the ideology of knowledge. It seeks to recover and explain the origins of works of art, to collect, catalog, and classify everything magnetized by its gaze and grant to these works legitimacy and authenticity.

Our world is rapidly becoming one where the force of knowledge, the desire to know, is a God-machine, omnipresent and equipresent. It is constituted of randomly interacting signifiers, messages, images, and representations. In his book *Simulations* Jean Baudrillard has examined the extreme consequences of this. The speed with which these signifiers, etc., are produced/reproduced is so rapid that a clear ordering of events can no longer exist. What is produced cannot be clearly distinguished from its reproduction. In our world all the values and objects which once seemed to have substance or solidity have become shades, they are weightless, not just floating around us but we around them. Everything worth knowing about them or us, every possible experience of them, must be inscribable in a code which will immediately be decoded and recoded. Because of this Baudrillard claims that we do not inhabit anymore reality but a completely synthetic "hyperreality" where "the real is not only what can be reproduced, but *that which is already always reproduced*."[47]

Baudrillard does not seem necessarily to like the world he describes, but he does suggest that its seduction is irresistible, that it is a terror which fascinates completely.[48] The real has been vanquished by the instantaneous repetition of its own image, by an infinity of realities. Nietzsche argued that the apparent is "evidence of the senses" and is falsified into the real by "Reason." However, the apparent has been undone as he realized it would be (see note 4) with the death of God and the ascendance of the God-machine. The hyperreal is the hyper-rational. Where Kant saw that there is a connection between what can be known and our human capacity for knowledge (i.e., a connection between the territory and the map we can make of it), we see that once such a connection is made it can only be a matter of time before the territory of that unknown, which is nevertheless ultimately knowable, disappears by becoming known and only the map remains. The world disappears and the museum remains.

Authenticity is a major problem for the museum. A multitude of hard questions arises when regarding the authenticity of an object. Walter Benjamin's observation on authenticity and politics quoted earlier in this essay is certainly indicative of the contemporary crisis of authenticity. There is today both a longing for the authentic in the work of art and a sense of its eclipse. And if authenticity can no longer reside in objects how do they acquire significance? Benjamin argued that it was through the practice of politics. Yet the notion of politics is itself in crisis, as was also established earlier in this essay.

For architecture the consequence of the hyperreal, the world of simulation is, foremost, the demise of traditional dialectical categories of urban and architectural legitimacy. These are inside/outside, fabric/monument, street/square, and particularly the tenuous relationship between public and private. They are the very ones which many historicists, rationalists, contextualists, regionalists, and others wish to recover in theory and practice. The irony is, as has been discussed above, that their recovery can only exist as simulation. Baudrillard argues that all such considerations have been invaded and their substance mutated by the statistical inquisition (which is neither dialectical nor discursive) of the public opinion poll, the market study, the mass media, the panoply of contemporary simulations of political action. But how, if politics has supplanted the authentic, can we speak of a simulation of politics?

The theoreticians discussed in this essay's text and notes (as well as others who have not been mentioned) have not been consciously complicit in this great leveling process. They certainly see themselves as fundamentally opposed to such developments for they are reformers, they have a true or truer vision, a vision which continues the message of the past into the present; theirs is a vision of a proper culture. But outside the comforting confines of the architectural culture, which is itself highly susceptible to the suasions of simulation, these visions are understood as other options in the giant statistically simulated politics of our world, the hyperreal universe.

In this world not only is the very notion of authenticity seen as invalid, and all attempts to recover it abortive, but critical reflective thought appears likewise to be irrelevant. It was this critical thought which once called into question the appropriateness of authenticity as a legitimate concept in the production of art and ideas. Why bother to reflect, why investigate, why take political action when all knowledge has become a matter of massaging or being massaged by the abundance of simulations and stimulations; when the rapidity of the hyperreal translates all thoughtful action into obsolescence? Daily we witness all this, and it is not really an issue whether it occurs with the global intensity that Baudrillard suggests. We are passive witnesses but virtuallly impelled to comply, to conform, to typify, to testify, and to participate; but above all to be neutral.

The untimeliness, the awkwardness, the inappropriateness, the otherness of authenticity seem now almost to be called for, the very notion of the authentic being both paradoxical and disruptive. To be authentic is to be removed from the field of forces which grant authenticity. But that is not all of it. If we look at the etymology of this word we find that it derives from the Greek word *authenteo* which meant both to have power over and to kill (the self or others). Thus the authentic may be interpreted not as a way to bestow legitimacy to things, but as a quality characterized by a continuous, active, thoughtful, and resistive engagement with the world. And in this way the authentic must be profoundly ethical. Consequently the authentic will not be found in models, types, codes, prescriptions, systems, religions, objects, original causes, or any other simulation. The authentic is a minority utterance which disregards the authority of the classifications and categorizations of prevailing culture. It disdains, laughs at, the neutralizing self-consciousness which is imposed by such culture, the State which superintends it and at the utter privatization of experience that this State's simulated politics affords. It makes its own gravity and counteracts it. It is true *ethos*, radically local but not regional, always on the move, searching, avoiding both the stable equilibrium of the universal and the metastable one of the relative.

Acknowledgements
I wish to thank two faculty colleagues, Ken Warriner and Nicole Pertuiset, for their discourse, constant challenges, and provocations to my own thinking. They are deeply ethical people.

Perhaps we cannot rely anymore on God or Nature or Heroes or Absolute Knowledge or the Essential Goodness of Humanity or the Text, but we can laugh the laugh that brings body and mind together and breaks them up. It is the laugh of "He," the other Diderot, who is not just Rameau's nephew, but who is also both Diderot and not Diderot. "He" is that sly "He," the joker, who when he first appears meets "I" with the laugh of recognition: "Aha, there you are Mr. Philosopher," and the "He" who, having the last (truly "last") word of this dialogue, ends as he begins saying "He laughs best who laughs last." "He" of course is the "He" "He".

David Bell is an associate professor of architecture at Rensselaer Polytechnic Institute. He is the author of numerous articles on architectural theory and was the executive editor of the *Journal of Architectural Education* from 1985 to 1989.

Garth Rockcastle

ETHICS IN PARADISE

1. *Andrew Leicester, Paradise, 1985. Fountain steps with silhouetted women.*
2. *Overview of the prison.*
3. *Overview with the trellis and watercourse.*
4. *Double-faced heads on the trellis.*

In the winter of 1985, the Art in Public Places program of the Colorado Council on the Arts and Humanities announced an open competition to artists interested in a commission to design and install works of public art at "Old Max," the maximum-security prison in Canon City, Colorado. The published request solicited proposals from artists for an artwork that would "ameliorate the imposing flat surface of the boiler house wall" and "create a focus for the area which will become a significant humanizing element within the walls (of the prison), an artifact with which all prisoners must empathise." [1]

The prison was undergoing a $12.5 million renovation and addition, and $125,000 was made available for Art in Public Places, the largest amount ever granted for a single project by the seven-year-old program. Some seventy

artists from across the country submitted their qualifications and slides of past work to the nine-member selection committee for review. Andrew Leicester of Minneapolis and Athena Tacha of New York were notified that they were the finalists on April 1, 1985. Each was paid $2500 to prepare a schematic design, narrative description and rationale, and a budget estimate for the larger of two commissions ($80,000), to be sited inside the prison walls. The other artwork ($35,000), sited outside the prison walls, was awarded to Chris Byars, a Colorado artist. On July 9, 1985, Tacha and Leicester presented their proposals to the selection committee. Thirty-eight-year-old Andrew Leicester was awarded the commission for a work entitled *Paradise*. He began work on his project in May 1986 and completed it in less than three months.

1
Page 2 in the "Art In Public Places" publication of the Colorado Territorial Correctional Facilities.

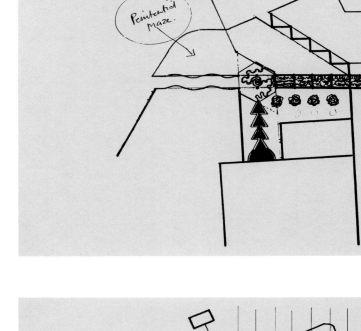

5. *Detail of gargoyle fountain.*
6, 7, 8. *Andrew Leicester.* Paradise. *1985. Design sketches showing the evolution of the design.*

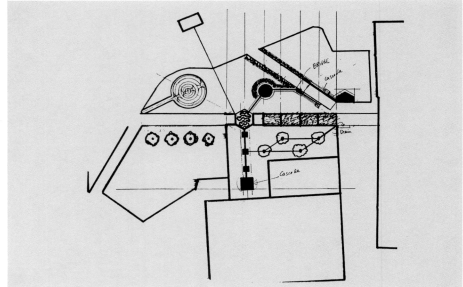

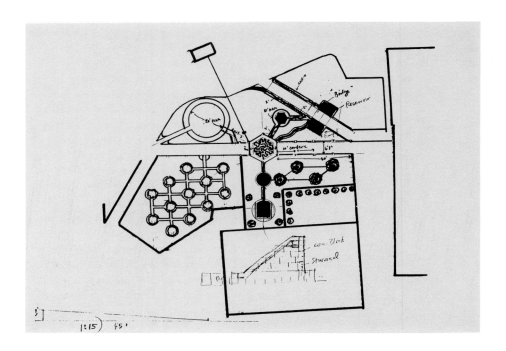

The idea of *Paradise*, from the ancient Persian *pairidaiza*, a walled garden, was an appropriately ironic starting point for Leicester and consistent with his interest in metaphoric irony in his projects. Leicester's early sketches (Figs. 6 to 8) show that he had consistently pursued the idea of embellishing (with a water feature, plantings, and decorative elements) the circulatory linkages between adjacent structures in the courtyard. Since this is an area of movement, prisoners are not allowed to sit or stand or congregate idly. The solar orientation of the space makes it very hot in the summer. The primary components of the initial schematic design (an arbor for vines and a water course) helped most to humanize the space and were immediately approved by the selection committee, the prison architect, and the prison authorities (Fig. 9). Leicester then began fabrication and construction of the project.

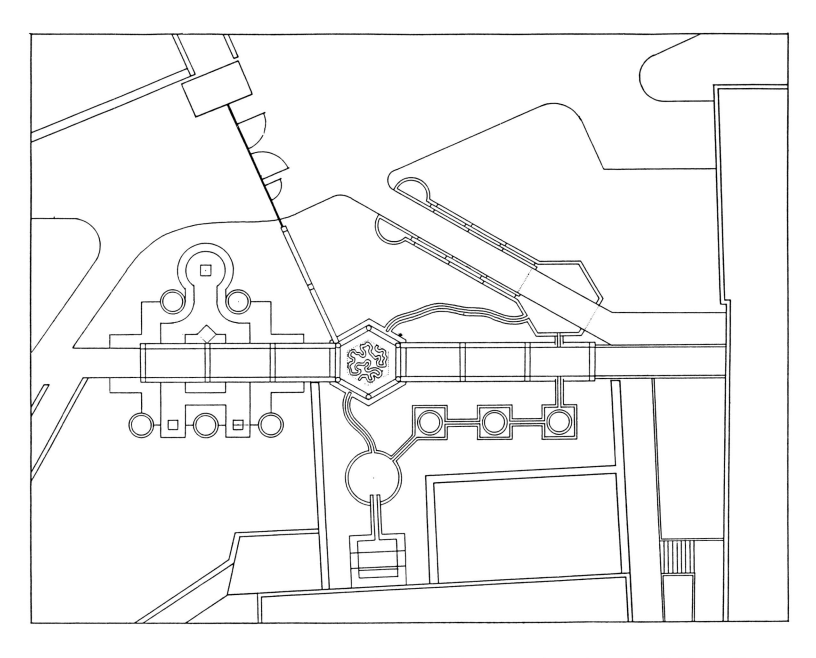

9. *Andrew Leicester, Garden plan submitted for the competition.*

Leicester's process has always placed primacy on assimilating and responding to the specifics of a site. Therefore, after winning the design competition, the artist developed and altered his design ideas. This can be noted in comparing the approved plan to the final photographs. While the plan evolved and changed considerably (see notes and changes on Figs. 10 and 11), various expressive features took shape in the final weeks of the project's implementation. Clearly some of Leicester's most keen understandings and resonant images emerged during his work inside the prison, weeks after the completion of the original design in Minneapolis. His daily experience of entering and leaving the prison, of talking to prisoners and guards, of reflecting simultane-

ously on prison and outside life, gave him new raw material to interpret and represent. This raw material resulted in several expressive features that were intended to express empathy for the imprisoned: (1) double-faced heads conveyed the contrasting perceptions of the imprisoned, (2) distressed gargoyles spewed forth their need for relief, and (3) silhouetted women (representations of those whom the prisoners left behind) stood in gestures of grief, longing, and betrayal. A pole-vaulting wind sock and the elusive footsteps of the Jailhouse Rock(er) conveyed sympathy for the prisoner's pervasive dreams of escape. Leicester's evolving reflection on these and other features are evident in the pages of his sketchbook (notes and Figs. 6 to 11).

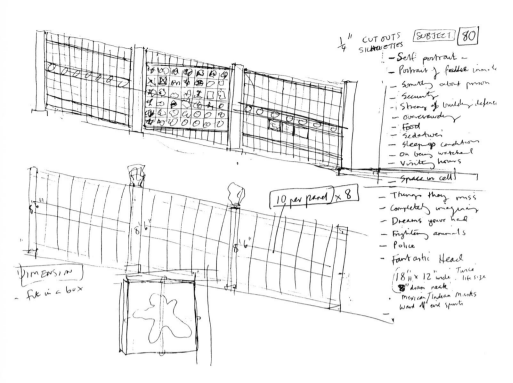

10. *Andrew Leicester, Sketch from field notebook.*
11. *Andrew Leicester, Sketch from field notebook.*
12. *Gargoyle fountains.*

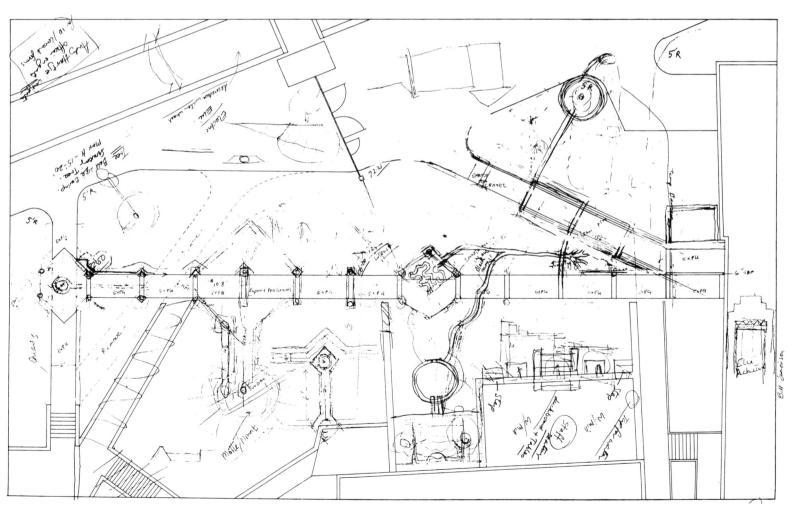

13. *Andrew Leicester*. Prospect V-III.

14. *Andrew Leicester*. Cobumora.

2
Several journals have featured Leicester's recent projects: *International Sculpture*. No. 11/12, 1986; *Arts Magazine*, No. 1, 1987; *Progressive Architecture*, No. 10, 1984; *Landscape Architecture* No. 1/2, 1986; among others.

In its conception and final embodiment, *Paradise* was consistent with the interests and process Leicester had developed since 1974. His interests over the past decade have evolved from an earlier fascination with the shifting kinetic perceptions of abstract forms ("Minnesota Highway" and "Diamond") to creative interpretation of contextual and narrative sources, such as the site's social and physical history, mythology, and reason for being. Because his later work is more germane to this discussion, I have included two of these projects to illustrate his development.

Prospect V-III (1982) is a miners' memorial in Frostburg, Maryland (Fig. 13). *Cobumora* (1985) is a sculptural courtyard at Washington State University (Fig. 14). Both projects set out to interpret and reveal to the visitor their respective reasons for being and their historic origins. Leicester uses highly charged, even literal, forms, spaces, and surface detailing in these works. Such direct and aggressive expression has become a hallmark of Leicester's work over the past several years.[2] His utilization of overt symbolic elements in a spatial, collage-like manner operates as both an index of quotations (most of them ironic or tragic) and a running commentary about them, through his use of juxtaposition and distortion.

In *Prospect V-III* Leicester's various rooms, or cottages, represent the noble but tragic progression of the coal miners' work-life from infancy to retirement along a ground-incising axis from beneath the earth to a tower and beyond. At *Cobumora*, an outdoor classroom or study area at the college of veterinary medicine at Washington State University, Leicester utilizes ancient and modern animal symbols and myths to comment and reflect on the peculiar relationship humans have forged with the animal world throughout history.

* * * *

While the work on *Paradise* was in progress, the site-inspired changes and embellishments Leicester made to the original design proposal received support and approval from the prison's superintendent, Mark McGoff, and the director of the Art in Public Places program, Gail Goldman. These two were the artist's official contacts on the project. On July 11, 1986, Goldman wrote a letter to the State Department of Corrections' physical plant manager announcing the project's near-completion. She inspected the site with McGoff and

Ellen Sollod, the director of the Colorado Council on the Arts and Humanities, and wrote about their impressions with glowing praise: "Wow, wow, wow! . . . very exciting . . . quality art, quality design, quality craftsmanship . . . Mark McGoff is delighted; [He] hopes to show slides of the project to his colleagues at the annual conference on state correctional facilities . . . I think you will be pleased . . . I think you will be impressed."[3]

On July 18, Bill Tripp, the department's facilities planner, wrote back to say that "the Department of Corrections is not pleased with the final product . . . Leicester went far beyond . . . what was agreed to . . . We are not impressed . . . Furthermore there are elements of the project that we will request be changed at no expense to the State of Colorado."[4] Several state legislators were notified about the work and invited to visit the site for an inspection. The press was then invited to record legislator and departmental objections and to bring the issue to the public's attention. The controversy compelled the Council on the Arts to reconvene the selection committee to review if there were any grounds for a breach of contract by Andrew Leicester for his embellishments. After considerable debate the committee accepted the project, requiring only a minor safety revision. Tripp and the disgruntled legislators soon discovered that this approval left them without the legal power to either remove the elements they disliked or to deny final payment to the artist.

Popular press coverage of the project routinely featured comments like "the whole thing just stinks,"[5] "it is so grotesque you can't imagine it,"[6] or "the grass and the trees are lovely, the rest of it is awful."[7] Journalists capitalized on the drama of the reaction story and simultaneously presented the artwork in a negative light. In a similar way, the largely conservative legislators spoke of *Paradise* in desperate and revealing social and cultural terms. Their public comments included: "People aren't put in prison to enjoy art"[8]; "Do you really think the average prisoner in the prison was going to reflect on medieval heads?"[9]; and "It's a very dreary looking piece of art, but I feel that's appropriate for a prison."[10] Some legislators argued that controversial art belonged more in the private sector and tax-supported artwork should be "more on the middle ground, reflecting the mainstream values of the culture and the institution where it appears."[11] Newspapers routinely showed only close-up and out-of-context photographs of its more sensational fragments, as well as these comments.

Public reaction followed in the form of letters to the editor, often contemptuous in tone and full of inflammatory banter. However, since the artwork itself was inaccessible, the public reaction was based entirely on press accounts. Such clamor, without any direct experience or firsthand knowledge, made impossible any balanced or healthy public discussion or understanding of the project. Leicester and art critics were inescapably put on the defensive.

Prisoner commentary was notably absent from popular press coverage of *Paradise*, presumably because prisoners might see the work as a victory over the society that oppressed them. Only *Muse, The Arts Newspaper for Colorado*, explored prisoner and guard reaction and artist intent. Members of the public would have been fascinated to discover that prisoners and guards were both split in their responses to the work. After only a few weeks of exposure, comments ranged from "it's obnoxious, it's racist, it's not art at all," to "I like it, it's different, it's not boring, and most of what's around here is set up to make sure you get good and bored."[12] When one prisoner was asked how he liked it, he humorously responded, "Not so much that I'd try pulling a bank job

DANCE #18: LATIN HUSTLE VARIATION
(HIS VERSION)

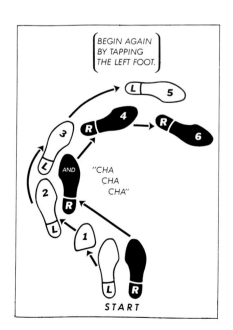

3
Letter from Gail M. Goldman to Ed Brown, Physical Plant Manager, Dept. of Corrections, on 11 July 1986.

4
Letter from Bill Tripp, Facilities Planner (18 July 1986), to Gail M. Goldman.

5
State Senator Cliff Dodge, quoted in Michelle P. Fulcher, "But Is It Art: $75,000 Sculpture at Prison Angers Lawmakers," *The Denver Post*, 23 July 1986.

6
State Senator Clair Traylor, quoted in John Sanko, "Prison Artwork Labeled Gallery of Horrors," *Rocky Mountain News*, 23 July 1986.

7
State Representative Bonnie Allison, quoted in John Sanko, "Prison Artwork Labeled Gallery of Horrors," *Rocky Mountain News*, 23 July 1986.

8
State Senator Raymond Powers, "Capitol Comments," *Fountain (Colorado) Ads & News*, 30 July 1986.

15. *Andrew Leicester, Photocopy of dance steps from field notebook.*

9

State Representative Bonnie Allison, quoted in Berny Morson, "Lawmaker Vows Changes in Arts Funding," *Rocky Mountain News*, 20 August 1986.

10

State Representative Elwood Gillis, quoted in J. R. Thompson, "Opposition Growing Against Tax Money for Art in State Buildings," *Rocky Ford County Gazette*, 31 July 1986.

11

State Senator Jim Rizzuto, quoted in J.R. Thompson, "Opposition Growing Against Tax Money for Art in State Buildings," *Rocky Ford County Gazette*, 31 July 1986.

12

Ed Quillen, "Paradise with a Prison View," *Muse, The Arts Newspaper for Colorado*, No. 10/11, 1986.

13

Ibid.

14

These comments by Leicester were made to me during October 1987.

16. *Footsteps of the "Jailhouse Rocker."*

when I get out of here just so I'd have the money to put one in my backyard. No way. But if it was in my yard, I'd sure leave it there. It's fun to watch." [13] These are important and revealing reactions for the public to have heard.

While Leicester explains that "any perceived racism is tragically misconstrued," he is also disappointed (though not surprised or troubled) that some inmates hold negative views of the work. "Some controversy and discussion among the prisoners about what the work represents is one of my objectives," he said. "I wanted to express my empathy while simultaneously making the pervasive and complex tragedies surrounding their imprisonment evident to all who cared to consider. Some, though, may not appreciate being reminded, while others prefer not to think about the prisoners in human or compassionate terms." [14]

* * * *

The difficulties facing projects like *Paradise* are becoming all too pervasive for controversial or provocative works of public art and architecture today. The hostility directed toward the work by politicians, presenting themselves as arbiters of public taste and watchdogs for public waste, was clearly fueled by the press. Local newspapers and national weeklies distorted the story by publishing only the negative comments and printing sensational headlines and eyecatching photos. The public was continually misled and denied a meaningful discourse or understanding of the project. Tragically, the

public was being sent only messages that attracted attention, leaving all others unspoken.

There are two equally extreme and perverse public perceptions of most public art and its artists. The first chooses to view the artist as an egomaniac and/or cultural subversive. The artist, in this view, is someone who should be prevented from getting public commissions (and restricted to the museum) or whose work should be regulated or edited to that which is acceptable. The second extreme public reaction is that any *real* artist can do no wrong, in private or in public. Good art is good art, no matter where it is or what it is about. This is the perception of the artist as visionary/priest. Here the artist is viewed as the automatic minister of aesthetic truth and enlightened work. Both public extremes are problematic because they view the artist as someone other than a legitimate or integrated citizen.

Likewise, contemporary artists often develop one of two extreme views to deal with the public's reaction to public art. The first is for the artist to work without regard for public reactions and challenges to his work. This view tends to regard the public as unworthy or incapable of appreciating art. The artist either becomes callous to public reaction or chooses to pursue only private or controlled settings for his work. This view can even find negative public reaction to be an indication of the work's aesthetic merit. The second extreme reaction is for the artist to pursue non-controversial imagery and subject matter in order to be popular or avoid public challenge. In this case the artist thinks of the immediate public as an omnipresent jury or market to be pleased. This reduces the artist to the role of public servant or seller of goods. Critical insights, worthwhile challenge, and artistic risk are generally absent in the work of such artists. All of these views of public art are unacceptable, since they stifle the numerous and critical opportunities for a meaningful engagement of the fertility of circumstance.

Leicester's inclination to work openly and directly with subjects, issues, and images that most artists either lack insight into or choose to avoid has provoked outrage from those who view the role of public art to be mere embellishment or abstract/minimal gesture. Interest in Leicester's site-specific public work naturally comes from those who view the artist's expressive rights and responsibilities to be broader than a sponsor's narrow interests, more far-reaching than a safe or conservative political agenda, and deeper than just aesthetic concerns. His sense of responsibility to these matters manifests itself literally in representational ways. The fact that the content of *Paradise* was so clearly evident in its appearance made possible the objections and negative sentiment expressed by those who objected to it.

Both the public and the artist have a responsibility to respect and maintain the ethics of a public/artistic discourse. While the institutional circumstances of *Paradise* are clearly unique, the opportunities and responsibilities surrounding its process and discussion are not. This project reveals the need to examine the ethical implications intrinsic to public works of art, including architecture, and to improve on the conduct of both artists and the public. Too often, the discussion of such matters focuses on the responsibilities the artist or designer has to the public. The inverse is also important. Vital public art can only grow out of an informed, open, and sincere public.

The artist and the public are pivotal because they comprise the essential figure/ground, or reciprocal, relationship for the success of any public work. Historic "publics" have given as much to the public art discipline as have its artists. The discipline in turn is able to contribute more to the artist and the public that invests in it. Sponsors of accomplished contemporary works of public art and architecture should be open to the aesthetic and public possibilities that extend beyond their personal vision. While the scale of public work rarely permits it to be completely free from acknowledging sponsorship, it must attempt to transcend it. Real artistic and public exploration of the goals for, and potential in, sponsorship of true public art, raises the probability of enlightening both the sponsor and the work.

Neither use nor the user should dictate artistic concern. Addressing use in a respectful, even direct (yet artful) way can offer creative potential. However, on occasion, a thoughtful challenge to provoke, even subvert, conventional or expected use can offer real artistic and cultural value. It is the ethical responsibility of the artist to seize the initiatives for creating artful use value, and the responsibility of the user to support artistic interest in use beyond mere accommodation. Any artwork is seen against an existing site and at the same time changes or remakes it. The artist and public have a responsibility to understand both what a site is and what it could be. These site conditions establish some of the best testing grounds for the exercise of these ethical responsibilities and standards.

It would be naive to link ethical practice or conduct directly to aesthetics in any case, but important relationships between the two do exist. The developed creativity and insight of the artist are critical to the success of any project. But, without the adoption of ethical standards of conduct toward the various constituents to guide and inform the artist or designer and the public, failure (i.e., trivial or destructive work) on some level is more likely. It is more possible, however, that the ethical and gifted artist could do compelling work even though the public constituents are irresponsible, than if the reverse were true.

The public artist shares with the architect the ethical challenges and conditions of working in the public realm. Any movement toward realizing our ethical responsibilities as artists/architects and as a public moves us to a more enhanced cultural condition within which aesthetic objectives (and higher ethical standards) can better thrive. Both ethical and aesthetic values hinge on such movement, not on those quantifiable measures. The professional artist and architect are granted the privilege of self-regulation in our society, which obligates us to maintain an ongoing discussion of the values that guide our disciplines and link us in meaningful ways to our culture. Each of us has the right and responsibility to determine the values upon which we base our work. This base is active, not static, and should remain open to revision and maintenance.

Leicester's *Paradise* is perhaps more important for the ethical commitment it demonstrates to pursuing empathy and insight into the project's unique circumstances than it is as an aesthetic masterpiece. Its capacity to render transparent the ethical challenges of contemporary practice is most remarkable. In any case, *Paradise* is a pleasant and provocative garden in an oppressive and deprived place. In imagining the potential demise of the program, Irene Clurman, art critic for the *Rocky Mountain News*, asserted that it was a shame that Leicester's project received more public attention than the visual pollution problems of the "state where visual awareness is so low that ticky-tacky commercial developments and garish signage sprout everywhere, unhindered and evidently unnoticed." [15]

15
Irene Clurman, "Let Us Praise Public Sculpture," *Rocky Mountain News*, 1 August 1986.

Garth Rockcastle received his B. Arch. from The Pennsylvania State University in 1974 and an M. Arch. in Urban Design from Cornell University in 1976. He is an associate professor in the School of Architecture at the University of Minnesota, where he teaches architectural design and theory and urban design. In 1986 he established *Midgard*, a new journal of architectural theory and criticism. Since 1981, he has been a principal in the firm of Meyer, Scherer and Rockcastle, where he has collaborated with sculptor Andrew Leicester and other artists on a variety of projects and competitions.

Ambrogio Lorenzetti, Detail from Good Government, *fresco in the Palazzo Pubblico, Siena, c. 1338– 1339.*

Francis T. Ventre

REGULATION: A Realization of Social Ethics

Ethics as Design

Ethics and design are so densely inter-twined, so intimately interactive, that ethical issues in architectural pedagogy are almost always arise in the context of a specific design situation. There is, of course, the obligatory acknowledgement of "professional ethics" in the equally obligatory "professional practice" course late in the undergraduate's career. Thus sequestered, however, professional ethics is exposed to not nearly as much scrutiny as is the moral dimension of design work. Moral development, in other words, is—or should be—an important subsidiary outcome of an architectural education. Nor is this emergence of ethics out of design discourse surprising, when one considers that the first comprehensive theory of design (and one that remains, to my mind at least, the most succinct amd intellectually coherent) issued from Aristotle's *Nicomachean Ethics*.[1]

Ethics and design share more than a common intellectual ancestor, for what I would like to call the "design attitude" appears in the works of the principal ethicists throughout the development of western philosophy. By design attitude I mean, following Aristotle and C. S. Peirce and scores of moral philosophers between them, the proposing, effectuating, and evaluating of any action in terms of its consequences.[2] In other words, design is the fore-thought of purposive, intentional action and the consequences of that action are evaluated against the purposes and intentions that precipitated the action in the first place.

Not all design theorists subscribe to this definition of design. Nor, for that matter, are all ethicists consequentialists, believing that ethical matters are utterly contingent upon outcomes or results.[3] Consequentialism entails a position on social values analogous to the secular economic theories of the eighteenth century Utilitarians and the more obscure seventeenth century Christian pacifists who proposed, in the words of Ralph Cudworth, that "the greatest benevolence of every rational agent towards all constitutes the happiest state of all, and therefore the common good of all is the supreme law."[4]

While the teleologically disposed ethicists claim that things are right or moral if they have good consequences, ethicists of the obligation-ist or deontic persuasion take the view that there are absolutes in ethics, that some motives or attitudes—honesty, promise-keeping, respect for persons, and (an example from medical practice and research) "informed consent"—are *in themselves* morally right, and transcendently so, making of ethics an un-flinching duty rather than an exercise of discriminating judgments about anticipated outcomes. (The distinction, though, may be only momentary because, as Dewey argues,

1
Aristotle, *Nichomachean Ethics*, trans. M. Ostwald (Indianapolis: Bobbs-Merrill, 1962), passim.

2
C. S. Pierce, "What Pragmatism Is," *The Monist* 15 (1905):161–181. This article is reproduced in many of the anthologies on Pragmatism. One such is H. S. Thayer, ed., *Pragmatism: The Classic Writings* (New York: New American Library, 1970), 101–120.

3
These metaethical categories are distinguished, although often with slightly different terminology, in virtually every reference work or text on ethics. A recent exposition and one closer to the subject of this paper is T. L. Beauchamp and T. P. Pinkard, eds., *Ethics and Public Policy: An Introduction to Ethics* (Englewood Cliffs, N.J.: Prentice-Hall, 1983).

4
E. Flower, "Ethics of Peace," in *Dictionary of the History of Ideas*, ed. Philip P. Wiener, Vol. III (New York: Charles Scribner's Sons, 1973), 441.

"When it is recognized that 'motive' is but an abbreviated name for the attitude and pre-disposition towards ends which is embodied in action, all ground for making a sharp separation between motive and intention (foresight of consequences) falls away."[5]

With these "metaethical" categories in mind, a rereading of the design-theoretical literature, both the abundant prescriptive exhortations and explanatory treatises and the infrequent descriptive accounts, might be instructive. Such a review exceeds the scope of the present article, but a consideration of one notable designer's deliberations allows us to examine the stability of these metaethical categories for architecture.

Alvar Aalto articulated his own design ethics in a 1940 article published in America, one that deserves more attention from Aalto's acolytes in the architectural academy.[6] (Perhaps it is because Aalto's completed works are so sensually gratifying, so compellingly beautiful, that we all slight him by not attending to what he wrote and said.) Aalto believed that the "only way to humanize architecture" was to use "methods which always are a combination of technical, physical, and psychological phenomena, never any one of them alone."[7] (This invocation of a mandatory method adumbrates an obligational ethic.) Moreover, continued Aalto, "technical functionalism is correct only if enlarged to cover even the psychophysical field." Aalto illustrated his argument with recollections, design sketches and photographs of the Paimio Tuberculosis Sanitorium (1929–33) and the Viipuri Municipal Library (1930–35). With a modesty emboldened by ethical belief, Aalto argued that the responsible designer must inflict no harm on building users or even provide environments unsuitable for their use. His specific example was the library's "indirect daylighting" using conical concrete skylights. Aalto was drawn to this design to preempt an ethically unacceptable alternative: "To provide [an unmodulated] natural or an artificial light which destroys the human eye or is unsuitable for its use means reactionary architecture even if the building should otherwise be of high constructive value." (Here Aalto appears, in ethical terms, to be a consequentialist.)

In this article Aalto exercised himself over the total effects of the library's lighting scheme and the sanitorium's patient rooms, and not on their visual appearance alone. Aalto acknowledged that "[t]he examples mentioned here are

very tiny problems. But they are very close to the human being and hence become more important than problems of much larger scope." Coming "very close to the human being" signifies Aalto's defection from the abstract utilitarianism promulgated by CIAM and which he had himself earlier proselytized among his fellow Finns. Aalto participated in the 1929 CIAM Conference on the Minimum Dwelling held in Frankfurt.[8] The very title of the conference suggests a utilitarian maximizing of total benefits (or goods) and minimizing of disbenefits (or harms), all at the level of total social aggregates. There was, moreover, in CIAM (and in *die Neue Sachlichkeit* (the "New Objectivity")) ideology of the time) the obligationist focus on a method that would override all other considerations, such as the evaluation of results. Returning from Frankfurt, Aalto conveyed these ideas in lectures, articles, and

5
Beauchamp and Pinkard, *Ethics and Public Policy*, passim.

6
J. Dewey, *Theory of the Moral Life* (New York: Holt, Rinehart and Winston, 1960), 6.

7
Alvar Aalto, "The Humanizing of Architecture," *Technology Review* 43, No. 1 (1940):14ff. All Aalto quotes are from this article.

Aalto scholar Richard Peters of the University of California, Berkeley, told me, while we were discussing this *Technology Review* article, that Aalto had expressed himself much more vividly on these distinctions in several unpublished writings.

2. *Alvar Aalto, Paimio Sanitorium, patients' room.*

8
Internationale Kongresse für Neues Bauen, *Die Wohnung für das Existenzminimum* (Frankfurt, 1930). This document provides comparative analyses of typical plans as well as articles and is reproduced, with plan annotations in English, in O. M. Ungers and L. Ungers, eds., *Documents of Modern Architecture* (Nendeln, Liechtenstein: Kraus Reprint, 1979).

9
Alvar Aalto "Rationalism and Man," lecture to the Annual meeting of the Swedish Craft Society, 9 May 1935, and condensed in W. C. Miller, *Alvar Aalto: An Annotated Bibliography* (New York: Garland, 1984), item 30, p. 15.

10
Pierce's later, more mature articulation of his consequentialism as it relates specifically to ethics takes this view. It may be found in Pierce's *Collected Papers*, ed. Charles Hartschorne and Paul Weiss (Cambridge: Belknap Press of Harvard University Press, 1960–66), 5: 411–437.

11
W. F. May, "Professional Ethics: Setting, Terrain, and Teacher," In *Ethics Teaching in Higher Education*, ed. D. Callahan and S. Bok (New York: Plenum, 1980), chap. 9, pp. 205–241.

12
May, "Professional Ethics," 238.

newspaper interviews as part of his early efforts to spur Finnish society toward its rendezvous with the modern sensibility.

Within ten years, however, Aalto would shift his attention (and allegiance) from CIAM's abstract statistical aggregates to specific users, seemingly one at a time.[9] Is this moving from one extreme to the other simply apostasy? Or is it the designer's ethical syncretism? The latter would be an axiological counterpart to the eclecticism of Aalto's architectural style, his coming to terms with the sense of place and tradition that the then-ascendant International Style aesthetic denied. I believe it is the latter because, as he did stylistically, Aalto in this case fused opposite tendencies into one. In metaethical terms, he adopted the consequentialist approach that renders evaluative choice or judgment according to results, but, going beyond that he appears to have said that even the least harm to the user should override any other consideration—for instance, "high constructive value," as he put it—and rule out the design action entirely. That seems to be an absolute obligational ethic—a designer's general duty, if you will—that overrides any specific consequentialist consideration.[10]

What concerned Aalto was the extent to which designers, whose professional acts after all bring consequences to others, should be accountable to those others (at Paimio, the patients and their technical agents, the acousticians; at Viipuri, the readers and their technical agents, the visual psychophysicists). This concern prescribed both a universalized obligation and a critical sense of consequences relevant to a specific situational context. Aalto's ethical stance, however, runs counter to some strongly held and long-standing beliefs of practicing or aspiring design professionals. Designers become designers, in part, because it is a professional role that provides a vehicle for personal fulfillment in a time when the organization of economic life threatens to relegate individual self-actualization to the nighttime and weekend fringes of a world that Wordsworth complains is "too much with us." If I read Aalto correctly, that fulfillment cannot come at the cost of harm to others. The proposition that the gifted and talented are exempt from such rules of proper conduct would have dismayed Aalto as much as it energized Nietzsche and his present-day epigones. But professional designers do submit to such rules; it is part of what distinguishes professionals from amateurs.

Professional Ethics

Universally accepted definitions of "the professions" all refer to the professional's concern with the welfare of the wider society in which the professional operates. Personal, individual advantage—even in the sublimated forms of aesthetic gratification or technical mastery—is not to be gained at the expense of the welfare of the larger social unit. Aalto, as we read, went further: for him, no single user should suffer. These sentiments are what distinguish the professional practice of design from, say, the amateur's pursuits in sculpture or woodworking (arts and crafts that have manifest similarities to the concerns of architectural designers). This might have been on Aalto's mind in the passages cited earlier. Most systems of ethics propose or at least address the normative criteria for dealing with moral problems such as the one just suggested: to what extent does the moral person maximize his own good and to what extent does he maximize the good accruing to others, whether Aalto's users one at a time, or to the greatest number? Here, indeed, is a contrast with a healthy egoism, an issue we take up again at the close of this paper.

Most discussions of professional ethics, whether in the classroom or in the professional society, address what William F. May terms "quandaries of practice."[11] The utilitarian calculus may be applied toward the resolution of these quandaries; its scope, however, would be much, much narrower than the "all towards all" referred to by Cudworth: it would be counting only the short- and long-term benefits or disbenefits to the professional transaction's immediate participants. Moreover, as May points out, "much [professional] behavior is far from exemplary, it is merely customary; ethics is not ethos; morals is [sic] not reducible to mores."[12] Codes of professional ethics offer guidance to the practitioner seeking to resolve the quandaries encountered in everyday work (for instance, candor in scheduling and cost-estimating or tergiversating to accommodate client preferences) reducing the backsliding that Professor May warns against. A code of professional ethics renders at this microscale the same kind of inspiration, guidance, and blessing to the commercially avantageous marriage-of-convenience of professional and client that an ecclesiastical ceremony might bring to a marriage. And peccadillos transpire in ethical firms even as they do in sanctified marriages.

To be sure, these codes of practice are revised from time to time, but not because ethical principles have changed. Rather, expanding technology and evolving social expectations present new dilemmas to the conscientious professional in design and construction.[13] And, it must be reported, many professional societies had changes in codes of ethics thrust upon them in the 1970s by a United States Department of Justice that had read into such codes a "subornation of collusion in restraint of trade" among the subscribing professionals. The American Institute of Architects' code, for instance, was ruled to be in violation of the Sherman Act by a U.S. court in a 1979 civil antitrust suit brought by a member it had suspended for a year.[14] In consequence, the AIA adopted in 1986 and promulgated to its members in 1987 a revised *Code of Ethics and Professional Conduct*. But within a year of its reissuance the AIA president, no doubt feeling harassed, wrote a "Dear Colleague" letter advising that "the AIA is at present subject of an inquiry by the Antitrust Division of the Department of Justice."[15] Legislating a collective

morality is, under the U.S. Constitution, a daunting challenge.

These new situations are familiar to attentive readers of the professional and trade press that regularly offer continuing commentaries by lawyers and jurists in addition to the regular reporting of pivotal court cases or arbitration decisions affecting professionals at work. Teachers of professional ethics courses in schools of planning, design, and construction or, more typically, teachers of the professional practice courses incorporating ethics education, make use of this case material also.[16]

The cases typically encountered in professional ethics discussions tend to focus on the private (in the sense of individual) success of morally responsible professionals. I believe there is a much stronger argument for moving ethical discussion away from the particularities of the individual resolving a moral dilemma. I would propose to move the discussion—and the search for May's "inspiration of exemplary performance"—away from the isolated conscientious designer as an individual and toward the institutions within which all professionals

13
The February 1988 *Progressive Architecture* "Reader Poll Report" (on p. 16) lists 25 specific actions that 1300 respondents ranked as ranging from "unethical actions" to "normal practices" in architecture. An interesting outcome of this poll of readers were the "several situations perceived as either unethical or as normal business practices by substantial portions of the respondents." P/A termed these six actions "split decisions." This ambivalence reveals the ambiguity of moral issues and underscores the need for continued ethical vigilance. For a general discussion of the emergence of novel issues in ethics, see G. Winter, *Elements for a Social Ethic: Scientific and Ethical Perspectives on Social Process* (New York: Macmillan, 1966).

14
"Ethics Code Walks Fine Line," *ENR* (formerly *Engineering News-Record*), 19 June 1986, 27.

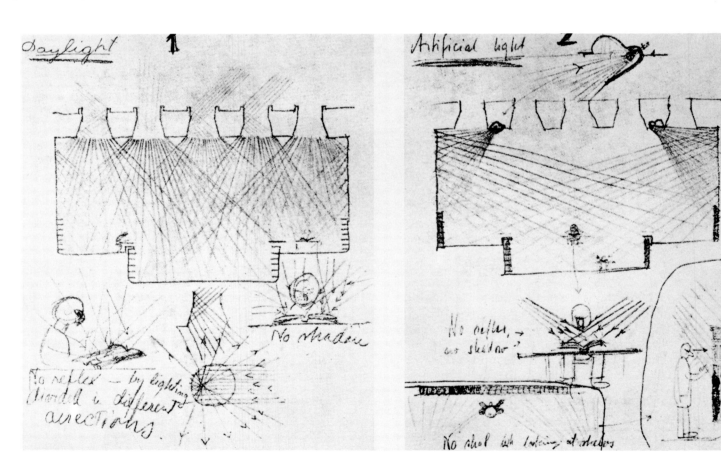

3. *Alvar Aalto. Rough sketch showing illumination with natural and artificial lighting.*

15
The new code is described in "Convention Approves 'Code of Professional Responsibility,'" *Architecture*, July 1986, pp. 11–12. The letter appears in *AIA Memo*, the Institute's office monthly newsletter, 2 September 1987, 3.

16
M. Wachs, *Ethics in Planning* (New Brunswick, N.J.: Center for Urban Policy Research, Rutgers University, 1985); A. E. Stamps III, "Teaching Design Ethics," *Architectural Technology*, May/June 1986, 17; H. D. Robertson, "Developing Ethics Education in the Construction Education Program," *Proceedings of the 23rd Annual Conference of the Associated Schools of Construction*, (West Lafayette, Ind., Purdue University, 1987):140–143.

Enterprising teachers at the University of Nebraska-Lincoln have enhanced the classroom ethical colloquies by introducing interactive videodisc methods that enable students (individually or in groups) to confront these dilemmas of conscience. See Robertson, p. 42. The Nebraska education effort in professional ethics is supported by a grant from the Peter Kiewit Foundation. Philanthropy from an industry that is reputed to be extremely "short-sighted."

The Truesteel Affair (Association of Professional Engineers, no date) presents these quandaries in film form. It is available through The Information Center, National Society of Professional Engineers, 2029 K. Street NW, Washington, DC 20006.

17
May, "Professional Ethics," 238.

18
This section's arguments, only outlined here, are amplified in F. T. Ventre, "The Policy Environment for Environment and Behavior Research," in *Advances in Environment, Behavior, and Design*, ed. E. H. Zube and G. T. Moore (New York: Plenum Press, 1989), 2: 317–342. Since submitting that manuscript I have discovered a similar argument, although one with religious overtones, in Winter, *Elements for a Social Ethic*, cited in Footnote 13.

—both the morally aware and the ethically obtuse—must operate.[17] This institutional approach would direct attention to the ethical values and power relations reflected in the very rule structures and modes of professional discourse within which individual decisions of conscience must work themselves out. All such cases occur and are resolved in a social reference larger and wider than even the most elaborate quandary that private practice knows. I propose that the morality of *social* as contrasted with *individual* ethics confronts the architectural designer (and indeed the entire building community) most vividly in the formation and execution of the public policies that frame and create the conditions for design and construction.

Regulation: Social Ethics Reified and Objectified

Societies, usually acting through governments, preempt entire classes of design decisions, restricting and sometimes totally removing areas of design freedom, reserving those decisions to society as a whole, acting through regulatory institutions.[18] This is now done routinely, in all the world's advanced economies. Less developed societies also regulate design and construction, but they tend to employ more diffuse, culture-wide mechanisms rather than special-purpose regulatory agencies.

Regulations, broadly considered, are the means by which societies, using the coercive powers of government, mediate the private actions of individuals. Of course, private actions know other limitations as well. Commercial transactions between informed individuals, for example, are limited by the mutually-agreed-upon contract. And it is usually these latter quotidian transactions that are grist for the professional practice course's "ethics case study" mill. But contrast those commercial transactions with regulation: the reach of public policy is broad where commercial law is limited; public regulations are coercive where commercial contracts are subject to mutual consent. Because they are intended to be universally and uniformly applied and coercively enforced, regulations must be carefully circumscribed either by statute, legal precedent, or (more significant for innovative designers) by technical knowledge. Design and construction are, in short, regulated industries and building regulations reflect, however imperfectly, a so-

ciety-wide understanding of what that society expects of its buildings and their environs. Only when that expectation is consensually shared does it become, at least in democratic states, a moral imperative enforced upon all. The operative term here is consensus, meaning more than a majority but less than unanimity. And here, exactly, is where postmodernism is most instructively contrasted with modernism. To a modernist (for example, the CIAM-era Aalto) a social ethic must be objectified; that is, it must "[attain] a reality that confronts its original producers as a facticity external to and other than themselves."[19] This modernist objectification renders ethical beliefs universal and accessible to rational method. Otherwise, the modernist argument continues, ethics would be merely a state of individual and subjective (and possibly solipsistic) consciousness.

Constructionists in philosophy and deconstructionists in literary studies, both of whom (but especially the latter) have influenced recent academic architectural discourse, have only recently separated fact from value and are dubious about separating knowledge from action.[20] Aalto, in his mature years, adopted what we now recognize to be this postmodernist program. He seems to have abandoned the search for universal solutions and sought situationally or contextually relevant standards for his own work. In so doing, Aalto anticipated Michel Foucault's arguments in *The Birth of the Clinic*.[21] Instead of evaluating behavior (or, one could say, candidate designs) relative to idealized, universalistic norms, Foucault proposes that situationally relevant standards be employed. But what keeps situationally relevant standards from degenerating into solipsism? A partial response (to be amplified later in this essay) is that designers do not work in isolation and are enjoined from self-indulgence by governmental fiat, by economic imperatives (referring both to tighter building budgets and more knowledgeable clients), by constituent and adjacent technologies, and by social sanction.

But who historically has assumed the task of inventing or interpreting what buildings and environments should do and be? Once that vision is articulated, who negotiates it through the wider public discourse that legitimizes emergent community values or public policies in democratic republics with representative governments? Table 1 shows a cursory chronology of nearly a century of community interventions into design and construction practice in America, providing some perspective.

Regulations have evolved (primarily) to meet newly sanctioned social needs and (secondarily) to take advantage of new technological opportunities. From the initial retributory penalities of the Code of Hammurabi (1955–1912 BC) that exacted a sentence of death from any builder whose building's failure resulted in the owner's death[22] through the Assizes of 1189 that proscribed the use of thatch in the densely populated portions of London,[23] the regulatory climate changed slowly. But the explosive growth of cities in the nineteenth century forced both a broadening of societal ends and an institutionalization of regulatory means from the 1880s through the 1980s. Table 1 reveals that the regulatory purview widened to embrace expanding notions of public health, safety, and welfare. These amplifications of the police powers of the state are traceable to both a deeper understanding of phenomena linking environmental stressors of various kinds to health effects and to the effective publicizing employed by public interest advocates near the turn of the twentieth century.

Although Archea and Connell have shown that the specific technical rationales for some of these Progressive-era reforms are erroneous in the light of current knowledge, the regulations promulgated at the time remain largely intact.[24] Some continue to be enforced. What might account for this persistence in the absence of supporting evidence? Is it sheer bureaucratic inertia? I nominate instead the potency of the initial images used by the Progressive-era pamphleteers. Let me illustrate: at the same session of the Environmental Design Research Association's 17th Annual Meeting that was addressed by Archea and Connell, David Hattis displayed Jacob Riis's nineteenth century photographs of New York City's notorious slums. (Indeed, it was Riis's images, including "Bandits' Roost" at 59½ Mulberry Street, taken on February 12, 1888, that bestowed on these dwellings their notoriety!) The effect on the EDRA audience of mature researchers was striking: after 90 years and more, those photographs still retained their shock value. So much so that it may be unlikely that the regulations they helped promulgate will soon be repealed. It is not bureaucratic inertia but persistence in the public will that keeps these regulations intact.

Are regulations reversible? In principle, they are; legislatures can formally repeal regulatory statutes and administrative agencies can achieve the same effect by selective enforcement.[25] But in practice regulations are all but irreversible. Allen Bloom's reading of the history of liberal political thought from Hobbes and Locke to John Stuart Mill and John Dewey concludes that

It was possible to expand the space exempt from legitimate social and political regulation only by contracting the claims to moral and political knowledge. . . . In the end it begins to appear that full freedom [to live as one pleases] can be attained only when there is no such knowledge at all.[26]

19
P. L. Berger, *The Sacred Canopy: Elements of a Sociological Theory of Religion* (New York: Doubleday-Anchor, 1969), 4.

20
J. Lave, *Cognition in Practice* (Cambridge: Cambridge University Press, 1988), passim; J. Coulter, *The Social Construction of Mind* (London: Macmillan, 1979), passim; A. R. Louch, *Explanation and Human Action* (Berkeley: University of California Press, 1966), passim.

21
Michel Foucault, *The Birth of the Clinic: An Archaeology of Medical Perception* (New York: Pantheon, 1973).

Table 1. An approximate chronology of the widening of the building regulatory purview in the United States

Date	Objective	Method	Initiating Advocates
1880	Curtail typhoid and noisome nuisance	Protected water supply; sewage treatment	Sanitary engineers, public health physicians
1890	Improve housing and health	Indoor plumbing	Housing reformers, plumbers
1900	Prevent conflagration	Sprinkler protection of individual structures and fire service to multi-building districts	Fire insurance underwriters
1920	Confine fire to building of origin	Fire endurance concept	Fire researchers, fire services, fire underwriters
1965	Confine fire to room and floor of origin	Fire zonation	Fire researchers, fire services, fire underwriters
1975	Energy conservation	Energy-use targets for overall building and/or components	Resource conservation groups
1978	Historic preservation	Alternative regulatory devices	Local and architectural history buffs (and professionals)
1980	Accessibility for handicapped	Performance requirements or prescriptive geometries	Architects (led voluntary efforts in 1950s), paralyzed veterans, disabled citizens, gerontologists
1990	Indoor air quality	Air management, real-time monitoring	Office worker unions, health organizations

22

Code of Hammurabi, trans. R. F. Harper (Chicago: University of Chicago Press, 1903), 834.

23

R. S. Ferguson, *The Development of a Knowledge-Based Code* (Ottawa: National Research Council Canada, Division of Building Research, 1974), 426:2. Citing Corporation of London Records Office (*Liber de Antiquis Legibus*), folios 45–58.

24

J. Archea and B. R. Connell, "Architecture as an Instrument of Public Health: Mandating Practice Prior to the Conduct of Systematic Inquiry," in *Proceedings of EDRA 17* (Atlanta, Ga., April 9–13, 1986), 305–310.

25

D. J. Galligan, *Discretionary Powers: A Legal Study of Official Discretion* (New York: Oxford University Press, 1986). How regulations operate in Chicago is described in B. D. Jones, *Governing Buildings and Building Government: A New Perspective on the Old Party* (University, Ala.: University of Alabama Press, 1985).

26

A. Bloom, *The Closing of the American Mind* (New York: Simon and Schuster, 1987), 28.

27

Sociologies of the professions convey this message. A comparatively recent review of the field is T. J. Johnson's *Professions and Power* (London: Macmillan, 1972). A sociological analysis emphasizing the primacy of autonomy in the architectural case is M. S. Larson, *The Rise of Professionalism* (Berkeley: University of California Press, 1979).

28

G. Gurvitch, *The Social Frameworks of Knowledge* (New York: Harper and Row, 1971); K. Mannheim, *Ideology and Utopia* (New York: Harcourt Brace, 1936); D. Bloor, *Knowledge and Social Imagery* (London: Routledge and Kegan Paul, 1976). W. J. Goode pointed out that no social mandate will be forthcoming if the profession's values are too far removed from the community's value con-

Regulation: Professional Values Collectivized

So it is the state of knowledge—moral and political knowledge according to Bloom; and practical knowledge, too, which according to Dewey has a moral force of its own—that drives regulation's juggernaut. But whose knowledge? The regulatory expansion after the 1920s seems to owe more to a public will rallied and given form by the cultural preferences and superior technical knowledge of articulate minorities who could link that preference and knowledge to wide social concerns.

Histories of the professions tell of their addressing the widely shared needs of the societies they have served.[27] Shared needs often began as latent, unexpressed, perhaps even unconscious tendencies or longings that were given form, reinforcement, and articulation by the profession with cognizance over that particular domain of ideas.[28] Rendering this service to society helps to reinforce the profession's status by evoking a social warrant for its existence on terms highly favorable to the profession. This drawing out of a latent societal mandate is a realization in the sociopolitical realm of (Jean Baptiste) Say's law that "supply creates its own demand," originally formulated to explain the dynamics of economic markets.

Modern-day occupations and professions express their specific concerns not only to their employers or clients but also to the social organizations or governmental agencies, usually regulatory agencies, that have cognizance over the activity in question. Working through the cognizant organization enables the prescribing profession to address all of society and not just those entities (either organizational or individual) with whom they are joined in a specific, contractually defined commercial relation. And the subject each of the prescribing professions addresses is a core value of the initiating professional (for physicians, wellness; for accountants, fidelity and accuracy; for airline pilots, safety of passenger and crew) that is then shown to be widely shared in the society at large. This enables the initiating profession to establish its hegemony over that aspect of social life: the entire society then becomes a collective client for the services of the collective profession.

However, the tactic of gaining wider public support for architectural values through congenial regulation is not likely to work today for three reasons: the first having to do with the

public's skepticism of government; the second, with the core values of the architectural culture; and the third, the widening gap between architecture and its public. A discussion of the first two reasons follows; the third recurs at the conclusion of this paper.

Regarding the public's skepticism of government: twenty years of Naderite public interest litigation has instructed consumers and even political liberals to an attitude once associated mainly with political conservatives: be more skeptical of regulatory agencies and, especially, the extent to which they may be "captured" by the very groups they were initially intended to regulate.[29]

The second reason that architects are unlikely to make strategic use of regulatory policies, even to advance their livelihoods, requires some elaboration. Architects are unlikely to employ this method not because it is manipulative and they are insufficiently cynical. Rather, a positive regulatory strategy to institutionalize the profession's core values would not be adopted because the furtherance of such an aggressive regulatory scheme (even if it were to materially benefit the architectural profession) is in fundamental opposition to a devoutly held aspiration of the professional designer: to realize one's own creative vision.

Architecture is singular among the professions in its pursuit of this aspiration. This could explain why transactions over which the designers nominally preside, and from which they earn their livelihood, are regulated by agencies largely responsive to others, principally the special interest advocates of the building products vendors and of the building-owning, -insuring, or -using groups in society.[30] It is these non-designers who have established and now maintain the rule structures and modes of discourse within which design is done.[31] Ironically, this situation, the circumscription of design freedom, has come about because of the higher value that designers place on the liberty to operate with less hindrance from socially imposed restraints, whether those restraints are in the form of codified knowledge of the world around us—which explains both the perennial deprecation of technical studies and its consequent, the only-recent emergence of research activities in architecture schools—or the more obvious hindrance visited upon them by regulatory institutions. This reluctance to discipline talent or, if you like, creative expression, is an inherited trait, a part of the profession's intellectual endowment, so to speak, and further conditioned by academic preparation and later professional socialization. Consider, for a start, the family tree. Architects are, in spite of themselves, siblings of Gadamerian aestheticism, children of Heideggerian existentialism, nieces and nephews of Nietzsche (an antiformal, anticlassicizing opponent of codified moral theories), and grandchildren of Schillerian Romanticism that sought through creative expression alone both truth itself and rescue from alienation. Little of our recent intellectual heritage is culturally conservative, and regulation is nothing if not culturally conservative.

Given this heritage it is little wonder that designers have ceded so utilitarian and rationalistic a thing as the building regulatory system to others, principally the agents of building products manufacturers and suppliers. Regulatory reform is a slow-moving, painstaking, cooperative endeavor performed anonymously and, consequently, is unlikely to attract the participation of those whose important secondary reference is to personal expression. Architects—who like to consider themselves artists but do not want to be paid like them—only reluctantly concede that they operate as a regulated industry within highly codified institutional structures and modes of discourse. In the architectural academy, the feeling is even stronger; there regulation is anathema, to be cursed, reviled, and shunned (except for that obligatory lecture in that same obligatory course in professional practice referred to in the first paragraph of this essay). This reluctance breeds alienation and withdrawal and designers, refraining from controlling the system, are instead controlled by it. There are exceptions. The late Fazlur Khan, a gifted structural designer at Skidmore Owings and Merrill in Chicago, was acutely perceptive about regulation and applied himself to regulatory reform efforts in that city.[32] But our Romantic heritage brings us, at worst, into obdurate opposition to or, at best, ambivalence toward the aspect of regulation that is, ethically speaking, its sinister side: paternalism, the "imposing [of] constraints on an individual's liberty for the purpose of promoting his or her own good."[33]

Regulations are in every way paternalistic and not the least deferential: the verb forms they employ are in the imperative mood, leaving no doubt about who defers to whom. With an appropriate preamble prevening, building

and development regulations really do tell one and all what is permitted in the built environment and, more emphatically, what is not. Moreover, these pronouncements are enforceable with the coercive power of the state. But because architects tend to follow the egoist-libertarian rather than the utilitarian-collectivist conception of social ethics (remember Aalto's warning) they are ambivalent about taking up anything like fundamental reform of an essentially imperative instrument. This means that regulatory matters—social ethics in action—are largely in the hands of others.

It was not always this way. The chronology of Table 1 reveals that designers have brought important issues into the public consciousness and then helped organize society-wide support for public policies of sound moral principle. Earnest instruction on architecture, its pleasures and its effects, was successfully imparted to large publics in America several times in this century. Where these matters bore on public safety, health, and welfare, the technically informed discussion was energized with an unmistakable moral fervor. And the regulatory powers of the state were subsequently guided by a specific moral vision that had first been articulated by designers and other building professionals and later endorsed by a much wider public. Consider California and how Sym van der Ryn and Barry Wasserman, in their successive tenures (during the administration of Governor Jerry Brown) made the Office of the State Architect a "bully pulpit" for climate- and user-responsive design policies and regulations not only for California but for the nation.

The Obscuring of a Profession's Core Values

Other professions have successfully proselytized their core values to the wider society and these engagements of the public have provided strong, if perhaps transient, boosts to each profession's welfare. Why then has the public embraced so few architectural values as a basis for public policy? Martin Filler, reflecting on the one-hundred-year effort to enlist a public constituency for architectural values through criticism in the public as well as the professional press, could identify only three recent successes: "historic preservation, ecology, and zoning."[34] What accounts for this lapse and, more important, how can it be remedied? Filler says:

sensus. In "Community Within a Community: The Professions," *American Sociological Review* 22 (1957):197.

29
P. Sabatier, "Social Movements and Regulatory Agencies: Towards a More Adequate—and Less Pessimistic—Theory of Client Capture," *Policy Sciences* 6 (1975): 301–342. A bimonthly update on the extent of regulatory capture and how to combat it is *Regulation*, published by the American Enterprise Institute in Washington, D.C.

30
F. T. Ventre, "Social Control of Technological Innovation: The Regulation of Building Construction," (Ph.D. dissertation, Massachusetts Institute of Technology, 1973).

31
A. D. King, ed., *Buildings and Society: Essays on the Social Development of the Built Environment* (London: Routledge and Kegan Paul, 1980); P. L. Knox, "The Social Production of the Built Environment," *Ekistics* 295 (July/August 1982): 291–297. Knox elaborated this view in an essay in *Architecture et Comportement* 2, no. 2 (1982); P. L. Knox ed. *The Design Professions and the Built Environment* (London: Croom Helm, 1988).

32
From personal communications during the years that Dr. Khan served on the National Academies of Science/Engineering-administered Technical Evaluation Panels that "peer reviewed" the programs of the National Bureau of Standards/Center for Building Technology.

33
D. F. Thompson, "Paternalism in Medicine, Law, and Public Policy," in *Ethics Teaching in Higher Education* ed. D. Callahan and S. Bok (New York: Plenum, 1980), 246.

34
M. Filler, "American Architecture and Its Criticism: Reflections on the State of the Arts," in *The Critical Edge: Controversy in Recent American Architecture*, ed. T. A. Marder, (Cambridge: MIT Press, 1985), 31.

35
Ibid.

36
For a sample of architecture interpreted in the manner of the literary art see *VIA 8: Architecture and Literature*, published for the University of Pennsylvania's Graduate School of Fine Arts by Rizzoli, New York, 1986. For an early view of architecture interpreted in the manner of semiotics, see G. Broadbent et al., eds., *Meaning and Behavior in the Built Environment* (New York: Wiley, 1980). The extent of semiology's popularity in the architectural academy may be gauged from recent annual volumes of the *Journal of Architectural Education*.

37
J. Derrida, *Margins of Philosophy* (Chicago: University of Chicago Press, 1983). In this work, Derrida says it is a "mistake to believe" that a text may be deciphered without a "prerequisite and highly complex elaboration." If you seek such an elaboration on Derrida and his relation to his antecedents and his contemporary Michel Foucault, look no further than A. Megill, *Prophets of Extremity: Nietzsche, Heidegger, Foucault, Derrida* (Berkeley: University of California Press, 1985).

How Foucault's structures and discourses play themselves out in planning and design is insightfully discussed in S. T. Roweis, "Knowledge-Power and Professional Practice," in *The Design Professions and the Built Environment*, ed. P. L. Knox, (London: Croom Helm, 1988), 175–207. I have found Foucault more provocative in his interviews. A good sampling of his ideas that illuminate regulation and regulatory institutions are the interviews, edited by Colin Gordon, *Power/Knowledge* (New York: Pantheon, 1980).

38
D. H. Fisher, "Dealing with Derrida," *Journal of Aesthetics and Art Criticism* 45 (Spring 1987): 298.

39
Random House Dictionary of the English Language, 2d Ed., unabridged (New York: Random House, 1987), 519.

One essential approach is to attempt to break down the wall of professional hocus-pocus that surrounds both the profession of architecture and much of the writing about it. To a greater extent than pertains in media that produce works that can be kept behind closed doors but still be enjoyed by people, architecture virtually demands the kind of consensus that can emerge only if the public is constantly instructed in the concepts and concerns that ought to inform architectural initiative and decision making.[35]

But the chief articulators and expositors of American architecture's "concepts and concerns" seem to be withdrawing from the concerns of public life. This is indeed ironic for just when the principal professional society, the AIA, actively sought wider public participation by creating both a new category of membership and a publication to serve it, architecture's wider conversation—as articulated by the profession's academic wing and then promulgated by the writers and critics who retail that message to the nation's cultural elite—has veered sharply away from the comprehensible ordering of the tangible, palpable, physical environment as its main topic and has turned instead into the forest of exotic conceits and arcana from such fields as literary criticism and, somewhat earlier, semiotics.[36] Highbrow architectural criticism was, until just yesterday, an exegesis on "deconstructionist" critics, notably Jacques Derrida and Michel Foucault.[37] Deconstructionism, by the way, does not mean tearing down or never erecting a building; it is a literary theory whose main message seems to be that literature can carry no message because the meaning of language is itself ultimately undecidable. Deconstructionism teaches that a

"secondary" or "supplemental" text is already implicit within a "primary" or "host" text, such that it becomes difficult to establish clear boundaries between the two texts so related.[38]

Under deconstructionism's method, texts, and by extension, buildings and their environs, are to be assayed by

eliminating any metaphysical or ethnocentric assumptions [?] through an active role of defining meaning, sometimes by reliance on new word construction, etymology, puns and other word play.[39]

The deconstructionist critical movement curtails the centuries-long (at least since Alberti) suzerainty of the creator, be it author or designer. Hermeneutics, the art and science of interpretation, of which deconstructionism is but a part, is now the locus of creative endeavor. Indeed, the "interpreter's creative activity is more important than the text," laments Allan Bloom in his thoroughly dyspeptic best-selling 1987 critique of American higher education, "there is no text, only interpretation."[40]

James Marston Fitch, in an *Architectural Record* article, several years ago decried this flight from immediately-sensed environmental data among architectural writers and thinkers at its incipience, and Michael Benedikt has recently argued for a "High Realism" that celebrates materiality over abstraction.[41] Jacques Barzun has attacked increasingly opaque literary analysis that is as far removed from the cognitive experience of the reader as hermeneutics is from the perceptions of people living and working in the environments that the architectural intelligensia has so recently deconstructed.[42]

So arcane and remote from palpable experience have architectural theory, criticism, and method become that the once-salutary dissimilarity between architecture (the discipline) in the world of the academy and architecture (the profession) in the world of practice is widening to the point of total discordance.[43] A signed editorial in *Architecture*, the AIA's principal periodical, made this point vividly, citing a "wide diversity between schools and practitioners in the very ways they look at architecture. They differ in their perspectives, their agendas, their points of emphasis."[44] Given the dynamic of university faculty recruitment, promotion, and retention and the search for academic and scholarly respectability on the one hand and the imperatives of commercial survival based on technical reliability, fiscal accountability, and clear-headed probity all wrapped in attractive packaging on the other, the divergence is likely to be even greater in the future.[45] This bifurcation is likely to induce an early cynicism among students, a truly regrettable outcome against which all teachers and practitioners must strive.

Not only is architectural discourse growing remote from the general public's experience of buildings and their environs; the turn toward the arcane has won neither adherents nor recognition from among those whom E. D. Hirsch, Jr. has called the "culturally literate."[46] John

Morris Dixon analyzed Hirsch's sixty-four-page list of terms that culturally competent Americans should know and was annoyed to find only three (none of them esoteric) from architecture's vocabulary.[47] Thomas Hines assayed over seventy articles in journals of opinion reacting either "positively" or "negatively" toward Tom Wolfe's attack on the prevailing values of America's architectural culture.[48] Hines found the controversy salutary and himself right in the middle, chiding Wolfe for "thin research and . . . reckless writing" and scolding the architectural intelligentsia for "self-defeating arrogance . . . toward the public or publics they are committed to serve."[49] So the architectural profession may find itself thrice alienated: from the world of commerce, from its academic wing, and from its primary patrons, the core (and corps) of reflective, cultured Americans.[50]

If the core values of the profession are to inform, instruct, and thereby insinuate themselves as the core values of the society—the path taken by other expansionist professions stoutly assisted by their academic wings—then some important changes need to be made. Needed, that is, if architecture is to take the offensive, enlarging its constituency by realizing Hines's hoped-for outcome of the *From Bauhaus to Our House* controversy; namely, a "greater public knowledge and awareness of architectural issues and a greater professional sense of responsibility to that public."[51] Is this a realistic expectation? Yes and no: the public is not so apathetic as before. But an apathetic public may be preferred to one aroused to hostility and cynicism; witness the reaction, both public and professional, to Prince Charles's philippics on postwar architecture, urban design, and planning in Great Britain.[52]

If the prospects for a positive strategy of professional proseletyzing are, at best, mixed, then what is the prognosis for a defensive strategy, for defending the profession's values, status and, ultimately, markets from encroachment by others? Take the last issue: encroachment. Architects sense that the interior designers, facilities managers, and other technical specialists are intent on poaching on the profession's territory.[53] A unified profession, of course, could muster a stouter defense. And, as the guilds of old assured themselves a monopoly of certain trades by presenting to the medieval burghers the promise of a guaranteed minimum level of competence, so do modern professions seek the same assurance by restricting (through licensing) access to the market for

building design and consulting services. So, we are back now to regulation, the subject of this essay.

A Course of Action

We confront the issue of *social* ethics: how should a society, and specifically its governments, be organized and what specific policies should those organizations pursue in the matter of the design and construction of the built and induced environment? And which of those design and construction concerns are central enough to that society's core beliefs and aspirations to be recast as moral imperatives and enforced upon all? Of course, the principal organizations representing the design and construction industries do address themselves to legislative bodies developing broad policies with respect to social practice of all kinds. The annual AIA conventions, for instance, have taken strong stands for nuclear disarmament and against racism. More to the point for the present discussion, however, is the extent to which designers and the organizations and the professional peers that speak for them will tackle policies that bear more directly on the central concerns and core values of the design community.

What are today's architectural core values, and what structures mediate the sustained relation between the profession and the laity? As for values, a new beginning may be at hand: in 1987 the AIA launched "The Search for Shelter . . . to confront the plight of America's homeless and dispossessed."[54] But where may the mediating structures be found? I submit that they are among the institutions that regulate all the parties affected by architecture, not only those involved in it professionally or self-consciously. Economic relations of the latter type are generally regulated by the commercial law enforced by the threat of criminal prosecution and civil litigation and by the conventions of business practice enforced by custom; these relations apply to the specific architectural professional—whether an individual or a firm—and a specific, fee-paying client that has engaged that professional. But what I am addressing here is something larger: a "meta-narrative" within which the entire society acts as a collective client for the services of the collective profession. More extensive relations of this type have been successfully initiated and then managed by other occupations in the past but much less successfully by the profession of

40
Bloom, *Closing of the American Mind*, 379.

41
J. M. Fitch, "Physical and Metaphysical in Architectural Criticism," *Architectural Record*, July 1982, pp. 114–119; M. Benedikt, *For an Architecture of Reality* (New York: Lumen Books, 1987).

42
J. Barzun, "A Little Matter of Sense," *New York Times Book Review*, 21 June 1987, 1ff.

43
Stanford Anderson elaborated the distinction between the profession and the discipline in "On Criticism," *Places* 4, no. 1, (1987): 7–8.

44
Donald Canty, *Architecture*, August 1987, p. 29.

45
Robert Gutman, "Educating Architects: Pedagogy and the Pendulum," *The Public Interest* 80 (Summer 1985), 67–91; L. Nesmith, "Economist Choate and Others Explore Economy and Market," *Architecture* (August 1987): 14.

46
E. D. Hirsch, Jr., *Cultural Literacy: What Every American Needs to Know* (Boston: Houghton Mifflin, 1987). "The list" runs from p. 152 to p. 215.

47
J. M. Dixon, signed editorial, *Progressive Architecture*, July 1987, 7.

48
T. Hines, "Conversing with the Compound," *Design Book Review*, Fall 1987, 13–19.

49
Ibid., p. 19.

50
L. Nesmith, p. 14 (see note 45), describes the current symptoms. Underlying causes are suggested in F. T. Ventre, "Building in Eclipse, Architecture in Secession," *Progressive Architecture*, December 1982, 58–61.

51
Hines, "Conversing with the Compound," 13.

52
H. Raines, "Defying Tradition: Prince Charles Recasts His Role," *The New York Times Magazine*, 21 February 1988, 23ff; P. Goldberger ("Architecture View" column), "Should the Prince Send Modernism to the Tower?" *The New York Times*, March 13, 1988, p. H33.

53
"P/A Reader Poll: Fees and Encroachment," *Progressive Architecture*, November 1987, 15–19. Analyzes fees and fears of U.S. architectural firms facing increasing competition from other providers of design services. The profession's response is documented in "Licensing Interior Designers: Tutorial on AIA position," *F. W. Dodge Construction News* (July 1987):35. The position itself is promulgated in a six-page "White Paper" drafted by the AIA Component Officers and Executives via AIA President Donald Hackl's 9 March, 1987, memorandum. Like all declarations of war, the President's memorandum combines high-minded pursuit of the common good with a grim-faced determination. The only rhetorical/polemical button left unpushed is the invocation of the Deity. Lawyers Carl M. Sapers and Jerrold M. Sonet, advocates, respectively, for the architects and for the interior designers, present arguments summarizing key points in the June, 1988, *Architectural Record*, pp. 37–47.

54
D. J. Hackl, "President's Annual Report," *AIA Memo* (January 1988): 1.

55
J. F. Lyotard, *The Postmodern Condition: A Report on Knowledge* (Minneapolis: University of Minnesota Press, 1984), xxiv.

56
"Prince Charles Criticizes City Planning 'Disasters'," *Christian Science Monitor*, 7 March 1988, p. 2. Said he, "Although there is no one who appreciates or values experts more than I do . . . it is important not to be intimidated by them."

Acknowledgements
Thanks to Professors Norman Grover, religion, and Scott Poole, architecture, both of Virginia Polytechnic Institute; and Ed Robbins, architecture, of Massachusetts Institute of Technology, who commented on an earlier draft of this essay.

architecture today for the reasons already specified plus one more: the postmodern sensibility that dominates academic architectural discourse today manifests an "incredulity toward meta-narratives."[55] This incredulity may lie at the base of the public's current skepticism—given voice by Prince Charles toward architecture and planning.[56]

The rules for tomorrow's design and construction are yet to be written. But these rules most certainly *will* be written, whether by enlightened and sensitive designers intent on the creation of environments that enhance human potential for knowing a good life or by others who do not share that aspiration. Ought not the core values of architecture then serve as a basis for a social ethic for the built and induced environment? The true test of our commitment to those values is in our readiness to share them widely. How to turn a universalistic, largely negative and coercive authority—the regulatory system—into a positive stimulus for achieving highly differentiated environments that inform and liberate is no easy task. Nor is it ever completed. But it will be difficult for society to get what it needs and wants from its architecture and just as difficult for architects to provide what is needed and wanted without undertaking these enabling actions.

Francis T. Ventre is a professor at the College of Architecture and Urban Studies of the Virginia Polytechnic Institute and State University. He holds a Ph.D. in Urban Studies from the Massachusetts Institute of Technology and a Master of City and Regional Planning degree from the University of California, Berkeley. He has written and lectured on building materials, practice, and the design and construction industry. Dr. Ventre spent ten years with the National Institute of Standards and Technology before forming his own consulting firm, which serves clients in government and industry.

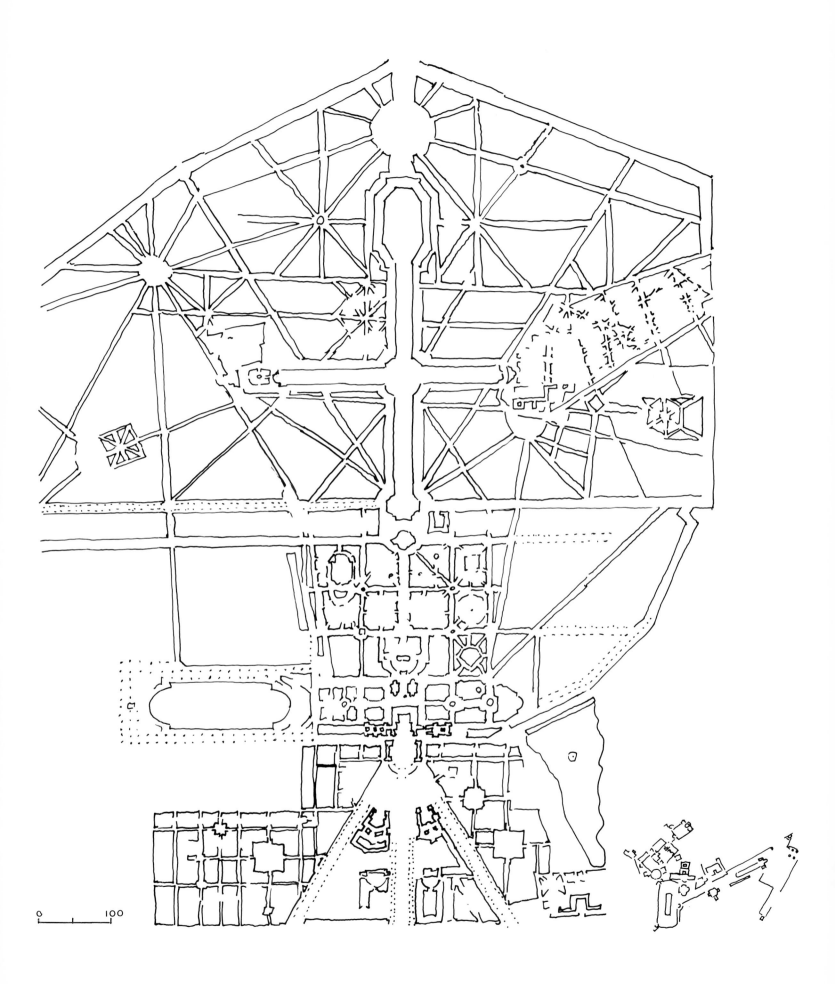

0   100

Jon Michael Schwarting

MORALITY AND REALITY: In Search of the Better Argument

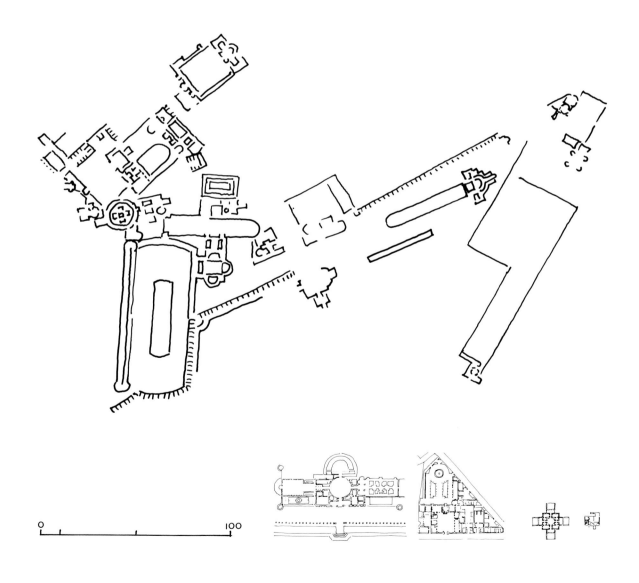

0   100

Architectural theories have not sufficiently examined those areas of the discipline that are not tangible or verifiable. Vitruvius sought to explain architecture with his three categories of *firmitas* (durability, construction, structure, materials, etc.), *utilitas* (use, function, cultural institution or type, etc.), and *venustas* (beauty, aesthetics, form/types, composition, space, style, etc.).[1] Aristotle explained being through his four causes: *causa materialis* (the matter or material in which change takes place), *causa formalis* (the form or shape into which the material enters), *causa finalis* (the end required of the form or matter), and *causa efficiens* (that which brings it about or means of production).[2] The first three causes relate closely to the Vitruvian terms. One area which is strikingly different is *causa finalis*, which has implications of aim, purpose and intention. *Causa finalis* has no clear parallel in the Vitruvian triad.

There are obvious intangible issues that define any intention to do something. Our opinions, attitudes and beliefs are reflected in all of our activities and thus impinge upon our intentions. Opinions, attitudes and beliefs are not based on absolute certainty or positive knowledge but on what seems to be true, valid or probable. These beliefs relate to choices one consciously or unconsciously makes or accepts about philosophical, social, economic or political issues. They are associated with our distinctions between right and wrong in conduct— our *moral* position. Once, through our beliefs, we form convictions that certain things are true or real, we are able to make distinctions between right and wrong. Therefore, convictions effect intention.

In making architecture, we can be as convinced about the truth of our beliefs as we are about which formal proposition or which structural system is appropriate to a problem. These convictions come together in an intention, which is defined as an aim that guides action.

Concepts of ethics and morality have appeared indirectly in most architectural theories. Any discussion of morality brings an aura of authority and correctness to the mostly practical discourse in architectural treatises. The "how" is given a sense of inevitability by introducing a "why" into the argument. Previous or alternative theories can generally be discredited by invoking a moral argument, which establishes good versus bad, right versus wrong, and virtue versus vice. Following this practice, the theoreticians of the Modern Movement called on moral justification to support their work. Contemporary theorists, in questioning the tenets of their predecessors, have similarly invoked arguments based on morality.

Starting in the nineteenth century, movements toward progressive political change were accompanied and supported by moral theories of society. For instance, Friedrich Engels's historicist theory, which maintained that society had evolved progressively from slavery through feudalism to capitalism, and would change naturally to socialism, had an implicit moral basis.[3] This theory was translated into real political movements which argued for a new ethical system within socialism, in which "the free development of each is the condition for the free development of all."[4] The Fabian movement in England in the 1890's, the Syndicate movement in pre–World War I France, and the Weimar Republic of post–World War

1
Marcus Vitruvius Pollio, Roman architect/engineer of the first century B.C.; author of the oldest extant treatise on architecture, *Ten Books of Architecture*, which states in Book I, ch. III, no. 2, "All these must be built with due reference to durability, convenience and beauty. Durability will be assured when the foundations are carried down to the solid ground and materials wisely and liberally selected; convenience when the arrangement of the apartments is faultless and presents no hindrance to use, and when each class of building is assigned to its suitable and appropriate exposure; and beauty when the appearance of the work is pleasing and in good taste, and when its members are in due proportion according to correct principles of symmetry." Translated by M. H. Morgan (New York: Dover Publications, 1960), 17.

2
Aristotle's well-known discussion of the four causes is given in *Metaphysics* 1.3 and is referred to in Martin Heidegger's "The Question Concerning Technology," in *Basic Writings*, ed. D. F. Krell (New York: Harper and Row, 1977), 289–292.

3
Friederich Engels, *Origin of the Family, Private Property, and the State* (New York: International Publishers, 1973).

4
Last sentence of Karl Marx and Friederich Engels, "Proletarians and Communists," Chapter 2 of *Manifesto of the Communist Party* (London: Pelican Books, 1970), 105.

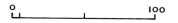

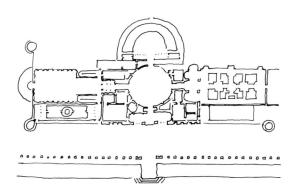

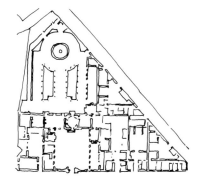

5
Siegfried Giedion, in *Space, Time and Architecture*, Part IV, "The Demand for Morality in Architecture," states:

Ambition revives and brings with it courage and strength to oppose those forces which had kept life from finding its true forms. . . . According to the easy explanation that was advanced later, the movement developed as the application of two principles: the abandonment of historical styles and—consequently upon this—the use of "fitness for purpose" as a criterion. The explanation is correct, inasmuch as both these factors were involved, but it does not go far enough. The movement took its strength from the moral demands which were its real source. The cry went up, "Away with the infected atmosphere" ([Cambridge: Harvard University Press, 1956], 291).

This is the only use of the word "moral" in the chapter; the issue raised here is not pursued further.

Giedion's and Pevsner's claims that the Modernist moral argument was primarily concerned with honesty to function and technique masked its political alliance with socialism and discredited its complex social agenda. This misunderstanding continues today.

Germany were the largest of many significant progressive political movements in this vein. Simultaneously, a related theoretical discourse developed in architecture with experiments in actual building. With the moral underpinnings of the social/political theory, these architectural theories argued that "good" or "right" meant putting architecture into the service of an evolutionary change toward a more egalitarian society.

The architectural discourse of the European Modern Movement called for an alliance between architecture and progressive political forces. Its sponsors believed that built form could work in the service of change. Critics argued that architects were morally responsible for providing social institutions with new techniques and images to address and represent a new, politically grounded, "spirit of the age."[5] The interest in mass production to achieve low-cost building, in public housing, in reevaluation of institutions and in a revolutionary urbanism were particular architectural manifestations of this belief.

Modern architects rejected the kind of "l'art pour l'art" arguments which had claimed that architecture was autonomous from politics. For example, Le Corbusier's "Architecture or Revolution," in *Towards an Architecture*, and *Une Maison, Un Palais*, articulated a social role for architecture by arguing for a certain quality of living for the common man.[6] Walter Gropius, Mies van der Rohe, and Richard Neutra described a similar social role.[7]

Since World War II, an opposite argument has been promoted in both politics and architecture. The desire for stability has replaced the desire for change. A new concept of morality has emerged, embracing these new conservative concerns of stasis and status-quo democracy.

By the 1960's, architectural discourse began to articulate these social changes. High Modern polemics were replaced by the idea that "architects cannot save the world" and that the architect's role was to "reflect" society, not to "criticize" it. The postmodern argument was that it was *wrong* for architects to believe that they could effect social change, and *right* for architecture to be autonomous, particularly from politics. As Paul Goldberger, critic of the *New York Times*, recently wrote, "They are not looking, as their counterparts were, . . . to remake the world; their attitude is evolutionary, not revolutionary. A belief in Utopia has been replaced by a contentment with what is, by a willingness to say that our culture is all right so long as it can make us comfortable."[8]

Perhaps the most articulate expression of this new sensibiltiy was contained in Robert Venturi's book, *Complexity and Contradiction in Architecture*, published in 1966. In its introduction, Vincent Scully said of the author, "Venturi is so consistently anti-heroic . . . It is this generation's answer to grandiose pretensions which have shown themselves to be 'destructive or overblown.'"[9] Venturi himself said, "The architect's ever-diminishing power and his

1. *Diagram showing canonical houses drawn at the same scale.*

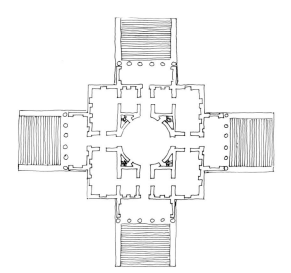
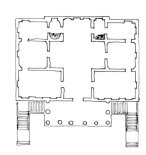

growing ineffectualness in shaping the whole environment can perhaps be reversed, ironically, by narrowing his concerns and concentrating on his own job. Perhaps then relationships and power will take care of themselves. I accept what seems to me architecture's inherent limitations and attempt to concentrate on the difficult particulars within it rather than the easier abstractions about it; . . . because the arts belong (as the ancients said) to the practical and not the speculative intelligence, there is no surrogate for being on the job."[10] In 1980, Robert Stern reinforced this attitude with a by-then-typical statement: "Post-modernism is not revolutionary in either the political or artistic sense; in fact, it reinforces the effect of the technocratic and bureaucratic society in which we live."[11] At about the same time, William Hubbard wrote, "An architect who has a firm handle on the actual, real-world consequences of architectural conventions would never think them so important as to declare, "Architecture or revolution.""[12]

Since both the modern and postmodern positions invoke a moral argument to support their theories, the current switch of moral positions leads us to consider the possibility that morality is not neutral and autonomous.

Ethics and Morality

The work of Plato and Aristotle established a dichotomy in the study of morality which has continued until this day.[13] On the one hand, the Platonic "Idea of Good" posed what has been termed a "non-natural" explanation, in which meaning in ethical terms goes beyond observable facts and thereby exists outside of nature. Plato's abstract "forms," Christianity's "will of God," the ideas of the intuitionists and later moral-sense theorists, are all related to some notion of an ideal.

On the other hand, the Aristotelian tradition of "naturalism" relates value to facts and defines "good" and related concepts in terms of observable criteria. The Aristotelian concept of fulfillment of natural tendencies and later concepts of satisfaction of desires (egoist, hedonist), as well as the "utilitarian" notion of production of pleasure for the greatest number, the conduciveness to historical progress (Marx), and the efficiency of means to ends, fit into the "natural" category.

Although there can be truth to certain fundamental physiological and psychological traits, our norms, which appear to be "natural," are considered by some to be controlled by

6
Le Corbusier, *Vers Une Architecture* (Towards an Architecture) (Paris, Editions Crès, 1923); Le Corbusier, *Une Maison, Un Palais* (Collection of L'esprit Nouveau) (Paris: Editions Crès, 1928).

7
"The ethical necessity of the New Architecture can no longer be called into doubt," wrote Walter Gropius in *The New Architecture and the Bauhaus* (Boston: C. T. Brandford Co., 1935), 112; he continued to explore this in his late book, *The Scope of Total Architecture* (New York: Collier Books, 1962). According to Mies van der Rohe, "Architecture is the will of the epoch translated into space," in "Architecture and the Times," *Baukunst und Zeitwille Der Querschnitt* 4(1924):21–22; and in Philip Johnson, *Mies Van Der Rohe* (New York: Museum of Modern Art, 1947) 186. Richard Neutra wrote *Survival Through Design* (London: Oxford University Press, 1954), whose title summarizes its contents.

8
Paul Goldberger, "Eighties Design: Wallowing in Opulence and Luxury," *The New York Times*, 13 November 1988, sec. 2, p. 1.

9
Vincent Scully, Introduction to *Complexity and Contradiction in Architecture*, by Robert Venturi (New York: Museum of Modern Art, 1966), 13.

10
Robert Venturi, *Complexity and Contradiction*, 21.

11
Robert A. M. Stern, "The Doubles of Post Modern," *Harvard Architectural Review*, 1 (Spring 1980): 82.

12
William Hubbard, *Complicity and Conviction: Steps Towards an Architecture of Convention* (Cambridge: MIT Press, 1981), 132.

13
Raziel Abelson and Kai Nielsen, "History of Ethics," in *The Encyclopedia of Philosophy*, Vol. 3–4, (New York: Macmillan Co., 1972), 81–117.

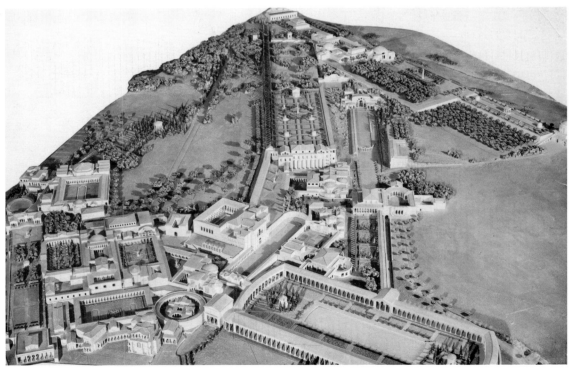

2. *Hadrian's Villa, view of the reconstruction model.*

dominating ideological forces. Both "non-natural" and "natural" ethical theories are now seen to be susceptible to ideology. Morality is seen as normative and defined differently by particular historical moments and cultures. We can look to recent discourse on the concept of meaning to examine this linkage of norms and ideology more thoroughly.

In the second half of this century, meaning itself has been scrutinized for its relation to ideology. Meaning had been generally assumed to be essential to communication and to the establishment of positive qualities of sociability and community. We have, however, come to be more skeptical of these assumptions. Jürgen Habermas, of the Frankfurt School defines what he believes to be a condition of "modern repression" as the situation resulting from the fact that prevailing relationships of power in society have not been "seen through," and therefore have become a means of domination. These relationships of power have determined the norms and attitudes that we maintain as our "world picture" or "social consciousness." We believe this to be *real* or *natural*, rather than seeing that it is artificial and imposed. "We believe them to be legitimate, and accept them as necessary, because of our relationship to a network of in-stitutions and practices of a repressive kind." Within the development of his theory of modern repression, Habermas argues that through repressive institutions and practices a "false consciousness" develops, which causes us to believe mistakenly that restrictive social arrangements are indispensable to our well-being.[14] Habermas's work has paralleled that of the structuralist and post-structuralist movements originating in the 1950's. Sources ranging from anthropologist Claude Levi-Strauss's work to that of French theorist Michel Foucault have focused on the concept of power, how it is maintained, and by whom.

For instance, in considering the issue of power, Foucault has suggested that "literal meaning, like proper usage, is the product of the application of norm, social in nature, hence arbitrary, rather than the result of the operation of a law."[15] From this, Foucault suggests that there is no such distinction as literal versus figurative meaning, except as a culture or an ideology defines it. "When we lose sight of the inherent error of a normative condition and believe that there is a real permitted vs. prohibited, rational vs. irrational, true vs. false, we are being managed by forces that have the power to decide what is real and unreal."[16]

14
Jon Michael Schwarting, "In Reference to Habermas," in *Architecture Criticism Ideology* ed. Joan Ockman (Princeton, N.J.: Princeton Architectural Press, 1985), 94–100.

15
Hayden White, "Michel Foucault," in *Structuralism and Since*, ed. John Sturrock (Oxford: Oxford University Press, 1979), 93.

16
Ibid., 95.

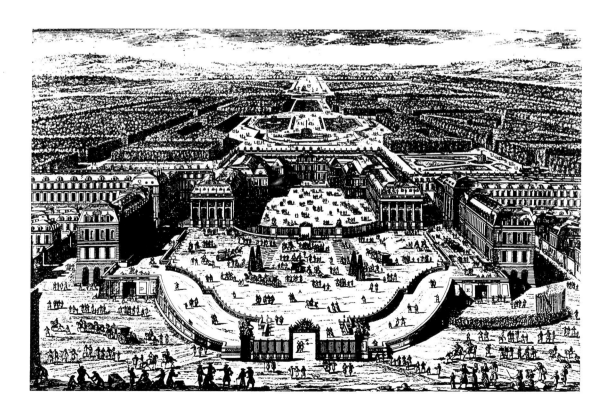

3. *Versailles, aerial view. Large scale work for autocrats deals primarily with simple axial and enfilade relationships.*

Habermas's concept of "false consciousness" is related to Foucault's definition of power and can be summarized as

"the capacity of a social group to realize its specific objective interests. In a process of realization of these interests, a society need not be reduced to pure domination by force or violence, but rather compromises a function of leadership and ideology by means of which social relations are founded on active consent."

Through a process of mythification these "interests" become natural and insinuate themselves in our mind as reality.[17]

By parallel argument we can conclude that morality is not just normative, but that there is a potential complicity between morality and ideology in which morality serves ideology. If we falsely assume morality to be above or independent of ideology and even serving as its critique, we run the risk of greater mythification of the struggle for power. Recent cultural criticism and its inquiry into meaning suggest that "natural" theories have the tendency to be conservative, in the defense of the status quo, if they are not utilizing rational thinking to uncover ideological constructs. Ideal theories also have the potential to hide reality by devising means to avoid it (i.e., inventing fantasies).

However, morality could be directed toward positive change and progress when motivated to analyze and demythify present conditions and to propose constructive alternatives or modifications. To do so, ideal or non-natural theories of morality would examine and analyze their intentions or reasons for being. This might be possible within Karl Mannheim's argument that the nature of utopia is a proposition transcending reality which, when it enters reality, tends to transform reality and in doing so, becomes transformed itself.[18] On the other hand, natural theories can engage in criticism only if they have the capacity to examine and analyze what is being defined as real and uncover the possible role of ideology and the struggle for power behind this definition. If one has faith in a particular moral position it is important to understand what this faith is ultimately supporting and suppressing. This understanding can bring about a more purposeful intention.

17
Demetri Porphyrios, "On Critical History," in Ockman, ed., *Architecture Criticism Ideology*, 16. He is also quoting N. Poulantzas here.

18
Karl Mannheim, *Ideology and Utopia*, (New York: Harcourt, Brace and World, 1936).

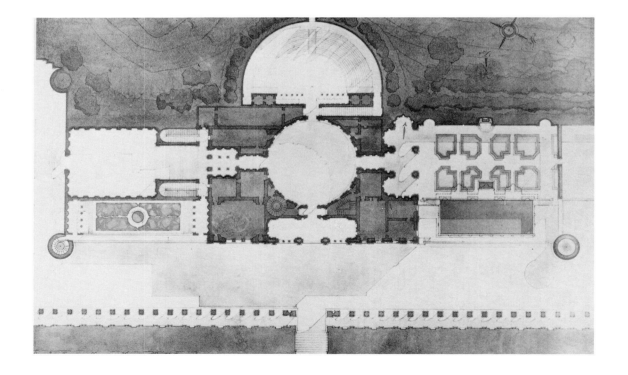

4. *Villa Madama, designed by Raphael, Antonio da Sangallo and Giulio Romano from 1516-1520, site plan. Reproduced by permission of Dr. Andreas C. Papadakis, from* Italian Gardens of the Renaissance *by J. C. Shepherd and G. A. Jellicoe. Published by Academy Editions, London.* ©

19
Ibid., 16.

20
Jürgen Habermas, "Modernity versus Post Modernity," in *New German Critique* 22 (Winter 1981): 3–14.

Morality In Architecture

As we come to understand that what is generally considered to be "reality" is in fact relative and influenced by the prevailing power relationships, we come to view architecture as a tool. "Architecture as ideology comprises not merely scattered elements of building knowledge and notions of design, but also the whole process of symbolization, mythical transposition, taste, style and fashion. Reality, therefore, gives to architecture a set of rules and productive techniques while, in turn, architecture gives back to reality an imaginary coherence that makes reality appear natural and eternal." [19]

High Modern theory argued that architecture should join forces with other social institutions trying to bring about more egalitarian conditions; that an overt moral commitment is required along with a formal and functional agenda. In these terms it did not, as most critics have stated, demand a break with history, but rather called for a reconnection to a general history of progressive change. The idealism of a better new world was founded on the argument for historical evolution toward an egalitarian society. Recent architectural theories that ad-

vocate the status quo might be analyzed as participating in, and contributing to, the conditions of a "modern repression" as articulated by Habermas.

Habermas proposes an alternative to the perceived modern repression in his proposition that the project of modernism is as yet unfinished. Weighing two moralities from two ideological arguments, Habermas claims that one will ultimately dominate through "the peculiar force of the better argument." [20] He recommends that, through *critical cultural analysis*, we will not only "see through" the "modern repression" but can also turn to theories of politics and presumably morality that withstand this form of examination and remain "virtuous." Neo-Marxist theory such as that of Habermas continues to champion the modernist project in this respect. Marx claimed that bourgeois moral principles represent the satisfaction of the interests of the ruling class. Marx appears to have combined aspects of the "naturalist" moral theories, through "historical materialism," with the "non-naturalist" proposal of an ideal "classless society." This same unlikely combination underlies the modernist "project." The ideal of a better new world was proposed as a natural historical evolution.

If we accept the concept that moral arguments are bound to ideology, then the moral argument is only as good as the ideological argument. However, the quality of a moral argument can be analyzed to reveal characteristics of, and possibly a means of judging, the ideological base it supports. As such, we must analyze both the modern and postmodern arguments, as they persist in architectural discourse today. One is based on the premise that architecture is affected by and affects society; that form and meaning interact. The alternate proposes that architecture is the result of society's determinations, and meaning is bestowed in this process. If the project of modernism is not complete, and has the potential to be the "better argument," it is important to analyze the issues of that argument. An examination of a particular issue might be made to reinforce this idea.

5. *Hotel de la Vrilliere, view in context. Planning in plutocracy involves more intricate sequences utilizing local symmetries and multiple axes.*

An Example of Critical Analysis

We can examine particular aspects of the history of architecture to understand the relationship of architecture to morality and ideology. The diagram presented serves to illustrate this analysis by presenting various canonical buildings at the same scale (Figs. 1–7). An argument can be made that a causal relationship exists between architectural patronage and formal invention. While not constructing an argument of historical determinism (such as that described by Friederich Engels's socio-historical theories), one can observe an evolution in patronage over time: from work for autocracies, later for plutocracies, and finally for democracies. This evolution is matched by a significant change in the scale or size of the architecture that is commissioned under each of these conditions.

The autocratic patronage that produced, for instance, the Villa Adriana (Tivoli, A.D. 180; 2400 ft. × 1600 ft.) or Louis XIV's Palace of Versailles (1678–1684; the building is 1420 ft. long and the garden is 2.5 miles square) is represented by planning on a very large scale. Raphael Sanzio and Antonio da Sangallo the Younger's Villa Madama (outside Rome, 1516; 213 ft. long × 146 ft. deep with the adjacent side gardens extending it to 500 ft. long) or François Mansart's Hotel Vrillière (Paris, 1635; 375 ft. × 375 ft. including the garden) are clearly more modest in scale, having been produced under more plutocratic conditions. Finally, if we compare these to Le Corbusier's Villa Stein at Garches (outside Paris, 1927; 61 ft. × 43 ft.) produced in a more democratic climate, we see an even more dramatic change in size.

While there is not a smooth or constant historical transition in social evolution toward greater human "virtue," the direction of change is obvious. The same holds true for architectural scale. As more people have had access to architecture, buildings have become smaller in size. In terms of visual form, no one of these buildings is *de facto* better, more elegant, more sophisticated, or more beautiful than the others. However, it is interesting to note the degree to which formal invention occurs under those conditions which force a reduction in the scale of construction. A conservative architect, one who would perpetuate the existing situation, would attempt to finesse the necessary change of scale by simply miniaturizing the old building organizations and images, or by using less costly materials or

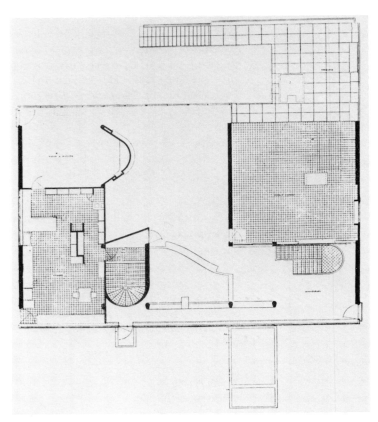

6. *Villa Stein at Garches, plan.*

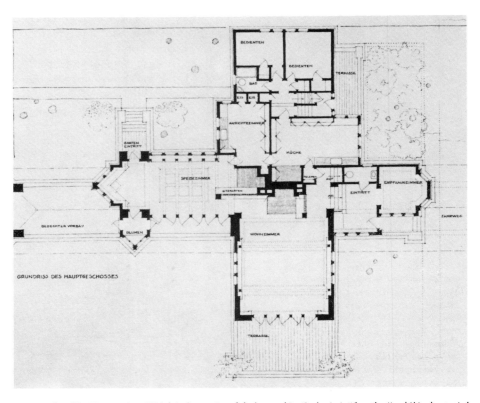

7. *Ward Willits House, plan. Wright's destruction of the box and Le Corbusier's "free plan" exhibit the spatial transparency of overlapping functional zones.*

21
Henry-Russell Hitchcock, Jr., *Modern Architecture: Romanticism and Reintegration* (London: Payson and Clarke, Ltd., 1929), 5.

22
Ibid., 160.

23
Giedion, in *Space, Time and Architecture*:

The historian, the historian of architecture especially, must be in close contact with contemporary conceptions. Only when he is permeated by the spirit of his own time is he prepared to detect those tracts of the past which previous generations have overlooked (p. 5).

24
Interestingly, his palazzi did not require such transformation.

techniques (e.g., faux marble). The progressive architect, on the other hand, would find ways to reconceptualize, to reorganize and to create new images and forms in recognition of change.

Henry-Russell Hitchcock, in his 1929 book, *Modern Architecture—Romanticism and Reintegration*, argued for a synchronic condition, in which more than one architectural value system could occur at the same time. He identified two positions which existed simultaneously at the turn of the century, which he termed the "New Tradition" and "New Pioneers." His argument, although primarily concerned with taste and style, had an implicit sociopolitical implication.

It is very clear that the New Tradition in architecture, the rationalistic manner of eclecticism of style beginning at the end of the 19th century and continuing still today is very essentially romantic in the large and non-historical sense of the term.[21]

But the new manner is fundamentally distinct from this version of the New Tradition in that it is based on principles of design not inherited from the art of the past.[22]

Rather than look to style as have many historians, such as Hitchcock, Pevsner, Giedion, and others, to discuss the importance of modernism, it might be more appropriate to examine other architectural issues or principles. The present discussion of scale, for instance, avoids the confusion caused by the commodification of style or popularization of particular styles or architects.[23] Numerous examples can be found to illustrate how spatial and formal invention have been put in the service of changing social conditions, through a reduction of scale.

In relation to the previous diagram, a comparison can be made between the High Renaissance "villa suburbana" and the Palladian farmhouse. The villa suburbana, described by Vitruvius as a country retreat, is represented by the Villa Madama, previously illustrated. Its room sequence is not particularly complex. It consists of corner "apartments," organized *enfilade* and separated by loggias on the principal axes. The elevations and plans are organized in typical proportional relationships to provide visual harmony. Local symmetries create a strong relationship between the landscape and building externally but have little relation to the internal spatial order (Fig. 8).

The Palladian villas of the Veneto also offered a retreat from the city, but they were principally created to resolve a specific economic crisis in the region. The economic shift of traffic from the East to the West had left the port of Venice in significant decline. Wealthy merchants opted to "diversify" by draining the Veneto marshes for farming. The Villa Rotunda is a statement symbolic of a prominent family's move onto the land and, as such, Palladio confronted a significant architectural problem of his day. This villa differed significantly from the Villa Madama of 50 years earlier in both size and program (the Villa Rotunda is about a third that of the Villa Madama and can thus fit into the latter's courtyard). Palladio's "conceptual" proportional system makes his villas revolutionary by creating a proportionally interrelated sequence of rooms. Thus the "whole" could be "understood" while one was involved with a specific "part." By having the whole act at an unconscious level simultaneously with the part, Palladio made what is small "seem much larger in the mind."[24]

8. Villa Madama, aerial perspective. Reproduced by permission of Dr. Andreas C. Papadakis, from Italian Gardens of the Renaissance by J. C. Shepherd and G. A. Jellicoe. Published by Academy Editions, London. © The Villa Madama measures 230 feet by 150 feet in building plan, with a 90-foot diameter court. The subtraction of a zone at the back of the building and the projection of a zone of front rooms beyond the garden walls recenters the asymmetrical plan.

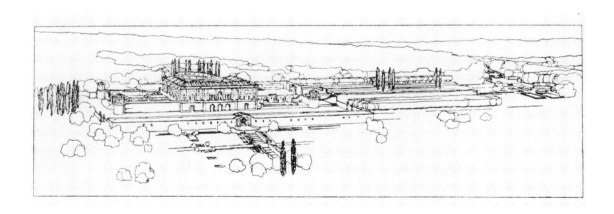

Although the typical French chateau is known to be very grand in scale and material richness, it was nevertheless quite simple in its spatial planning. The chateau was situated outside of the city, but by the early seventeenth century certain factors favored urban dwelling. Henry IV's choice to move the court to Paris from the Loire Valley, and the rising social standing of the urban bourgeoisie, brought about a demand for a new building type: the urban hôtel. Mansart's Hôtel de Vrillière is one tenth the size of Le Vau's Vaux-le-Vicomte of 1661 (Figs. 10, 11). Its *cour d'honneur* in front and its *cour de logis* behind follow the basic organization of the chateau. However, a high level of formal invention is required to accommodate the extreme contraction, and the assembly of basic parts on often erratic sites. A shift of the main axis re-centers the plan and sequence in relation to an unaligned exterior, which permits the service section to be placed along one side. This axial shift begins to increase the complexity and dynamics of internal spatial planning and sequence. For instance the stair hall, which had been an almost insignificant element in the chateau, became an active participant in the hôtel, interrelating the floors spatially. As with the Palladian farmhouse, the French produced formal inventions in the face of apparent adversity.

9. *Villa Rotunda, aerial view. The main block of the Villa Rotunda, with a 35-foot diameter central drum, could be placed into the court of the Villa Madama.*

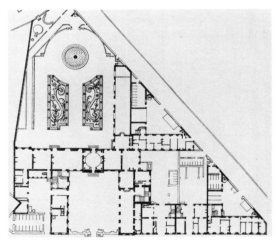

11. *Hotel de la Vrilliere, plan.*

10. *Vaux le Vicompte, aerial view. Vaux le Vicompte, designed by Louis Le Vau in 1661, is a 250-foot by 125-foot building. The garden from the forecourt to the first canal is 3,750 feet long, and the garden as a whole is 15 by 85 miles. This suitably reflects the attitude of "L'etat c'est moi."*

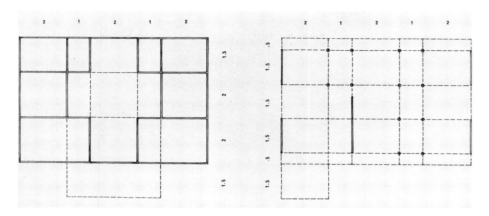

12. *Colin Rowe demonstrated the formal similarity with this diagram.*

13. *Immeubles Villas, plans and interior. The four-part plan with one quadrant devoted to the ground lifted into the air and the double-height section.*

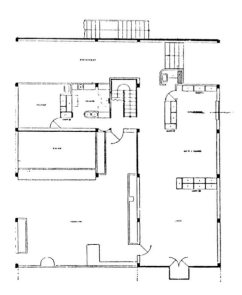

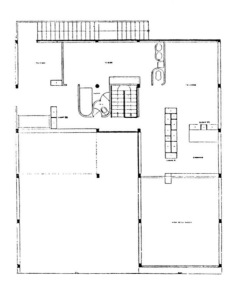

A third example, involving Modern architecture, examines the concept of the "free plan," illustrated by Le Corbusier in 1914 with a structural diagram of the so-called "maison domino." This was further articulated in his 1926 polemic, "Les 5 Points d'une Architecture Nouvelle." The free plan is perhaps one of the few real inventions in Modern architecture, and it is most often discussed as a formal, space-making or stylistic (cubist simultineity) device.

The plan of the Villa Stein ("Les Terraces") at Garches, is a classic use of Corbusian free-plan principles. The building (61 ft. × 43 ft.) happens to be nearly the same size as Palladio's Villa Foscari at Malcontenta (73 ft. × 51 ft.); this suggests that there are no arguments to make regarding scale and invention in this case. We must, however, look more clearly at Le Corbusier's intentions (Fig. 12). The *Oeuvres Completes 1910—1929* is dedicated principally to the issues of housing and not simply the opulent house. The 1922 "immeubles-villas" housing, for the Ville Contemporaine ideal city project, is significant among the various housing proposals that constitute about three quarters of the book. This duplex unit (30 ft. × 30 ft.) is formally divided into quadrants. One quadrant is a terrace, or "the ground raised up" (Fig. 13). Two quadrants employ the "maisonette" section and free arrangement of activities and contain the basic elements of the "maison standardisée" or the "maison minimum." All of the best known early Corbusian houses, for example, Villa Meyer (1923–24), Maison Cook (1927), Villa Stein at Garches (1927) and Villa Savoy at Poissy (1928–29), can be argued to be variations on the "immeubles-villas" theme (Figs. 14–17). They are essentially based on a four-square division of space (using the square of the golden rectangle), they have a mezzanine section, they devote a quadrant of space to an exterior raised terrace, and they are party-wall schemes (arguably including Poissy). One could speculate on a thesis that these houses are demonstrations and studies on the theme of the "esprit nouveau-immeubles villas" house for the "common man" (Fig. 18).

This hypothesis suggests that we view the free plan to be in the service of public mass housing. The free plan makes a literal visual transparency of that which was a conceptual spatial transparency for Palladio. Like the objects in a cubist painting, activities are overlaid in this scheme (living with dining, with library, etc.), thus reducing space requirements.

It provided Le Corbusier's particular studies of the "maison minimum" with qualities rare even for a conventional middle class dwelling.

The relationship between *intention* and *production*, proposed here, can be further specifically illustrated in my work with the New York based Karahan/Schwarting Architecture Company. The development of these arguments concerning morality and reality presented in this discourse stem from a concern for the human condition which requires articulation in built form as well as theoretical and polemical discourse. The work of Karahan/Schwarting over the past decade reflects an awareness of the slow movement of society toward egalitarianism, which necessitates a reduction of space for most residential private commissions. This problem has created the need for new spatial and formal invention directed toward its resolution. Although this awareness and concern has not been articulated in socially significant projects, it has been explored within the bounds of commissioned projects.

Expanding the idea of simultaneity of space of both Palladian conceptual space and the "free plan," our work explores a concept of *implied* or *virtual* space: an organization and space that can exist in the mind and be other than that which exists physically. The architecture of many cultures has employed the concept of implied space. The Italian Renaissance architects manipulated the ambiguities of shallow space and deep space, while the Baroque interest was in the articulation of "false" perspective. The High Modern enthusiasm for cubist overlap or "iridescence" is another example. Our work has specifically tried to redirect these devices to provide a sense of space that can be "seen" mentally in a different way from that which exists literally. This may appear to be an attempt to create a surreal space through the contradictions of the virtual and the real, but our *intention* goes beyond aesthetic interest to a concern for the quality of the living and working environment. In addition to resolving the program with the necessary division of space, we have been able to imply a different spatial organization by changing materials, texture or color. This order may be seen to counteract the organization of enclosing walls.

14. *Villa Meyer, sketch. This space in the four-part plan of the house is remarkably similar to the Immeubles Villas.*

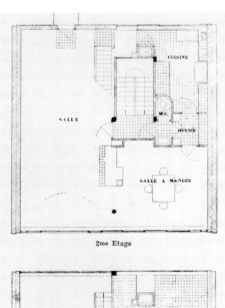

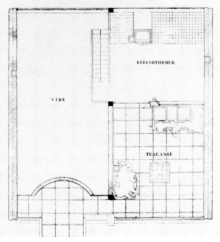

15. *Villa Cook, plans. The Villa Cook also has the four-part plan and double-height living room. In this case, the garden is in a quadrant at the top.*

Morality and Intention

Historically, the "new traditionalists" either worked in the service of the upper class, continuing to design large houses, or attempted peculiar miniaturizations or de-materializations of past models. The "new pioneers," on the other hand, devoted themselves to spatial innovations necessitated by their acceptance of prevalent moral criticism emanating from the culture. These two alternatives persist today. The so-called postmodern movement varies little from Hitchcock's definition of the New Tradition, as it ranges from desires to resurrect the past—or myths of it—to seemingly more progressive attempts to find new ways to preserve tradition (i.e., work which is merely romantic about progress, reducing it to a popular commodity as, for instance, the "Five Architects," reveals an unconscious traditionalism). A pioneer must critique present society or culture as well as its architecture. Change for its own sake is merely novelty leading to commodification.

The units of "immeubles villas" contained 2000 sq. ft. of area on two levels. United States Federal Housing Authority standards, which have dominated the American housing "program" since the 1940's, allots 900 sq. ft. for a two-bedroom apartment. If housing is to continue to be one of the important socio-architectural issues of the twentieth century, those who believe that every person is entitled to an affordable house must recognize and be involved with contemporary problems, as were Palladio, Mansart, and Le Corbusier. It is hard to believe that we can go back to historical forms and images, whether "classical" or "constructivist," to solve these problems realistically. A traditionalist attitude suggests a lack of concern for the problem of housing, one of the critical problems of our time.

Palladio, Mansart and Le Corbusier were not radically progressive. They did, however, see and address the problems of their day with an eye toward progressive change. As they sought ways to accommodate a changing world which was seeking reform, their work took a moral position. Clearly, it cannot be argued that a progressive architect pursuing issues of social moral development will automatically, as a consequence, be formally innovative; or that formal invention comes from, or is related only to, moral consciousness. However, an argument can be developed which centers on the issue of *intention*. In a design, the issues which the architect addresses and the hierarchy into which they are organized will have a significant impact on the essence of the building. Intention, if not conscious, will develop unconsciously. A sincere moral concern can assist in the formation of a complex, concentrated and compassionate intention. Significant architecture is possible when a clear intention is developed by an architect who is also capable of formal and visual profundity.

Arguments for a moral intention in architectural production are not concrete enough to enter into common discourse regarding "design formulae" or "design methodology." However, this same kind of intangible argument is made by philosophers affirming the necessity of morality in society. The distinction between right and wrong is valuable only when it is believed in and can be recognized as improving society. In the same way that we hold a belief in morality to be crucial to the perfection of the world, we can give importance to morality in the making of good and appropriate architecture.

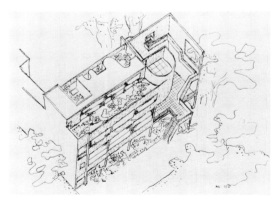

16. *Villa Stein at Garches, view from the south.*

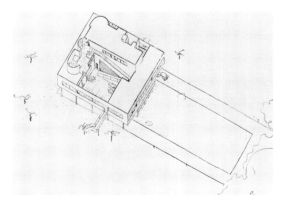

17. *Villa Savoye, aerial view. Again, one quarter of the plan is devoted to a raised terrace overlooking private property, revealing Le Corbusier's double agenda.*

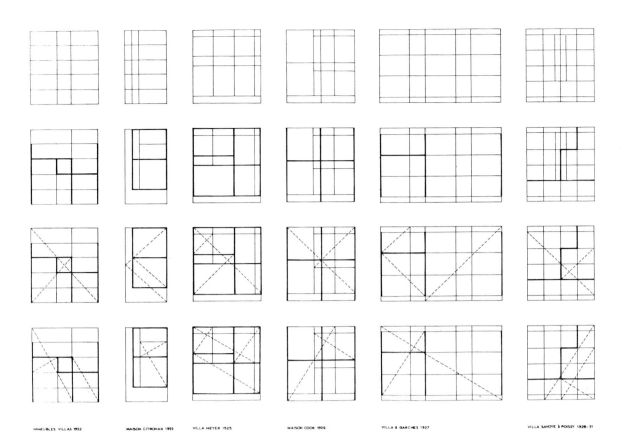

| IMMEUBLES VILLAS 1922 | MAISON CITROHAN 1922 | VILLA MEYER 1925 | MAISON COOK 1926 | VILLA A GARCHES 1927 | VILLA SAVOYE A POISSY 1928-31 |

18. *Like the Wittkower diagram of Palladian villas, this diagram reveals Le Corbusier's manipulation of theme with variations.*

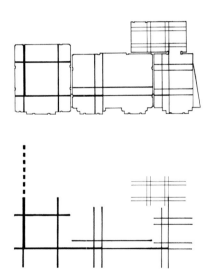

PARK AVENUE APARTMENT, NEW YORK

This apartment renovation leaves the rooms in their existing locations. However, the passages between them are altered to create an implicit spiral. This spiral is then made explicit by a *system* rather than a spatial sequence. The system is a "tartan" grid, made manifest in the aluminum expansion strips necessary in the new terrazzo floor. They are thin near the entrance, delineating a small-scale grid, and grow wider as the grid expands in each successive room. The spiral enhances notions of growth, expansion, and continuation. Other elements in the design relate to and reinforce this idea.

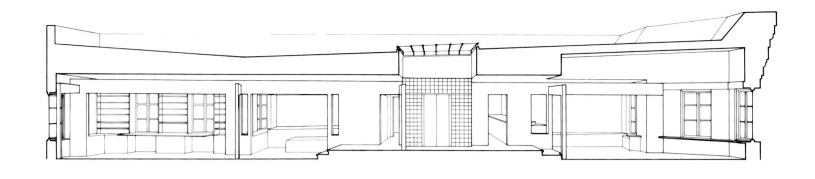

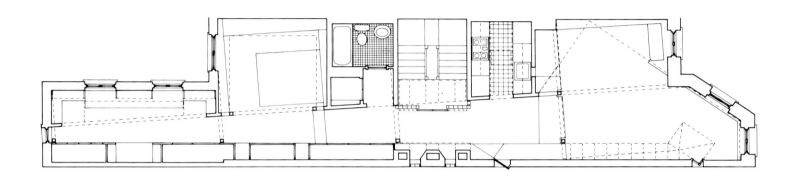

HAMER RESIDENCE, NEW YORK

In this small (720 sq.ft.) floor-through apartment a continuous plane runs diagonally from front to back. It is open at the public end and closed at the private end. Moving along this wall heightens the contrast of intimate versus expansive space. The sense of expansion and contraction imply the infinite. The diagonal through the orthogonal is also intended to relate to the way Broadway passes through the grid on the upper west side of Manhattan.

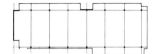
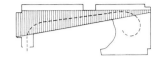

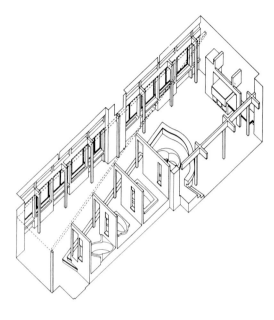

KALLISTA SHOWROOM, NEW YORK

This showroom employs a forced perspective distortion to make the experience of coming in very different from that of leaving. The displays are open to the entry sequence and more enclosed to the sequence of leaving. A light-to-dark color progression is employed to reinforce the false perspective.

FASHION INSTITUTE OF TECHNOLOGY, NEW YORK

The *Campus Walk*, on a New York street, uses continuous linear elements to define the street edge and to create its volume. A series of lateral, implied "cross walls" then subdivide this volume into systematically varying spaces. These "cross walls" of steel, stone and glass begin thin as planes close together, and grow thicker into volume as they become objects spaced farther apart. This expanding grid establishes a condition in which the linear space is seen entirely differently from either end. The conceptual false perspective expands the space in one direction and contracts in the other. The actual space is different from the one perceived, creating a dynamic condition for the participant and a distinction of its ends as unequal entry gates.

Jon Michael Schwarting is a partner in the Karahan/Schwarting Architecture Company and associate professor and chairman of the architecture program at the New York Institute of Technology. He received the Prix de Rome in Architecture in 1968, after receiving bachelors and masters degrees from Cornell University. He has taught at the University of Pennsylvania, the Cooper Union, and Yale and Columbia Universities. His writing has appeared in *Architecture Production* and *Architecture Criticism and Ideology* and in his forthcoming book *Rome: A Study of Urban Formation*.

Museum of Pre- and Early
History, Frankfurt am Main:
Courtyard Elevation

Joseph Paul Kleiheus

ARCHITECTURE IS RARE

Nichtsahnend,
  zumeist humorlos, zuweilen wohl auch böse,
wird Architektur in Nichtgkeit zerredet,
  wird mediokrem Konsens das Wort geredet gegen
  Architektur.
Architektur ist selten:
Architektur als Ermunterung
  gegen eine zunehmend verwaltete Welt, in der
  Bauherr un Architekt aus Verantwortung und Engagement sich entlassen.
Architektur als Widerspruch
  gegen unpolitischen Technizismus und eine instru-
  mentelle Art zu denken, die das Planen und Bauen
  zur Routine pervertieren.
Architekture als Beispiel
  gegen vordergründige Erfahrungs und Funk-
  tionsgläubigkeit und einen utilitaristischen
  Rationalismus, die jede Poesie negieren.
Architektur als Poesie
  gegen die blinde Ordnung zweckrationaler
  Überheblichkeit.
Architektur zurückblickend
  scheu und begeistert.
Architektur als Lernende
  in den klassischen Landschaften, aus Bergdörfern des
  Nepal und von Las Vegas.
Architektur als Erneuernde
  in Dialektik mit Alberti, Palladio, Schinkel un allen
  Heiligen.
Architektur als mögliche Kategorie des Neuen
  in Erkenntnis des immer gleichen, unter stets neuer
  Hülle.
Architektur auf der Suche nach erweiterter Autonomie
  liebevoll distonieren, Attribute sammeln, gegen den
  moralischen Terror reiner Vernunft und empirischer
  Realitäten absetzen, dem Markt un Verschleib sich
  entziehen.
Architektur als Sehnsucht
  grenzenlos.
Architektur
  auch zum Vergügen auf der Seite des Betrachters.

Unsuspecting,
  usually humorless, now and then even malevolent.
Architecture will be talked into nothingness;
  the mediocre consensus will have the last word
  against architecture.
Architecture is rare:
Architecture as encouragement
  against an increasingly administered world in which
  client and architect relieve themselves of responsibility and commitment.
Architecture as contradiction
  against unpolitical technicism and an instrumental
  way of thought, where planning and building are
  perverted into routine.
Architecture as example
  against a superficial belief in experience and function
  and a utilitarian rationalism which negates all
  poetry.
Architecture as poetry
  against the blind order of arrogant expediency.
Architecture looking back
  humble and enthusiastic.
Architecture as learning
  in the classical landscapes, from Nepal's mountain
  villages and from Las Vegas.
Architecture as renewer
  in dialectic with Alberti, Palladio, Schinkel, and all
  the saints.
Architecture as a possible category of the new
  recognizing what is always the same within always
  new wrappings.
Architecture in search of broadened autonomy
  distoning lovingly, gathering attributes, against and
  separate from the moral terror of pure reason and
  empirical realities, withdrawing from the market's
  wear and tear.
Architecture as yearning
  boundless.
Architecture
  also as pleasure on the participant's part.

In the fall of 1979 an open competition for a new Museum of Pre- and Early History was announced by the City of Frankfurt am Main. This project was awarded First Prize and was built in the years 1986–1989.

CUT STEEL
NAILED STONE
MEMORIES RUSHING AHEAD

More museums are constantly being built. New programs are being developed and expectations broadened; the demand can hardly be satisfied. The "socially" defined expectations of a museum are for the most part confusing. The discussion is of temples for the fine arts, of educational spaces for the study of the historical development and social conditions, of "environment" museums, and of museums for interdisciplinary activities.

But perhaps an archaeological museum can be just a place of perception and recollection, particularly since a greater awareness of history has been noticeable within the last few years.

The concept and practice of remembrance supported the planning, detailing, and the choice of materials for this museum. Memories sometimes rush ahead, because the concept of remembering is originally dependent upon the relationship between the rational and the historical, while the prerequisite of the rational is independence.

This relationship of recollection, rationality, and independence, as indispensable and inseparable as it is, is uniquely defined by the practice of remembering: the ability to remember, the willingness to remember, and the intention to remember.

This example is a recollection of the Frankfurt Stock Exchange, built 140 years ago by F. A. Stüler and destroyed in the last war: its distinguished hall of columns, and its striped facade of reddish-brown and greenish-yellow sandstone.

Recollection is a process of dialogue or, to be more precise, the relationship of the traditional to the modern is diction and contradiction:
- Expedited parts of old foundations are reflected in the design of the floor tiles.

- New dimensions are combined with the floor plans of the historical church.

- Structure in cut steel opposes the restoration of the stone vaults.

- The toothed pattern of the stone brick reflects the setting of the nails.

This museum is a quiet, provocative dialogue between the traditional and the modern, and a space for intellectual and sensual enjoyment.

Josef Paul Kleihues has practiced architecture in West Germany since 1962. He studied at the Technische Hochschule of Berlin and the Ecole Nationale Superieure des Beaux-Arts in Paris. From 1979 onward he was director of planning for the International Building Exhibition (IBA) in West Berlin, which showcased housing projects by most of the world's leading architects. He initiated the IBA's publication series, *Dokumente und Projekte, Die Neubaugebiete* in 1984. He holds the chair for design and urbanism at the University of Dortmund, West Germany, and is Irwin S. Chanin Distinguished International Professor at The Cooper Union.

We thus find that one of the most characteristic features of the theory of modern architecture has been its concern with morality, whereby the ethical bases of architectural design have obsessed modern propagandists in a way formerly unknown. Why this change should have occurred in the middle of the eighteenth century is not entirely clear, but it is evident that as soon as architects became aware of architectural history, and of the architecture of exotic civilizations (and hence of architectural "style"); as soon as they became uncertain as to which of a wide variety of tectonic elements they might appropriately use; they were obliged to make basic decisions involving moral judgments, and so to discuss fundamental problems which their fortunate forbears had disregarded because in their ignorance of history, and the security of their traditions, they did not know that these fundamental problems existed, and hence were blissfully unaware that there were any ethical decisions to make.

—Peter Collins, *Changing Ideals in Modern Architecture*

Caspar David Friedrich, Der Mönch am Meer, *1808–1810*.

Robert Fripp

THE ACT OF MUSIC

I

The act of music is the music itself. Here are two ways of looking at the act of music:

1) Experientially, in which there is no separation between the elements within the act of music; and
2) Analytically, in which each role is other, or seemingly other, for each of the elements participating in the act.

In the first, the multiplicity of participants honors the unity, but does not *seek* the unity because there is no real separation. From this perspective, any apparent separation occurs only to emphasize the ultimate unity. In the second, we honor the separation and seek connection.

In the first we proceed by an act of *experiencing*. In the second we proceed by *argument*.

In the first, music is one with those who perceive it. That part of us which recognizes music as a friend is not apart from music. In the second, the music is the music, and the audience is the audience.

The first way is *synthesis*. The second is *analysis*.

In *knowing* we learn the parts. In a moment of *understanding* we know an aspect of the whole; there is participation. Our mental habits, the verbal approach to thinking, the Western scientific and philosophic tradition, encourage us to take apart all the bits and look for their connections. Perhaps, because of our ingrained way of thinking, we forget that we are already connected. A technique for facilitating thinking in wholes is therefore more likely to lead to understanding, seeing the complete picture and being part of that complete picture.

Language is what language does, and there are languages which speak of function, languages which address essentials, and languages which speak equally and to all. These languages are different: functional language, which refers to things and physical acts, can establish canons of reference and definition. But when we speak of our essential natures, of the patterns upon which and through which we live our lives, words of *doing* attempt the work of words of *being*. Generally, we assume that words bring us together. In a world of functioning, of doing things together, this may be so. But in a world of being, where we already are together, probably silence is better syntax than learned argument. *One language of being is music.*

In the qualitative world there is no separation. In the world of organization, or essential patterns, there is a separation of roles, or agencies. In the world of doing there is a multiplicity of operators; a profusion of agents.

The multiplicity of operators is only a seeming multiplicity: the number of operators does not increase the number of roles being played. All musicians are simply aspects of the single role of musician. At the point where the individual musician honorably fulfills the role of musician, he acts on behalf of all musicians. Essentially, they are all the same creature. Similarly, the multiplicity of audiences is only one pair of ears. Similarly, one note is all notes, that have ever been and will ever be.

What we hear is not what we are hearing, but the way that we hear. In other words, what we hear is the quality of our listening. And listening is intentional.

Music so wishes to be heard that it calls on some to give it ears and some to give it voice. It is difficult to argue for the intentionality of music, to ascribe to music the capacity of volition, the power of willing itself to be. But when one experiences this musical intentionality, it is the gentlest necessity. Discovering this by the process of rational argument may be very difficult. It is simply experienced, often in unlikely places: perhaps on one's feet in a sweaty rock club. The musician can attest to familiarity with the creative impulse of music's willingness-to-be, and, no doubt, so can many audiences. It is where our lives change irrevocably; we become vital, alive to life. This shift in experiencing the act-of-music is a creative leap in which *music*, the *musician*, and the *audience* become the same person, without reservation, without separation. This experience is available to us all, directly, or through the presence of a person who has had this experience. The sceptic may find this presence more convincing than argument.

II

What is music? Here are two definitions:

1) Music is the cup which holds the wine of silence; sound is that cup, but empty; noise is that cup, but broken.

2) Music is a quality organized in sound.

The first definition is more poetic; the second more precise. They say the same thing, but inversely. The quality of music, this impulse to be clothed in sound, is universal and eternal. It is invariable and unchanging in all cultures and in all times. Forms of organization, patterns through which music appears, vary from culture to culture and from time to time. Some patterns are eternal; some are not. The sound in which music is expressed varies through time and place.

Music is the placement of sound at critical, and necessary, points within a field of silence. A structure of sound is placed within a field full of emptiness. The organization of music is the architecture of silence. There is the organization of sound, and the sound of organization; there is also the organization of silence, in sound. This is close to the sound of music, but the sound of music is not the music, merely a representation of the music.

The difficulty of speaking of creativity is that it does not exist, per se. This does not mean that creativity is not real; simply that it does not belong to the world of existence. *The working of creativity can only be experienced by a creative act*: creativity requires an instrument through which to express its nature.[1] Perhaps, this instrument is the *musician*.

What, then, is the musician? The musician sounds the note, or gives music voice, and perhaps even organizes the unfolding of the sound. Is this enough?

1
Similarly, creative insight requires an instrument. The practice of holding symbolic images in the visual imagination provides mental instruments of synthesis, i.e. drawing together relevant components into wholeness. Systematics is a technique for engaging the active intelligence in fashioning synthetic symbols which function as instruments for creative insight. Where the symbolic figures are natural, i.e. reflecting natural law, or principles of the Creation, they are structural reflections of the creative impulse. This implies that their nature is sympathetic to the nature of creativity.

The notion of correspondence implies that we can only know that which is a part of us. If this is so, then part of the musician corresponds to, or is in correspondence with, the quality of music. Perhaps we may call this the quality-of-musicianness. If we view the act-of-music as a *unity*, in which there is no real, but only apparent, separation, we should also conclude that there is something inseparable in the nature of *musician and music*. A tentative definition of musician might be, then, a quality patterned in flesh.

The question for the practicing musician is, "How can I experience this essential unity for myself?" This is the question which leads one to a discipline. The discipline of the musician is three disciplines: those of the hands, the head, and the heart. These three disciplines are actually one. The discipline begins with the acquisition of craft, and craft begins with obedience. Generally, if we are fortunate, our instructor in craft is a craftsman. In the acquisition of craft, we seek to establish discipline. For this the student needs a teacher who understands his personal needs, and is prepared to accept him as he is. If we manage to establish a personal discipline, our teacher may become music itself.

The acquisition of musical craft begins with the musician addressing the multiplicity within himself: "Am I myself a unity?" We approach our unity by attempting to function as musicians.

The hands, and by extension the whole of the body, the head, and the heart, may be viewed as, first, the musician's instruments of insights, or ways of experiencing, the different worlds of music: music as quality, music as an unfolding pattern, and music as a phenomenological event. Our instruments operate variably, fulfilling their potential and capacity only more or less. The degree to which they fulfill their potential is the degree to which we fully

experience, or fail to experience, that which is possible in our musical lives.

Whenever we make an unfamiliar demand upon ourselves, the ways in which we behave, we discover the remarkable power of habit. For the guitarist, this is often the recalcitrance of the little finger of the left hand, the inability of the right hand to coordinate with the left, and the reliance upon visual contact with the hands. Are we able to hold the pattern of the music in our mind's eye while playing the notes and feeling the mood of the piece? If we wish to discover how we habitually function, the rule is to alter our tempo of operation, whether faster or slower. The mighty being, guitarist-as-musician, convinced of his volitional power, may find himself unable to play and count while breathing and smiling. The harmony of the head, the hands, and the heart is our aim, however difficult in practice.

This point of discovery, however, is a change of state, a change in the quality of our perceptions. Before, we were creatures of habit; now, we are perceiving that we are creatures of habit: we are in contact with what we are doing, perhaps even what we are thinking and feeling. Aware of our perceptions, we make contact with the world around us, as well as the world within us. This is a state of alertness, or vigilance, in which our attention is engaged and in touch with ourselves and the world. The guitarist experiences the flow of blood and the pulse in the left hand; the touch of the fingertips on the string, the string on the fingertips; the delicious sense of fluency in constantly releasing necessary pressure when it becomes unnecessary. Or the discomfort and struggle of misapplied effortfulness. And the triumph of ceasing to make the effort and finding in this point of letting go: the achievement of effortless effort.

When we are in contact with a situation, our perspective is partial, limited, restricted.

Sensitivity to ourselves, our guitar, our environment (musical or otherwise) is subjective. How can we see the situation integrally, as a complete event, from outside our limited terms of reference? How can we know a piece of music as one present moment extended in time, rather than as notes, bars or sections, that is, a succession of moments? Part of the answer lies in aspiration; part lies in commitment. We may not be equal in talent, but we may be equal in aspiration; we may be equal in commitment. Part of the answer lies in the quality of the techniques, whether of hands, head, or heart. Techniques with this approach to extended perspective are quantitatively efficient, compatible in nature and sympathetic in feel to a holistic approach. Necessary information is part of these techniques. The rule of quality is: honor necessity. The rule of quantity is: honor sufficiency. Aspiration directs our aim, commitment ensures our movement toward its realization, and technique provides the means. Talent is of little value.

The alert musician will be in contact with the note sounding in the moment. But to be in contact with all notes in the piece, while playing one particular note, is a quite different order of experiencing. The master musician becomes an instrument available to music. He is efficient and sensitive, and also reliable. He has craft; he has detachment; he sees the world and what it requires, and responds to the requirement, regardless of personal interest. He can answer for himself, but not for music. To answer for oneself is mastery; to answer for music is artistry.

When the musician learns a piece of music, playing it well goes beyond sounding the notes. Music and musician are joined in this act of musicking. It is easy to detect when the notes are being played on the outside of the musician: there is a hollowness within the sound which fails to move or convince us. To add resonance to the mere presentation of sound, the musician brings the music within who he is, by accepting it. As the notes are not

the music, but the phenomenological appearance of the music, so the musician is not the person, but the appearance of the person. If the music is to be sounded rightly, the blending of the essences of both music and musician is necessary, and probably inevitable. Arbitrary music, poorly conceived or springing from a bright idea, brought to the inside of a musician is, at best, unhealthy. The professional musician, whose daily work generally involves him in the acceptance of any music without question, is at risk.

But there is also hope in this: music invents itself through musicians working on behalf of music, rather than themselves. This is healthy music, and can be experienced as such. After listening, or playing, one feels stronger and cleaner. No elaborate metamusics is needed to demonstrate this, for it can be simply experienced. The question for the musician is this: do I become alive playing this? For the audience, it is: do I become alive listening to this?

What is the *audience*? The human agent will conform to the humanity of the musician, but the nature of the agency will differ. The quorum for audience is one, so our tentative definition of the audience is also a quality patterned, or organized, in flesh.

III

The *act of music* is a sacrament in which an outward, audible, and usually visible event expresses phenomenally an inward and qualitative action. This silent, invisible, noumenal, and qualitative presence is nevertheless quite real. Music itself is a sacrament, a quality organized in sound.

The note which is sounded is not the note; it is a representation of the note. The note is not the quality of the note; it is the manifestation in sound of the idea of the note. When we sound the note, A, we are sounding, not a quality, but a representation of the idea of the quality, A. This is the name we give to a universal quality, recognizable by us when it is presented to us in sound.

The quality of music, the musicness of music, accepts the constraints of form and restraints of sound, in order to be brought into the world of sounding and hearing. This musicness sacrifices its possibilities in the world of immanent silence in order to become actual. This sacrifice makes possible the transformation of sound into music by a process in which the sound is ordered, and brought into a relationship with the possibilities present within silence. Without this sacrifice, the sound would remain sound. And if the sound refused to accept ordering, it would degenerate into noise.

So, sound is upgraded by providing a vehicle for the presence of a more subtle world, the creative world, coming into the world of actualities. The relationship between the two is mediated by organization.

The act of music is a musical act. The act of music is also a social act. It is a personal act, a psychological act, perhaps a spiritual act. It takes place in time, perhaps even in eternity. The act of music is an aesthetic act. The act of music is also economic, political, personal, idiosyncratic, universal. The act of music is inherently unlikely, a daily event.

IV

What, then, is the meaning of this unlikely act?

Music is inseparable from the performance of music, where performer, audience, and music come together in a particular place at a particular time, and re-enact this eternal event.

In seeking the meaning of *music* within the *act-of-music* we are seeking meaning and meanings in the presence, conflicts, relationships, activities, potentials, hazards, completenesses, individualities, and processes within the so-

ciety of contributors to this eternal act. Generally, all this is within our experience in the event of performance.

In a moment when a performance comes alive, we experience this presence of the eternal and our place within it. In this creative moment we know this for ourselves, directly, immediately, undeniably, and unprovably. Then, we fall to earth, reach for our manuscript books, scores and pencils, and attempt to analyze the structure of reality. This experience of the eternal, and the following fall from grace, often results in despair and may prompt questions which are always present for the performing musician, whether he wishes them to be or not; whether he considers them or not; whether he answers them upon reflection, or answers them in practice, thinking on his feet while performing to audiences in clubs, theaters, stadia, parks and marquees, at bar mitzvahs, dances, celebrations, communions, carnivals, concerts, entertainments, parties, presentations, or in privacy. These questions are also present for the audience.

Within the act-of-music there is no separation between what music is, does, and sounds like. Within the act of *criticism*, there *is* a separation between what music is, does, and sounds like.

What is the meaning of music? The meaning of the music is the music itself, from which we are not apart. Perhaps. There is meaning in the sound, meaning in the organization, meaning in the quality. And each contains the other, inseparably. The sound is a phenomenological event, the sound has a pattern, and the sound has a quality. The organization has a pattern, and a distinctive quality, and may be phenomenologically represented, by indication or by symbol. The quality is a quality, real but not existent, yet tangible and recognizable within phenomena, and has a pattern which exceptionally gifted individuals, the innocent, and fools can sometimes see.[2]

2
1.   i) The sound of the sound has meaning;
   ii) The pattern of the sound has meaning;
  iii) The quality of the sound has meaning;

2.   i) The sound of the organization has meaning;
   ii) The pattern of the organization has meaning;
  iii) The quality of the organization has meaning;

3.   i) The sound of the quality has meaning;
   ii) The pattern of the quality has meaning;
  iii) The quality itself has meaning.

Musicians use indications, generally in musical notation, for the depiction of sound. This has its limitations, and sometimes other symbols, even gestures, are used to represent the organization of sound. Iconic music I have never seen visually represented; this is not its medium. Iconic music is present, real but not existing, within the act of music.

Assuming all the elements of sound, organization, and quality to be present, we will have full and rich, yet perhaps quite simple, music. But these elements may not be fully present in the audience, or the musician. Although meaning may be present in the music, it may not be present in the musician or audience. This leads us to communication.

Assuming the musician is competent, and has intention, can he communicate? Does he have anything to communicate, that is, what does he communicate? How does he communicate? If the musician does, as is said, have something to say, why should an audience listen to it? Or, can the audience listen to what is being said? If it can listen, does it understand what is being said? The syntactic and semantic content of the music may be very sophisticated; does it matter, in terms of the language of music, that the audience is without comprehension?

Consideration of what music says-itself-to-be is a consideration of the *musical language* of a particular piece of music. This is generally the approach in the Western tonal-harmonic tradition. By analogy, we might say that this presumes the meaning to be contained within the syntax of the musical language: the shape of the relationship between the notes, the indications of what is to be played, and how it is to be played, expresses, determines, contains, or simply is, the meaning. In this view, the structure not only determines the quality of the music; the structure *is* the quality of the music. Within this tradition, this form of consideration is referred to as musical analysis. However, what is analyzed is actually a musical score. Structured, notated, the music does not have to

be sounded for a literate audience to discover, quietly, the meaning of the piece. A successful musical score generates the sense of immediacy of the musical insight. Otherwise, the score is a record of labor. We may ask whether the meaning of music is different in a musical tradition which has no notation, or a restricted notation where small indications are developed between musicians in a personal context. Does a literate musicality change our musical event?

The *history* of music is the history of the development of musical forms of organization, where one technical solution leads to another. This is the act-of-music as a sequence, as progress, as unfolding in time, revealed by the studying of scores. A score *represents* the language of music, and the sounding of that language. The score describes what the composer has seen, not the seeing. The seeing is an eternal moment, in the moment: it is an act-of-seeing, creative, unified and unifying.

Experience is our access to the quality of an event, and we can discover the history of music which has never been notated within the creative performance. This moment is unchanging: it is the act-of-music as a process within which we participate. Within this unchanging moment we understand how it has always been for musicians and audiences in that moment. Where there is no score, there is no history, but there may be eternity. In the *creative leap*, the history of music waits outside. In a sense, all creative leaps are the same: *the* creative leap. This single creative leap at all times and all places by all people is our place in eternity, and where we meet.

Music is a society of the imagination in which relationships of the perfect world are ordered and presented for examination, experiencing, and participation. This perfect world is a temporary affair, but the moment of experiencing is an eternal moment, the future reaching back to pull us towards it, the present repairing the past, the past preparing its future. Perhaps, the perfect world can only be in the moment: not a structure to be reified and deified, and applicable to all occasions and situations, but limited by the extent of our willingness and capacity to be in the moment.

The audience, as witness, recognizing the music and musicians of quality, can connect hearers with listening and with music worthy of their aspirations. An understanding audience can exert an influence on the musician by supporting him, but by also making a demand of him. Similarly, the understanding musician will not accept the audience's demand to entertain, other than as a means of leading the audience to something more.

What is the meaning of the musician? Obviously, the executant produces sound, but this is not necessarily the musician who writes or directs the production of sound. What are the intentions of the composer, or writer, or arranger? Of the bandleader or conductor? Or the player, perhaps in the rank and file of a symphony orchestra, or the session player doing jingles sessions under rigid control, or the gigster playing cover versions in lounge bars around West Virginia?

The *pragmatic* musician, the practicus, is concerned with solving problems within sound, rather than within the organization of sound. Often, the main semantic problem of the working musician is earning a living. The *theoretician* is concerned with the knowledge of music; the practicus with the use of music. Both seek the quality of music, but in different places. There is music, and there is the *use* of music. In the use of music, the music changes. The practicus is concerned with organizing his experience within the act-of-music; the theoretician is interested in organizing music. Both can help each other. In a perfect world, both inhabit the same body.

The musician, at moments of understanding, has insights into his relationship with music which are surprising. Where the musician consents to the action of music upon him,

without reservation for wherever this may lead, the life of the musician changes. Before, the musician used music. Now, music uses the musician. Perhaps the musician has a sense that his involvement with music is not arbitrary, and that music has guided his life from birth. Perhaps a large pattern of his life unexpectedly presents itself. To begin with, feeling like this may seem imaginary, accidental, or coincidental. And it often is. But in time, with discrimination, one learns to trust this sense, and to believe in it. Belief becomes faith and trust grows to reliance: music is a benevolent presence constantly and readily available to all. The unexpected appears, and one sometimes follows promptings for no rational reason. There is simply a feeling of rightness, even when this seems to run counter to the situation of one's life. There is a resonance to rightness, and rightness has its own necessity. The musician calls constantly on music for help; sometimes, one wakes in the night and finds oneself calling silently to music, our friend. Sometimes, one finds our friend calling quietly to us.

If the meaning of a particular piece of music can be simply found in an analysis of its sonological, syntactic and semantic properties, is the meaning of the music itself altered by the intentions and motivations of the audience and performer, or promoter? If motivations and intentions alter behavior, or our perceptions of behavior, will the behavior of the musician and audience affect the meaning of the music? We may ask the intention of music (if we can attribute intentionality to music) and what it intends for us.

Assuming intention, in performance the intention of the performer is limited by his competence. Assuming intention, in performance the intention of the audience is limited by its capacity to listen. How is our musical event affected by capacity?

A reasonable, intelligent, discerning and enquiring musician, or listener to music, will consider the meaning of music, in general and particular. He will perhaps consider the possibility that music is a doorway to the world of qualities, and then look for the meaning in a piece of music. Unfortunately, this reasonable, intelligent, and discerning enquiry will almost certainly close the door.

The doorway which opens to a finer, more subtle world is closer to me than the air I breathe. Strangely, it is a doorway to myself. It may be roughly hewn, even of poor materials; but if it is seen to be a doorway, it may be used as such. To go through this door to myself all that is required is that I leave behind my baggage; this doorway is exceptionally small. And, surprisingly, on the other side of the doorway I find myself. For just a moment. Then I am called back by my notions of fine art, the meaning of art, even sacred art.

The audience which can make contact with the music as it is occurring is in the moment, but the moment is short; the listening is only partial. How does one hear a piece of work in its entirety, as an integral event, at any point within it? This is an equivalent to the master musician, and its numbers are likely to be limited. We might call this a conscious audience.

If the artist is *silent*, responding directly to the creative impulse of music as it flies, what is to be said of the *audience* which is one in this creative act of music? What might we call this audience for the architecture of silence-in-sound? Perhaps, a creative audience.

The musician and the audience available and in contact with music-in-the-moment have a perspective, albeit a partial and subjective one, of the moment. The music is music, but subjective music; beautiful music, but a distraction from going further.

The master musician and the conscious audience are in-the-moment, but the extended moment of a complete event: they are committed to this act of music beyond their per-

sonal, limited interest. This music is true, and therefore common to all. This is true, or objective, music.

The genius and the creative audience are the parents to new music. This new music may only be heard once, in the flying leap of the improviser; it may be iconic, where the recording of the event is the event that it purports to be: The Beatles' *Sergeant Pepper's Lonely Hearts Club Band* is a notable example. The transmission by symbols of one great creative leap may enable the re-creative musician and the creative audience to return in innocence to an earlier moment of the same conception: Mozart, Beethoven, Bach, Bartok.

What is the music of the noisy musician and the deaf audience? Probably, muzak. Muzak is aural imprisonment. Within the prison we remain responsible for our responses, and, although limited, they may be creative. But real music not only permits us the freedom to make our own creative response; it is the springboard for that response. This is the point where our lives change; they will never be the same again. When this current turns on we have no way of rationalizing, or describing, or proving, what we know for ourselves: that music is a benevolent presence, constantly, freely, readily available to all and that there is no separation between us. The act of music *is* the music.

V

And yet music is a product, a commodity, for sale in the marketplace, the act-of-music a commercial transaction. The art is in selling; the quality of artistry in the quantity of sales. To our participants within the act-of-music— music, musician, audience—let us add a new contributor: the music industry.

The musician aspires to music; the professional musician aspires to earning a living. The life of the musician is difficult; the life of the professional musician is difficult, and more

Paul Klee, Gebrige im Winter, *1925.*

complex. The relationship, music/musician/audience, accepts direction in order to discover itself in activity. Within this particular activity-of-music, the professional activity of music, the direction is given by the music industry. The capacity of any agency to discharge its role within any particular structure depends upon a cohesion between the components of the agency, that is, between the agents. The clarity of direction in the professional activity-of-music is contingent on the unity of the music industry. Similarly, the strength of this activity-of-music is determined by the unity of common aim between the industry, musician, and audience. *Is the aim music?* The assumption is affirmative; the experience is mixed.

The musician knows music is a gift, and that a gift is the outcome of an act-of-giving. For the gift to continue as an act-of-giving it must remain in motion. If the act-of-giving becomes a thing, the gift is separated from the world to which it belongs. So, the musician is only able to receive the gift-of-music for as

long as music is kept in motion: the musician is as rich as the music he has given away.

The professional musician takes money for music; even claims to create music. This is called composition, or authorship. Music created by this musician is probably recorded, and its quality is meaured in *units*. It will be published, copyrighted, and become the property of the copyright owner. The right to listen to this recording is owned by the audience, which has paid for this right by boosting the "unit quality" of the record. Otherwise, it will assemble in a public place to become an audience for this music, or musician, in a *musical event*. The quality of this event is measured in the number of operators meeting to discharge the agency of audience. This music is an asset, bankable, and something to be relied upon; but it has no rights, no volition: and no impulse from itself is accounted for.

What is the source of tension between the musician/audience and the music industry? For the musician and the audience, music is inseparable from the performance of music: this is a process, whether the performance of music is live, or recorded. For the music industry the performance of music, whether a primary or secondary experience (or even a tertiary experience via notation), is an object. Music as process is communal, hazardous, malleable, dynamic, changing, and inseparable from its contributors. Music as object is reified, collectable, product, private, static, and controllable, a record of the process but not the process itself, the property of its owners, and probably expensive. So, here are our two main sources of tension:

1) A difference in the perception of the nature of music, as separable and inseparable from performance;
2) A difference in distribution of the results of performance in its varying forms, whether separable or not.

This is an example of a relationship of variable quality which the professional musician will necessarily, and inevitably, address.

The main components of the music industry are record manufacture and distribution, artist management and direction, music publishing, promotion and plugging, and live performance services. The communications media are independent but closely linked in operation; they perform the sounding of music and depiction of musicians. Although they are not actually a part of the music industry, it is not possible to discuss the conventional assumptions of the industry without reference to radio, television, and the press, the way these media work, and their governing assumptions.

The effect on musicians of their interaction with the media is to stress their *celebrity*, their appearance, and their opinions, rather than their musicianship. For musicians whose interest lies in celebrity and use music as a vehicle, this will be satisfactory. For a musician who wishes to present himself musically, the clear

implication is that one must learn the vocabularies of fashion and presentation of self. The music industry sells both music, in various forms, and the *producers* of music.

Radio and television sell advertising, and generally papers and magazines survive on their advertising revenue rather than the direct sale of copies; the sale of copies attracts advertising. Similarly, radio and TV advertising is sold on the basis of the size of the audience. The assumption is that the audience is attracted by the presentation of recorded music and music videos. The music industry supplies radio and TV with its sources of sound and vision freely and without cost (although this is changing, and disputed) in exchange for audibility and visibility: exposure to a large audience. Press are also supplied with free records/tapes and publicity material. There is a significant correlation between the size of single sales and radio/TV play. Album sales reflect singles sales. So:

1) The most significant factor in recording music, for record company promotion, is to get radio/TV play (preferably TV).
2) The most significant factor in getting video/TV play is to get radio/TV programmers to play the record/video.
3) Significant factors in enlisting the support of programmers are:
    a) The belief that the record/TV play will attract a large audience;
    b) Provision of a free product;
    c) Reminders of the symbiotic relationship between the communications industry and the music industry (pressure, favors).

Therefore, the most significant factor in making an album is to make a single which will appeal to programmers, or those that influence programmers.

How does this affect the musician? There is, within the industry, a conventional assumption that

1) It is not possible to tour without a hit record.
2) The musician cannot perform without a hit.
3) The musician cannot have a hit without performing.

The rationale is based on the high costs of touring. From the record company's viewpoint, ticket receipts from live performance are only of relevance if they enable the performer to go on the road and promote the record. If there is a projected loss on the touring budget, this is the subject of negotiation between interested parties (record company, artist, artist management, concert promoters, and performance agent). Often the touring performer is unpaid for his live performances; his record and publishing royalties being considered his payment.

This assumption locks recording and performance together, but with recording in the prime position. However, live performance is quite different in nature to recorded performance: one is *in* the moment; the other is *fixed in* the moment. For the musician, live work is the way to discover the music one is playing; it only comes to life before an audience.

What solutions to this dilemma can the industry advance? What solutions can the audience or musician advance? The confusion can be resolved to a considerable degree if one resolves the aim: if the aim is *music*, then the reward is the *music*. If the aim is a successful music *product*, then the reward is *success*.

If music is inseparable from the performance of music, we must include *performance* in our commercial considerations. In this sense, performance is the outcome of the demands and responses of the *music, musician, audience, and music industry*. A representation of a performance, as in a record or video, generally lacks the presence of the audience, other than in the imagination of the performer, or the ability of another element to play the role of audience. In the immediacy of live performance, something

becomes possible which would not be possible otherwise: the audience can respond in the moment to the music and musician, the musician to music and audience, the music to audience and musician, and change the course of the performance. This is why live performance will always offer more potential than could the record: possibilities are present which otherwise could not be.

Performance, as an act, speaks several languages at once which are received in parallel by the audience. The musician learns that these other languages may be as, or more, important for the audience than the musical one. In performance, there are visual, verbal, and musical codes interacting between the audience and musician. The visual codes are kinesthetics, dress, and stage set. Gesture is a more concrete language than music, and a sumptuary code more immediate. If the musician has no awareness of his body movement or appearance, this is a clear statement of his nonawareness. The verbal code includes lyrics, which may or may not be *en rapport* with music, announcements, and introductions. This language is concrete. If music is a language, it is abstract.

Anything within the performance has significance, whether intentional or not. In performance the musician becomes a performer, whether he wishes to or not. The performer can hide nothing, even the attempt to hide. One is revealed, and revealed completely. This is humiliating. The part of the musician which experiences humiliation is the part which gets in the way of that music reaching directly into the heart of the musician: egotism. The brave, committed, and egotistical musician will recognize this as a reliable way to approach more closely to music, if he can bear it. This is a hard education for the aspirant musician, and subtle.

The experiences of performance as an event, and as a commercial event, are quite different experiences. It is difficult to conceive of the music industry affecting the course of the performance while it is under way, although we must allow that this is part of the possibility. The best examples, in the context of performance, of the music industry assuming the role of *direction* while *sharing the aim* of music are probably in the free festivals of the 1960s. At one of these, the Rolling Stones' Hyde Park concert of 1969, I played as a member of King Crimson. The remarkable sense of optimism might be better described as a sense of possibility in the occasion: we felt we could change the world. If one of the contributory elements fails to share the same aim, the possibilities shrink. Practically, a large and expensive performance has less possibility than a large performance where the audience gives what it can, and to a charity. The most notable recent example is the Live Aid concerts of 1985.

The relationship between recording and performance becomes possible through proportion: where the scale of each is fitting as regards the other.[3] The music industry rarely distinguishes between scales of operation; fails to acknowledge that some relationships are governed by size. (This changed considerably during the 1980s, as typified by the formation of small independent record labels. Often these have been formed by musicians who have been excluded from recording and performance by the functional dilemma, and who have adopted a second role to make music possible.) In discussion of scale, it would be unfair to suggest that the industry is the only component which suffers confusion of scale; performers with mistaken beliefs in their drawing power can budget records, and tours, of impressive unrealism.

VI

Probably most of us have experienced at some time in our life a sense of unity with music, or perhaps with a musician, or being at one within an audience. And yet we honor the separation, seeking connection. Why?

Firstly, this is a partial way of looking at the whole of things, which is well established: in our culture, it has become habitual. And what we believe to be happening is more important to us than what is happening. What we see is the way that we see: the world we perceive is not our sense impressions of the world, but our interpretation of our sense impressions. For the audience, there is more to hearing than meets the ear. To a considerable degree this results from our cognition being based in language. If we were to say, "the act of music contains three elements: music, musician, and audience," we would envisage the act of music as three distinct elements trying to come together. If instead we found a way of saying:

"Act-of-music"
music
musician
audience
"   "

as one word, we would begin to have a feel for the unity in the act, rather than the components of the act. Unitive cognition requires a different way to thinking, for example: visually, symbolically, simultaneously, in synthetic images; rather than verbally, sequentially, and analytically. Since our thinking, at least in the West, is automatically verbal, only when our attention is engaged and present in our thinking is there any likelihood of us seeing the connections rather than the separations. Both ways are valid, and complementary: one way sees the inside, the other the outside. Seeing the separation while honoring the unity, the unity knows itself more fully.

Secondly, this can be a full way of looking at things where the seeing is misplaced. In the person, this is an assertion of individualness at the expense of individuality. Moral philosophy of a theological bent has referred to this as a fall from grace, a separation from the power within connection. In the act-of-music, this is the musician who believes himself to be the creator

3.
This should come as no surprise to the musician, knowing music's role in the quadrivium as the branch of mathematics dealing with ratio theory: the reflection of qualities in the relevance between quantities.

of music, the inventor of the audience, and the originator of the act. Yet, egotism is not far from individuality. What is involved in replacing this viewpoint, moving our seeing from egotism to individuality?

Let us pose this question: to what must we attend? The question provides its answer: we attend to what we must. Then, we can say, there are different qualities of attention. We may have no attention, attention which is attracted and distracted, and attention which is under our direction. The quality of our attention is who we are, where we live, and who we know ourselves to be. To be who we are, we attend to our attention.

Responsibility is present only where attention is present. Without attention there is no contact; without contact there is no mutuality; without mutuality there is no responsibility. When there is contact, the nature of the responsibility is governed by the nature of the contact.

There is quality of attention and placement of attention. If our attention can be brought within ourselves, we begin to experience ourselves from the inside; the sensation of living within a body, the thinking of thoughts, the feeling of feelings. As our contact with ourselves grows, and the quality of attention changes, so does the nature of our responsibility. We begin with accepting responsibility for our organic state: our health. Then, we are responsible for our thoughts, and our feelings. At this point we can do nothing but make the contact and accept the responsibility. With practice, we take responsibility for our behavior, our thinking of thoughts and our feeling of feelings: we assume the active role toward our human instruments. In experiencing our directing of these instruments of human operation, we experience ourselves as separate from what we do: we experience who we are. I am not my thoughts, neither am I the thinking, I am the thinker. I am not my feelings, neither am I what my body does, I am the director of

the body. Who I am is not three (thinker, feeler, doer) but one: I am a unity in the act-of-humanity. When we contact who we are, there is another part of us that is making contact. We can never see this part of ourselves directly: it would be like the eye seeing itself. But we can know it indirectly, and we can discover it through understanding others. If we understand others in this way, there is no separation between who you are and who I am. I may even find myself behind your eyes looking at me, feeling your feelings, seeing things the way you see them, experiencing you experiencing me: I am you and you are me. This is known in a moment.

Contact is the outcome of a mobile attention. If our attention is fixed within ourselves, we are separateness incarnate. This is alienation, and is unnecessary. The alienation may be habitual, or clear, or conscious, even creative. It is a denial of who we are, of both you and me.

It is necessary for the musician to attend to his musician-ness, to the audience, and to music. The professional musician will also give attention to the music industry, and to performance; perhaps, even the performance place. If the musician's quality of attention is such that he experiences the essence of his humanity within the role he plays, he will also make contact with the humanity of the audience, in which there is no difference. This incurs *responsibility*. In this contact, the spirit of music is not apart. The highest quality of attention which can be given is love. If grace is a gift given freely and without reservation, then the act of music is an act of grace. Within the unity *act-of-music*, grace is an invisible contributor which maintains the connections between the functioning of the agents. The separation is, as we have seen, only apparent. The *act-of-music* is an intentional *act-of-giving*, and graceful music the invisible glue which maintains the unity.

Perhaps, the *act-of-loving* is love itself.

Robert Fripp is a rock guitarist based in Wessex, England. He has collaborated with, among others, Brian Eno, David Bowie, and Peter Gabriel; but he is best known as the leader of influential and controversial rock band, King Crimson, which he founded in 1969. In 1974 he met the late J. G. Bennett, a disciple of the Caucasian thinker G. I. Gurdjieff, and disbanded King Crimson to study at Bennett's school in Sherbourne, Gloucestershire. In recent years he has concentrated on teaching guitar through his Guitar Craft Workshops and currently directs Guitar Craft courses worldwide.

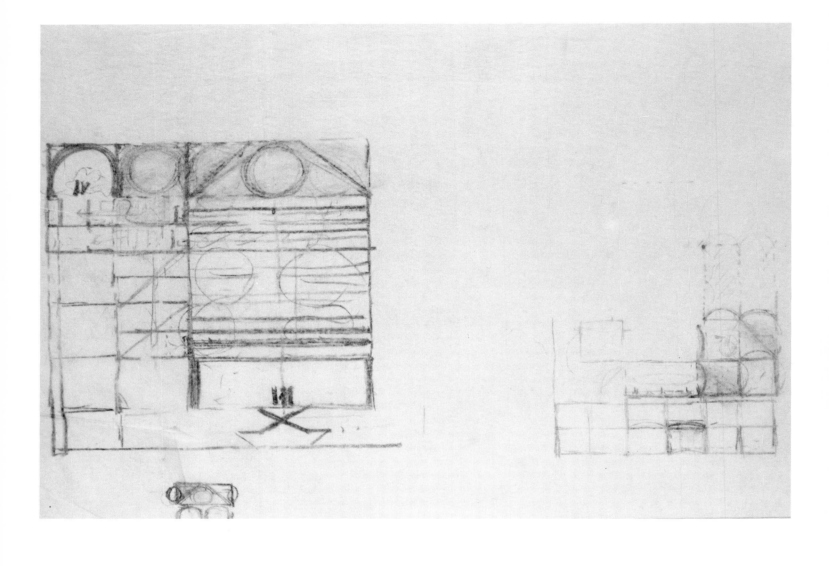

Peter Kohane

LOUIS I. KAHN AND THE LIBRARY:
Genesis and Expression of "Form"

1
See Vincent Scully, Jr., *Louis I. Kahn* (New York: Braziller, 1962), 18.

2
Other building types in Kahn's work could be fruitfully analysed to reveal a similar change. For instance, the museum, where the interrelationship of two grand public spaces with galleries, libraries, etc., at the Yale Center for British Arts and British Studies, New Haven, 1969–74, replaces the open loft spaces of the Yale Art Gallery, New Haven, 1951–53; or the laboratory, where the plaza and cabins of the final phase of the Salk Institute for Biological Studies, La Jolla, 1959–65, provide a dimension to the nature of scientific work not present in the prosaic spaces of the Richards Medical Research Laboratory, Philadelphia, 1957–60.

1. *Louis I. Kahn, Phillips Exeter Academy Library. Section; L.I.K. 710.91 in the Louis I. Kahn Archive of the University of Pennsylvania.*

Louis I. Kahn founded the design work for an architectural project on a meditative inquiry into the essential characteristics of the particular institution. In his view, the nature of the institution belonged to a realm of ideas which transcended the interests of the individual architect and the immediate requirements of each commission. By studying Kahn's various schemes for a single building type—in this case the library—one can discover the way in which Kahn sought to give fundamental human concerns, such as reading and learning, a concrete architectural shape. This approach is particularly valuable in identifying a major and hitherto rarely explored change in Kahn's work.

In general Kahn's mature phase has been dated to 1950–51 when, as a fellow at the American Academy in Rome, he was inspired by ancient architecture.[1] However, a comparison of a library designed soon after that time with those commissioned in the 1960s and 1970s reveals a further transformation in his thinking. Kahn maintained the monumentality and integrity of structure attained in the buildings of the early and mid–1950s, but explored a greater variety of spaces, bringing them together in a new manner.[2] The source of this change was a profound insight into human nature and society that acknowledged the importance of an individual's private and public life, the interconnections between each realm, and the relationship of both to a spiritual existence.

This investigation draws upon the collection of personal sketches held in the Louis I. Kahn Archive at the University of Pennsylvania.[3] A unique resource, the Archive is the result of Kahn's expressed hope that the material in his office should not be dispersed upon his death, but should remain intact as a public collection. In this wish, he was guided by his conviction that a building was more than simply the finished product. Rather, it comprised on the one hand the architect's creative process, as revealed by sketches and models, and on the other the materials and techniques by which it was constructed.[4]

Kahn designed three self-contained libraries, all for schools.[5] The first, was a competition entry for Washington University, St. Louis, in 1956. The jury found fault with that design and passed over it in favor of that of another architect. The second was the Phillips Exeter Academy Library, built between 1966 and 1972, and considered by many to be one of his most successful works. The last library was a project for the Graduate Theological Union at Berkeley, commissioned in 1972. At Kahn's death in 1974, a final scheme had been determined and documented in a model, perspectives by Kahn himself, and a number of office drawings, but no final working drawings had been prepared.[6] The sketches for these schemes included brief ideograms, close statements of a first response to the nature of a library; drawings that conveyed his search for appropriate spaces for human use; and plans, perspectives, etc., that, like the elaborate models, described the completed phase or project. Complementing the drawings and models were his pronouncements on the meaning of the institution of the library.

Kahn's designs for, and comments on, the three libraries are succinct and profound, yet they cannot express the full nature of his difficult search and achievements. An awareness of his theory of architecture and its place within his philosophy is also necessary. Kahn's beliefs can best be outlined by introducing his key concepts and explaining them with reference to his own analysis of the conception and realization of the First Unitarian Church, Rochester, N.Y., commissioned in 1959.

2. Silence to Light. *From bound sketchbook; L.I.K. K12.*

Kahn's theory is broadly encapsulated in the dichotomy of *Silence* and *Light*.[7] *Silence* contains our desires: the desire to learn, to meet, and to achieve a state of well-being; that is, all those attributes which define our humanity. The essential meaning of an institution, which is termed its *"form,"* exists in this realm. In the famous "Silence and Light" diagram (Fig. 2), *Light* refers to the tangible representation of the realm of ideas. The transformation from Silence to Light occurs through the act of *"design,"* which exists between, in the realm of shadows.

Kahn carefully defined "design" in relation to "form" in his explanation of the sequence of sketches for the First Unitarian Church (Fig. 3)[8]. The "form" was his intuition of the meaning of the institution: a Unitarian church. For Kahn, Protestantism differed from Catholicism, with its stress on faith and ritual, by stimulating people to search and question. A central sacred space for communal worship and discussion, with surrounding ancillary spaces

to be used for school rooms and other social and educational activities, was therefore proposed. "Form" thus defined the hierarchical and reciprocal relationship between these two kinds of activities. The upper sketch in Fig. 3 is a close representation of the "form" idea. Kahn's diagrammatic drawings were not conceived in response to a specific building program, but addressed such issues as activities, relations, and hierarchies. They were the first visual representations of a deeper reality, one which could only be experienced intuitively. Thus, the "form" was the generating idea, which guided the initial sketch, and to which all further design decisions relating to specific requirements had to refer.

By contrast, "design" was the circumstantial part of an architect's work, involving consideration of available materials, costs, and specific requirements of the client. During this process, Kahn was careful not to override his initial commitment to the "form." Thus, while engaged in the act of designing (the "how to do it"), he constantly asked: "Am I designing what I intended?" At Rochester, for instance, various specific "design" factors led to the plan at the upper right-hand corner. However, this plan conflicted with his initial intuition, and therefore was rejected. Finally, he devised a plan which both accommodated the specific requirements and reinforced the original "form" (see the lower left-hand plan).

The Rochester drawing primarily conveys the role of "design" in terms of the imposition of specific requirements upon the "form"-idea. To understand the creative process of arriving at the "design," one must refer again to the meaning of Silence and Light, particularly in relation to the creation of a space, such as the central hall at Rochester. Kahn believed that the material world was spent light.[9] It was in these terms that the rationale for the activity of "design" was conceived: materials and structure were essential to the revelation of light:

A great American Poet once asked the Architect, "What slice of the sun does your building have? What light enters your Room?" as if to say the sun never knew how great it is until it struck the side of a building.[10]

As this comment and the sketch of "The Room" upon which it is inscribed (Fig. 4) indicate, such a vision was predicated upon the assumption of a discrete unit of space. Kahn

3
The Louis I. Kahn Archive, comprising personal sketches, working drawings, models, and office files, is jointly administered by the University of Pennsylvania and the Pennsylvania Historical and Museum Commission.

4
To date, scholars have not fully exploited the opportunity to investigate the conceptual stages of Kahn's architecture which is provided by the Archive's holdings. The present study is therefore intended to demonstrate one of the ways in which the Archive can be used to trace the genesis and evolution of Kahn's design process.

5
Important libraries designed as part of larger institutions include those at the Indian Institute of Management, Ahmedabad, India, 1962–74, and at the Philadelphia College of Art, 1960–66.

6
The Graduate Theological Union Library was ultimately completed in 1987 by two California firms, Esherick, Homsey, Dodge & Davis and Peters, Clayberg & Caulfield. These architects altered Kahn's design in response to changing client requirements. Joseph Esherick and Richard Peters were both friends of Kahn, and sought to complete the project in the spirit of his work. The completed building is discussed by the architects in an unpublished pamphlet prepared for the opening ceremony in April 1987. It is held at the Graduate Theological Union Library.

7
The terms Silence and Light were introduced in the late 1960s. For analyses of Kahn's theories see Scully, *Louis I. Kahn*, 32–34; and Alexandra Tyng, *Beginnings: Louis I. Kahn's Philosophy of Architecture* (New York: John Wiley and Sons, 1984), chs. 2, 4. Kahn's major theoretical essays include "Remarks," *Perspecta* 9/10 (1965): 303–335; "Structure and Form," The Voice of America *Forum Lectures*, a series on Modern American Architecture in 1960, in Scully, *Louis I. Kahn*, 114–21; "Architecture: Silence and Light," in *On the Future of Art*, ed. A.

Toynbee, (New York: Viking, 1970), 20–35.

Parts of these and other writings can be found in Richard Saul Wurman, *What Will Be Has Always Been: The Words of Louis I. Kahn* (New York: Access Press, Ltd., and Rizzoli, 1986); J. Lobell, *Between Silence and Light: Spirit in the Architecture of Louis I. Kahn*, (Boulder: Shambhala, 1979); Tyng, *Beginnings*; H. Rohner, et.al., *Louis I. Kahn Complete Works*, (Boulder: Westview Press, 1977). Many tapes of Kahn's lectures are held in the Louis I. Kahn Archive.

8
See J.C. Rowan, "Wanting To Be: The Philadelphia School," *Progressive Architecture* 42, no. 4 (April 1961):134. This is also discussed in Tyng, *Beginnings*, 43–44.

noted that "the light that enters the room should be the light of the room itself."[11] He also assumed the necessity of a coherent structural solution. Drawing on the legacy of an established theoretical position now termed the Graeco-Gothic ideal, he argued that the structure must respect the "order of nature."[12] Kahn's insight lay in his belief that the theory of designing a rational structure was inherently linked to the creation of light and the meanings this conveyed. To "grow" a room was to bring the meaning of an institution, the "form," out of the realm of Silence into Light.

In the early fifties, Kahn couched the search for meaning appropriate to a particular institution in his question, "What is the nature of space?" His well-known comment, "in a small room one does not say what one would in a large room,"[13] reflected this approach to conceiving context. A sketch for the section of the theater in the Fine Arts Center, Fort Wayne, Indiana, 1959–73, reveals further aspects of his thinking. In this drawing, Kahn labeled the concrete auditorium space, "violin," since it resonates with sound like the musical instrument; and he surrounded it with a brick "violin-case."[14] This analogy between music and space draws upon German Romantic theories, which stressed the similarities between music and architecture, both being capable of acting directly upon the soul.[15] Indeed, the very notion of space was first formulated in late nineteenth century German intellectual circles. For Kahn, however, it was light, not music, that filled space and served as the representation of the meaning of an institution. Light had a tangible presence in a space and was inseparable from the order of materials and structure. A particular nature of space thus required a particular conjunction of material and light. In the the First Unitarian Church, light entering the central space through four

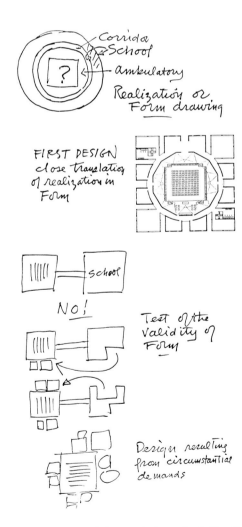

3. *Left: Kahn's explanation of "form" and "design" for the First Unitarian Church, Rochester, New York, 1959–67. Right: Skylights in the church's sanctuary.*

4. The Room.

hoods at the corners takes on different qualities in response to the configuration and materials of the surfaces with which it interacts (Fig. 3). The structure of the room gives substance and value to light. With its endlessly changing effects, the interior exists in a flux of natural light and shadow, in which Kahn located the significance of the institution.

While the "form/design" sketches for Rochester do not convey all dimensions of the search for appropriate spaces, they indicate how the rooms, once "grown," were integrated to ensure that the overall "form" was never compromised. For Kahn, the resulting plan was a "society of rooms."[16] The relationship between these discrete rooms was conceived in terms of "served" and "servant" spaces. Periph-

5. The Street is a Room.

eral rooms of the First Unitarian Church, for instance, serve the central space, just as the foyer of the Fort Wayne theater serves the auditorium. This concern to create hierarchical sequences reflected Kahn's philosophical understanding of order. In architectural terms, he did not conceive of space as universal and undifferentiated; rather, unity was created from the coming together of unequal parts. Such a division of roles extended from the smallest to the largest constituent element: from the gathering-up of mechanical services, to the grouping of school rooms around a central hall, to the role of a building within the city. Hence the note accompanying a sketch for an urban setting, stating that the "street is a room" (Fig. 5). Elaborating on this elsewhere, he observed, "a street wants to be a building equally organized as to space and structure as any other piece of architecture."[17]

In explaining his approach to design, Kahn was skeptical of the formalistic implications of the term "composing," preferring to stress the idea of "growing" spaces.[18] Although the emphasis on the role of discrete spaces hierarchically ordered and linked is reminiscent of the Beaux Arts method, he also drew on an organic theoretical tradition in which space was a response to the promise of function. A comment made by Colin Rowe in a letter to Kahn of 1956, now in the Kahn Archive, acutely highlighted this difference.[19] Recalling a previous and often impassioned debate with Kahn over the merits and demerits of "composition," Rowe observed: "You deplored composition because it appeared to be no more than a manipulation of forms for the sake of effect. You wanted to grow a building."

To summarize this investigation into Kahn's theories, then, the "form" of an institution is that intuition into its essential meaning which, through "design," is represented in spaces determined by material and light. The meaning an individual experiences in such spaces is this idea of the institution. Perhaps the most striking feature is the blending of structural rationalism with the notions of light and space. The former ultimately derives from the French Enlightenment, while the latter belongs to the tradition of Romanticism especially strong in German circles. For Kahn, the meaning of space was an intuition suspended in a light that was derived from a rational structure.

* * * *

9
Quoted in P. McLaughlin, " 'How'm I doing, Corbusier?' an interview with Louis Kahn," *The Pennsylvania Gazette* vol. 71, no. 3 (December 1972):23.

10
The poet is Wallace Stevens. See Tyng, *Beginnings*, 23. The "Room Sketch" is in Tyng, *Beginnings*, 131. She dates the drawing as approximately 1971.

11
Ibid.

12
See K. Frampton, "Louis Kahn and the French Connection," *Oppositions* 22 (Fall 1980):21–53.

13
Quoted in Lobell, *Between Silence and Light*, 38.

14
See Tyng, *Beginnings*, 98.

15
For Kahn's connection to German Romanticism, see J. Burton, "Notes from Volume Zero: Louis Kahn and the Language of God," *Perspecta* 20 (1983):70–90.

16
See "Room Sketch," Fig. 3.

17
See L.I. Kahn, "Order in Architecture," *Perspecta* 4 (1957): 62; Scully, *Louis I. Kahn*, 27.

18
Although the term "growth" was replaced after the 1950s by other theoretical terms such as "form", the basic concept was maintained.

19
See the letter from Colin Rowe to Louis I. Kahn, February 7, 1956, L.I.K. Box 65.

20
For a perceptive analysis of the building, see Scully, *Louis I. Kahn*, 26. The building appeared in the literature of the time; see "Murphy and Mackey Design Wins Washington University Competition," *Architectural Record* 120 (July 1956):16; and "St. Louis Architects Win Washington University Competition," *Progressive Architecture* 37 (July 1956):76–77.

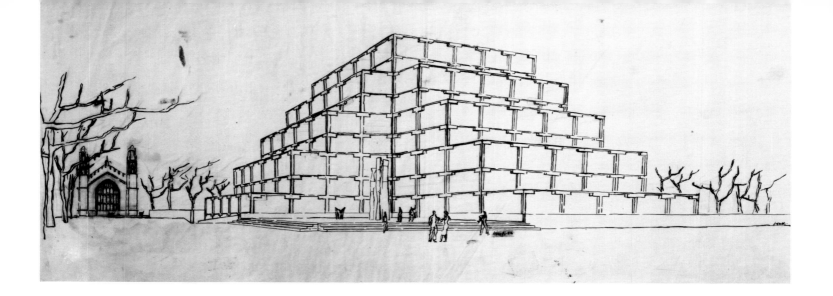

6. *Competition entry for the Library of Washington University, St. Louis, Mo., 1956. Perspective; L.I.K. 465.11.*

21
All plan levels are published in Rohner, et al., *Louis I. Kahn Complete Works*, 102–104.

22
L. I. Kahn, "Space Form Use: A Library," *Pennsylvania Triangle* 43 (December 1956):43–47.

23
Ibid., 43.

24
This was made clear in an essay by the librarian T. Williams, who noted that the inner workings of the library were a "wonderful and complicated machine." See T. Williams, "Plans for the Library building of the University of Pennsylvania," *The Library Journal* (August 1888):240. For Furness, see J. O'Gorman, G.E. Thomas, and H. Myers, *The Architecture of Frank Furness* (Philadelphia: Philadelphia Museum of Art, 1973).

25
Kahn, "Space Form Use: A Library," 43.

Kahn's first library project, a competition entry for Washington University, St. Louis, in 1956 (Figs. 6, 7, 8) had a cruciform plan and pyramidal massing.[20] A reinforced concrete structure formed a three-dimensional repetitive grid. The basic structural unit was a single-height cell. However, variations were introduced without disruption. Double height spaces resulted where alternate floors ended one bay from the perimeter and, less consistently, bays of the second floor were cut away. Within this trabeated frame Kahn freely located the stacks and rooms for particular uses. The reading areas were at the periphery and services such as stairs and elevators were near the center.

While the structure was fixed, the plan was relatively open. This conflicted with central concerns of Kahn's theory, namely that the "form" should generate discrete units of space disposed hierarchically. Unlike the plan of the First Unitarian Church, which clearly derives from the "form" diagram, the library could not have been founded on an intuited "form" comprising stabilized hierarchies and relationships. One senses an insecurity in the definition of generating ideas. Certain activities were almost randomly located within the all-pervasive structure.[21] Perhaps this can be attributed to a failure of imagination. Intuitions that could delineate an appropriate hierarchical order had not yet crystallized. For instance, the "desire to meet" was not deemed to be essential to a library; consequently, no grand space devoted to public activities galvanized the design.

Nevertheless, at this stage Kahn was struggling with substantial issues that undermined any stable ordering of discrete parts. These were specifically addressed at the beginning of an important published essay on this project, entitled "Space, Form, Use: A Library."[22] He began by perceptively questioning the then-accepted notion of a rationally organized library. Instead, he sought a more profound human organization:

A library building should offer a system of spaces adaptable to the needs in time; the spaces and their consequent form as a building should originate from broad interpretations of use rather than the satisfaction of a program for a specific system of operation.[23]

Evidently Kahn was considering an alternative to libraries organized on the stacks system. A product of the nineteenth-century interest in standardization and efficiency, the gathering together of all the library's holdings in isolated and self-contained stacks was to become a common method of organizing large libraries. Kahn would have been intimately familiar with this arrangement from the library of the University of Pennsylvania, at which he was then teaching. Designed in 1889 by Philadelphia architect Frank Furness, the building was conceived of by both architect and client as an efficiently functioning machine, organized to facilitate a fluent circulation of workers, readers, and books.[24] Instructed by the example of the University Library, Kahn sought to avoid what he saw as an arbitrary division of the building into two entirely separate realms.

A space order for a library which encompasses many possible relationships between books, people and services could possess a universal quality of adjusting to changing human needs, translatable into an architecture. A library designed around the incipient influences of a standardized book storage and reading devices could lead to a form with two distinct space characteristics—one for people, one for books. Books and the reader do not relate in a static way.[25]

Such a statement reflects Kahn's maturity as an architectural thinker. Since 1950, he had been searching for an alternative to formulaic functionalism, in which the client's brief was addressed too prosaically by the architect. This kind of approach primarily involved the rational separation of stated functions and their direct and simplistic expression in forms. Yet, while rejecting the reductionalist functionalism of nineteenth and twentieth century modernism, he did not abandon all modernist premises. For instance, it is likely that he looked to the polemics of the 1920s (De Stijl and Le Corbusier) in his recognition of the necessity for freedom of movement in a design.[26] Only by refusing to restrict and codify human action, he believed, could modern buildings attain a universal and timeless value.

The free plan was, however, antithetical to his essentialist thinking. A "broad interpretation of use" was founded on a careful consideration of activities:

In the . . . design for [the] building . . . thoughts were centered around the desire to find a space construction system in which the carrels were inherent in the support which harbored them. Reading within a cloistered space with natural light in nearness to the building surfaces seemed good.[27]

This statement reveals a central aspect of his theory: that connection between an activity, in this case reading, and its expression through structure and light. The placement of reading spaces at the periphery of the library, so that they are bathed in natural light, demonstrated his search for the appropriate environment.

At the same time, Kahn was inspired and supported by a distinctive reading of history. In rejecting conventional functionalism he founded "form" on the origins of the institution. For the library, Kahn was drawn to an account in Russell Sturgis's *A Dictionary of Architecture and Building*, on the origins of the post-antique library. Here he attentively read of the aspirations that generated the medieval library: "During the early centuries of the Christian era, literature was kept alive by the ecclesiastics. Libraries were slowly gathered in cathedrals and also in monasteries . . . they were at first so small that a single room, or oftener part of the cloisters held all the books

7. *Washington University Library Competition. Section, plans, perspective; L.I.K. 465.2.*

26
Perhaps Kahn's respect for Le Corbusier, as expressed in his question, "How'm I doing, Corbusier?", is particularly relevant to his work at this stage. It is as if Le Corbusier challenged his assumptions of a stable hierarchical order. For Kahn on Le Corbusier, see McLaughlin, "How'm I Doing, Corbusier," 22.

27
Kahn, "Space Form Use: A Library," 43.

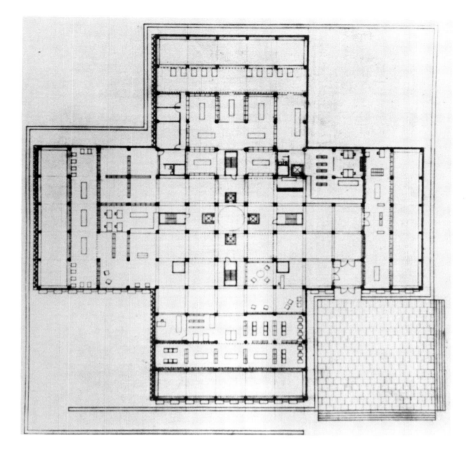

8. *Washington University Library Competition. Plan of entrance level.*

and all the readers."[28] Sturgis also included a contemporary chronicler's description of the twelfth century library at Durham, which so fascinated Kahn that he quoted it in his own essay:

The North syde of the Cloister . . . was all fynely glased from the hight to within a little of the ground and in every Wyndowe iii Pewes or carrells, wherein . . . the Monks dyd resort. And in every carrell was a deske . . . And over against the carrells against the church wall did stand great almeries (or cupboards) of waynscott all full of books. [29]

Such a lucid depiction of reading space, defined by privacy, light, views, and adjacency of books must have either inspired Kahn's design or provided a historical confirmation of the appropriate nature of space which he had already intuitively felt.

Reference to Kahn's later terms, Silence and "form," further clarifies his theoretical position. The realm of Silence contains both human desires—in this instance to learn—and historical architectural examples, such as the medieval carrel by the light, which serves as a

28
Charles C. Soule, "Library," in Russell Sturgis, *A Dictionary of Architecture and Building*, vol. 2 (New York, Macmillan, 1901), 750.

29
Kahn, "Space Form Use: A Library," 43.

30
Ibid.

31
All quotes Ibid.

32
Ibid.

concrete statement of the originating desire. Consequently, historical examples must be acknowledged as an integral aspect of his realm of Silence and its related concept "form." Through intuition, and with assistance from history Kahn derived the generating impulse from which it was possible to "grow" a spatial unit. This was how he addressed the problem of "What the space wants to be."

At this stage, Kahn must have considered the integration of these units, understood in structural terms, with others to comprise the whole:

Then from the smallest characteristic space harbored in the construction itself, the larger and the still larger spaces would unfold. [30]

Stating his central theme, he argued that "this pattern of spaces, if inherent in a construction system, would closely approximate what the architect thought the space 'wanted to be,' and how they could be made." The actual project, however, did not consistently reflect such connection of different spaces. Even the primary variation within the concrete structure, the cutting away of bays of the floor to introduce what he called "high spaces" and, in the case of the periphery, clerestory lighting, was not the manifestation of consistent ideas. His dictum that "high spaces exist for undivided areas and low spaces for small rooms and divided areas" was rarely supported by the quite-open distribution of activities. This is exacerbated by the peripheral penetration of light. Kahn described a "clear story light" illuminating "the high interior spaces and the intermediate levels looking out over these high spaces."[31] Thus, the same light and structural system "makes" two different kinds of space, a situation which does not reflect his belief that the meaning of spaces inheres in the conjunction of use, construction, and light. As a result, the overall building does not "unfold" with the consistency of the stated theory.

While specific spaces were the foundation of Kahn's method, he perceptively rejected the functionalist's technique of defining these at the beginning of his essay: "Spaces for books and for reading are not distinguished from each other."[32] However, the only space imaginatively analyzed was that for reading. The nature of other library activities had yet to be creatively felt and studied, with the result that they found their place in a fluid, yet ultimately arbitrary, manner within the structural frame.

A comprehensive order could not alone be based on an insight into the desire to read. Only by considering the relationship with the desire to meet and the need for well-being could a substantial architectural synthesis arise.

Kahn had thought deeply about the nature of reading. His ideas, the beginnings of a profound understanding of the "form" of the library, led to a critical assessment of the concrete frame. The remainder of his text reflected upon the use of materials and constructional systems eschewed in the project. With this he returned to a theme first introduced in an essay, published in 1944, entitled "Monumentality."[33] There, he acknowledged a respect for the buildings of the past while also recognizing the necessity for coming to terms with the materials and constructional processes of the modern age. Yet the utilization of current technology should not be allowed to destroy the humane quality of earlier spaces. Ultimately, Kahn adopted a positive position, arguing that the new materials could be equally responsive to human needs.

This meditation on the tension between past and present reappears in the discussion of the Washington University Library:

Wall-bearing masonry with its niches and vaults has the appealing structural order to provide naturally such spaces [for reading]. Concrete and steel, the obvious economical form making system of our time, are natural to big openings, not harbored little spaces.[34]

He continues, introducing a parallel problem:

But the needs of sun control challenge the large openings, and the exterior walls must be sensitive to orientation. A search for a high order of construction which could embody the appropriate sun protection and the little harbors of reading would, if found, sing out joyously as architecture.[35]

His solution, elaborate metal devices on the south and west sides, could perhaps be considered to be integral to the structural system, but did not relate to the search for an appropriate spatial order. The result suggests that it was not possible to employ a modern structure that was the basis for both the control of sun and the order of space.

The intention to "make" the unit of space with modern construction was equally problematic. On the one hand, the exterior's vast agglomeration of concrete modules was criticized by the competition's jury: "the tremendous bulk above the ground and aggressive pyramid shape . . . [was] . . . incongruous with the grace of the old campus buildings."[36] On the other hand, from historical examples Kahn had observed the sense of intimacy characteristic of spaces created by "masonry construction with its niches and vaults." At issue was the realization that his designs were animated by the same essential human needs that had inspired the historical examples he valued. Yet he had to acknowledge the tradition of technological invention that separated the perceptions of the modern world from those of the past. This was less a dilemma than a statement of the complex predicament of the modern architect and a stimulus for design. Nevertheless, although poignantly present in his text on the Washington University Library, such complexity did not creatively inform its design.

By this time Kahn had firmly rejected the functionalist method. His concern to allow freedom of relationships, however, was in conflict with his search for the meaning of those discrete spaces that would be integrated to facilitate an appropriate hierarchical order. Such ambiguity would be overcome when the commission for the Phillips Exeter Academy stimulated fresh insights into the "form" of a library. Materials, space, and light would there attain a new synthesis.

* * * *

33
L. I. Kahn, "Monumentality," in *New Architecture and City Planning*, ed. P. Zucker (New York: Hubner, 1944), 577–588.

34
Kahn, "Space Form Use: A Library," 43.

35
Ibid.

36
"Murphy and Mackey design Wins Washington University Competition," 16.

9. *Phillips Exeter Academy Library, Exeter, N.H., 1966–72. Plans, elevation, form sketch; L.I.K. 710.36.*

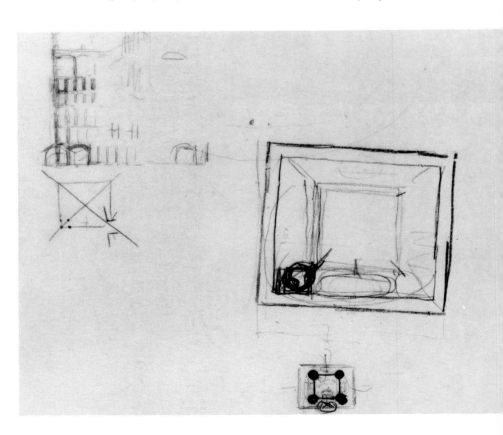

In 1966 Kahn began to design a new library building and, slightly later, a dining hall for the Phillips Exeter Academy, a preparatory school for boys. An early drawing of the library shows Kahn's "form" sketches, diagrammatic efforts to arrive at appropriate relationships (Fig. 9). The two sketches on the right show his plans based on a concentric organization with four servant spaces. Such sketches illuminate the initial stages of Kahn's approach, when he sought to define the archetypal "form" of a library.

Kahn's formative assumptions regarding the activities to be given architectural expression are spelled out in the following comment:

I see the library as a place where the librarian can lay out the books, open especially to selected pages to seduce the readers. There should be a place with great tables on which the librarian can put the books, and the readers should be able to take the book and go to the light.[37]

Kahn stated the idea from which he would "grow" three different spaces: one where students come together in the presence of books, another for the storage of books, and a third for reading in the light. Metaphorically, one can extend the persuasive role envisaged for the librarian to Kahn's sense of his own rhetorical purpose as architect, displaying the books to inspire the students, who will then move to the light with a chosen volume. As a statement of relationships and movements, this observation clearly belongs to the realm of "form."

A second comment clarifies the "form" by mentioning such "design" concerns as the choice of materials and construction:

Exeter began with the periphery, where light is. I felt the reading room would be where a person is alone near a window, and I felt that would be a private carrel, a kind of discovered place in the folds of construction. I made the outer depth of the building like a brick doughnut, independent of the books. I made the inner depth of the building like a concrete doughnut, where the books are stored away from the light. The center area is a result of these two contiguous doughnuts; it's just the entrance where books are visible all around you through the big circular openings. So you feel the building has the invitation of books.[38]

Returning to the "form" sketches (Fig. 9), one now perceives that the concentric organization was the representation of the three zones: the

37
Quoted in Lobell, *Between Silence and Light*, 100.

38
Quoted in "The Mind of Louis Kahn," *Architectural Forum* 137, (July/August 1972):77.

10. *G. E. Lind, Peabody Institute Library, Baltimore, Md., 1875–78.*

11. *Frank Furness, Library of the University of Pennsylvania, Philadelphia, Pa., 1889.*

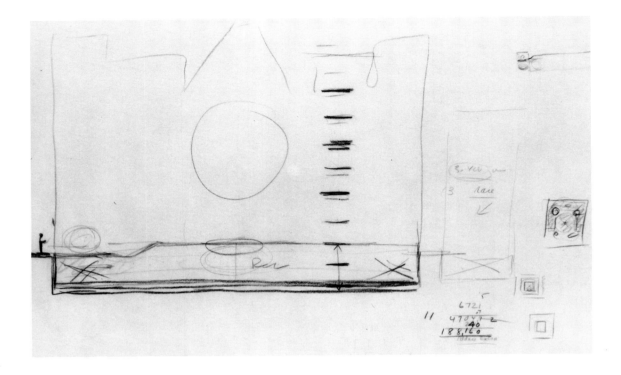

12. *Phillips Exeter Academy Library. Section; L.I.K. 710.99.*

peripheral doughnut for reading, the inner doughnut for books, and the center as the place to meet and acknowledge "the invitation of [the] books." Four servant spaces, containing stairs, bathrooms, air exhausts, etc., were already firmly located near the corners.

In its fixity and clarity this conception differed from the flux of ideas worked through ten years earlier in the Washington University scheme. Here Kahn articulated a hierarchical order. A major new insight was involved: the desire to meet was introduced and recognized to be as important as the desire to learn through private reading. A grand central communal hall is the result. Around it are the less important servant spaces and stacks which serve both hall and private spaces at the periphery.

Adjacent to these sketches is a view of an

39
William Jordy, *American Buildings and their Architects: Progressive and Academic Ideals at the Turn of the Twentieth Century* (Garden City, N.Y.: Doubleday, 1976), 321.

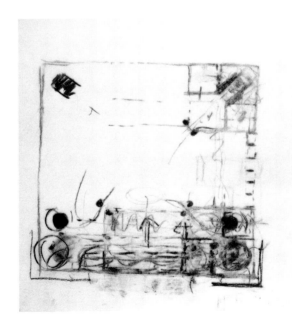
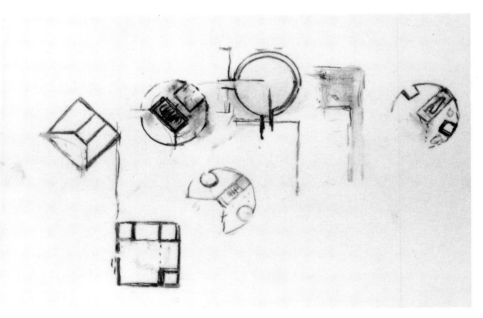

13. *Phillips Exeter Academy Library. Plan detail; L.I.K. 710.39.*

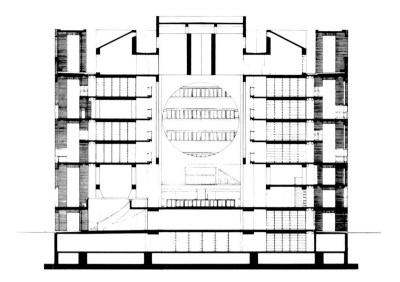

14. *Phillips Exeter Academy Library. Section, final scheme.*

40
Quoted in I. Shenker, "Kahn Defines Aim of Exeter Design," *New York Times*, October 23, 1972, 40.

41
Louis I. Kahn, "Room, Window, and Sun," *Canadian Architect* 18, (June 1973):53.

internal hall (Fig. 9, left), probably from an actual building. To find it on this early sheet of "form" diagrams is not surprising. The chosen building surely conformed to the intuited idea of a central space where the reader discovers the books laid out. Many seventeenth, eighteenth and nineteenth century libraries, such as the university libraries at Harvard and Yale and Sydney Smirke's library at the British Mu-

seum, include a large central space surrounded by books, intended to impress upon the reader the accumulated knowledge of centuries available for study. One example that Kahn would have found inspirational is the library of the Peabody Institute at Baltimore (G.E. Lind, 1875–78), which has a five-story central well surrounded by book stacks, presenting the reader with what William Jordy has aptly termed imposing "cliffs of erudition" (Fig. 10).[39] The grand public space of Furness's University of Pennsylvania library, although separated from its book stacks, was surely also an influential example for Kahn when he made the sketch (Fig. 11).

These "form" sketches and related historical examples provide some idea of what Kahn believed the Exeter library "wanted to be." In the design stage, the "form" was given shape and size. Taking into consideration materials, technologies, costs, etc., he sought to conceive individual spaces and to combine them without contradicting the concentric and geometric framework. A plan (the sketch to the left in Fig. 13) shows him studying the organization of servant spaces and their relation to the corner. Figure 12 conveys an early spatial formulation of the grand central hall, surrounded by the stacks and reading spaces.

As a feature of the particular commission, the site was addressed in the realm of "design." The decision to use brick on the exterior, for instance, rather than concrete as at Washington University, was motivated in part by the surrounding neo-Georgian brick buildings (Fig. 16). The negative comments of the Washington jury were surely in his mind:

At Exeter I didn't try to make something that stands out. I honored the buildings around me and I chose brick to sympathize with them.[40]

A further connection with the surrounding environs was established by the inclusion of a plaza. This stemmed from his recognition of the necessity of giving architectural shape to an aspect of "form," a fundamental human need, "the desire to meet."

The libraries of all university schools sit well in a court entrance available to all the students as a place of invitation. The entrance courts and the gardens and paths knitting them together form an architecture of connection.[41]

Here Kahn restated the principle of devoting

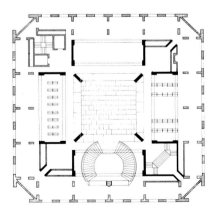 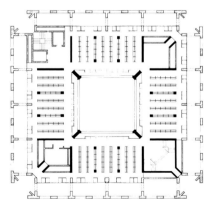

15. *Phillips Exeter Academy Library. Plans of first and second floors, final scheme, showing brick and concrete structures.*

16. *Phillips Exeter Academy Library. Perspective of exterior.*

the same care to the design of external spaces as to internal ones, noted before in the "street" sketch (Fig. 5).

Placed to the north, the plaza was to be made of brick and granite and surrounded by stone benches and a low hedge.[42] In the site plan (Fig. 17), the library appeared above the dining hall, connected to the rectangular plaza and to paths leading across the lawn to the corners. These would draw one into the arcade surrounding the building, through the entrance and stairs to the central hall. With its connections both outward into the campus and inward to the library, this plaza was a first "invitation" proffered to the students. By providing a place where the "desire to meet" could be fulfilled, the external spaces would have been made an essential part of the meaning of the library.

Passing through the exterior arcade to reach the foyer, the visitor to the building is confronted with a monumental stair whose ceremonial function is explicitly denoted by its white travertine marble facing. Although the foyer is entered to the side, the reaching arms of the baroque-inspired stair sweep one onto the central axis. Ascending the stair, massive concrete trusses obscure the view ahead;[43] the gradual unfolding of the central space creates a strong sense of anticipation. Having traversed the intricate entrance sequence, one responds

with all the more intensity to the perfectly ordered geometries of the light-filled hall (Figs. 18, 19, 20).

Like the plaza, the central hall grew out of the "desire to meet." Both are public realms acting as invitations to students to congregate. The section (Fig. 14) illustrates the dramatic change in level which expresses the honorific function of the central space as a container of cultural memory. It is a place to pause, to reflect upon the knowledge, history, and tradition embedded in the books. Visible behind the monumental circular openings, the books in their stacks comprise the ornament of the interior. Founded on pure geometries and using the books themselves as ornament, this conception of a library subordinates particular functional determinants to the statement of a higher meaning.

For Kahn, the library had a timeless and universal value. In this respect, the eighteenth century theorist Etienne-Louis Boullée was a major influence. In 1952 Emil Kaufmann's long essay,[44] dealing in part with Boullée, was published in Philadelphia, where Kahn was then working, and attracted a great deal of interest from architects. In 1968, Kahn wrote a poem to preface an American exhibition of Boullée's designs.[45] Kahn admired Boullée's own library project for its expression of the essence of the institution (Fig. 21).

42
See A. LeCuyer, "Kahn's Powerful Presence at Exeter," *Architecture* 74 (February 1985):78; and working drawings dated 8 November 1967 and 20 November 1967 in the L.I. Kahn Archive.

43
As occurs in the open vestibule of the Richards Medical Research Laboratory, the reinforced concrete structure is revealed to the entering visitor.

44
Emil Kaufmann, *Three Revolutionary Architects: Boullée, Ledoux and Lequeu*, Philadelphia: American Philosophical Society, 1952.

45
L. I. Kahn, "Twelve Lines," in *Visionary Architects: Boullée, Ledoux, Lequeu* (Houston: University of St. Thomas, 1968), 5.

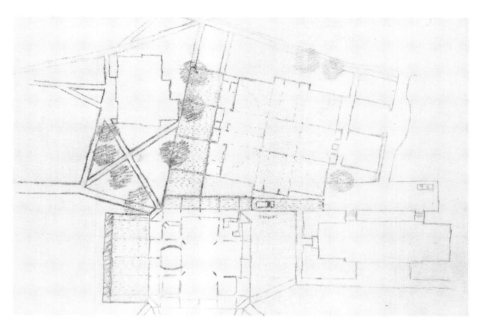

17. *Phillips Exeter Academy Library. Site plan; L.I.K. 710.3.*

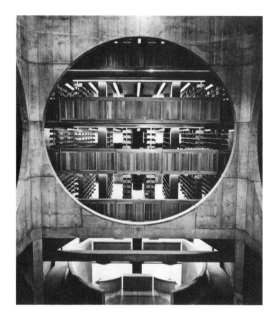

46
Quoted in Wurman, *What Will Be*, 182.

47
Letter from Colin Rowe to L. I. Kahn, February 7, 1956. Rowe sent a copy of the second edition (London: Tiranti, 1952). While pure geometries organize the hall at Exeter, there is no attempt to create an intimate human scale. As is often the case in Kahn's work, sublimity in eighteenth century terms was achieved, not that consonance of form and body that was the Renaissance, humanist ideal.

18, 19, 20. *Phillips Exeter Academy Library. Progressive views of main stair, central hall, and concrete cross beams.*

There is one illustration of the library in which there are no tables. It is a great imperialistic room, and there are people handing down books from on high to people who are lower. There are no tables to read on, just a feeling of what a library should be—you come into a chamber and there are all the books.[46]

The central hall at Exeter is a re-presentation of Boullée's library.

Kahn's emphatic use of the circle and square in this space reads as an object demonstration of the way in which surface planes generate volume. In the visitor's perception, the circle and square of the four walls is ineluctably translated into a space ordered by the sphere and cube. The cross beams of the roof unify the whole and introduce the triangle inscribed within the square. In Kahn's theory, geometric order resided in the realm of Silence, and had as its corollary the correctly ordered material building, existing as Light. In 1956 Kahn debated his ideas with Colin Rowe, who subsequently sent him Rudolph Wittkower's famous study of the meaning of geometry in Renaissance architecture, *Architectural Principles in the Age of Humanism*, as a historical discussion which he believed would be of interest to Kahn.[47] The historian's argument that the Renaissance buildings were believed to be microcosms of a divine order would have complemented Kahn's notions of Silence and Light and reinforced his respect for those deeply symbolic geometries of past monuments. For Kahn, the geometric forms of Exeter's hall were connected with a transcendant realm. Such meaning was universal, but was particularly relevant to the institution of a library, where meditation, stimulated by books, was a kind of ascension into the realm of ideas.

At the same time, these geometric forms were also conceived in terms of a rigorous structural logic.[48] The concrete walls, whose shapes are defined by the cutting away of inscribed circles, brace the corner piers. Efficiency is attained by the elimination of unnecessary weight. Similarly, the concrete cross beams in the ceiling stabilize the piers.

Natural light enters the hall laterally, through the surrounding two doughnuts and from above. The light passing through the high clerestory windows is more dramatic, since it plays off the material of the cross beams and the walls.

In the central room I chose the kind of structure which shields the light so it is not pouring down . . . a clerestory light gives you light from the sides of a beam.[49]

Careful deliberation determined the size of these cross beams. Rational technology was only one factor; equally significant was the centralizing focus of the cross shape within the geometrically ordered space. More complex and demanding of creative energy was his investigation of the nuances of light. The purpose of the deep beams was to bring material and light together. Natural light strikes the concrete surfaces of beam and walls and is thereby subtly transformed, becoming tex-

tured and diffused within the contained volume of the hall.

The Washington University project never convincingly embodied Kahn's theory, whereby material and light would interact such that the light entering the room became the light of the room itself. In Exeter, theory and practice were brought together. Behind this achievement lay more than a decade of experimentation, as witnessed in the First Unitarian Church, the Erdman Dormitories at Bryn Mawr College, Bryn Mawr, Pennsylvania (1960–65), and in a major project contemporary with Exeter, the Kimbell Museum in Fort Worth, Texas (1966–72).[50] In all these designs, Kahn sensitively explored the ways in which materials reveal the quality of light, and light reveals the nature of materials.

At Exeter, the meaning of light is a demonstration of Kahn's most profound philosophical beliefs. As a result of ever-changing exter-

48
Kahn related the cut-out circles to the structure of column and beam. See his comment in Wurman, *What Will Be*, 180.

49
Quoted ibid.

50
For interpretations of Kahn's use of light see Vincent Scully, "Light, Form, and Power: New Work of Louis Kahn," *Architectural Forum* 121 (August-September 1964): 162–170; and Tyng, *Beginnings*, 140–155.

22. *Phillips Exeter Academy Library. Perspective of reading area; L.I.K. 710.140.*

21. *Etienne-Louis Boulée*, Proposed New Hall for Expansion of the National Library, c. 1788.

51
Kahn believed that "the room is not only the beginning of architecture: it is an extension of self." Quoted in Lobell, *Between Silence and Light*, 38. Also see L. I. Kahn, "Architecture: Silence and Light."

Kahn discusses the "psyche" in essays, such as L. I. Kahn, "Remarks;" L. I. Kahn, "A statement by Louis I. Kahn: A Paper Delivered at the International Design Conference, Aspen, Colorado," *Arts and Architecture* 81 (May 1964):18–19. Also see Rowan, "Wanting to Be," 133; and Tyng, *Beginnings*, 18,19,129,130.

23. *Phillips Exeter Academy Library. Section detail; L.I.K. 710.93.*

nal conditions, the interior space comes alive with a constant flux of light and shade. The room exists in the realm of shadows, that is, between the Silence of ideas and the Light of material reality. This is also the realm in which we live our lives: a continuous alternation between spiritual and corporeal states that defines our humanity. Through this interpretation of the blending of spirit and matter, in the room as in human nature, one can begin to perceive the content Kahn wanted to give his design: space is the representation of the human psyche.[51]

To conclude, the meaning of the central communal space derives from Kahn's desire to "grow" a room from the idea of the institution, synthesizing a range of themes: the dramatic experience of orchestrated movement up the stairs into the center; the visible location of the books acting as a literal statement of accumulated knowledge and an inspiration to read; a

feeling for the connection of light and material; belief in the symbolic value of pure geometries.

Having been "invited" to read in the central hall, students make their way through the stairs in the servant spaces to the stacks, where books may be selected (Fig. 22). Noting that books want to distance themselves from the light, Kahn placed them in an inner doughnut between the zones defined by natural light. Reinforced concrete was chosen for its capacity to carry the heavy load of books; its austerity in comparison to the warm textured brick of the reading doughnut denotes its prosaic function. Servant spaces, acting like enormous hollow columns, spatially frame and structurally support the floor slabs of the concrete doughnut.

Despite the use of brick, the reading doughnut was not presented as a purely load-bearing entity. Evidently Kahn was responding to the plea, made in the essay "Monumentality," to realize the timeless qualities admired in past

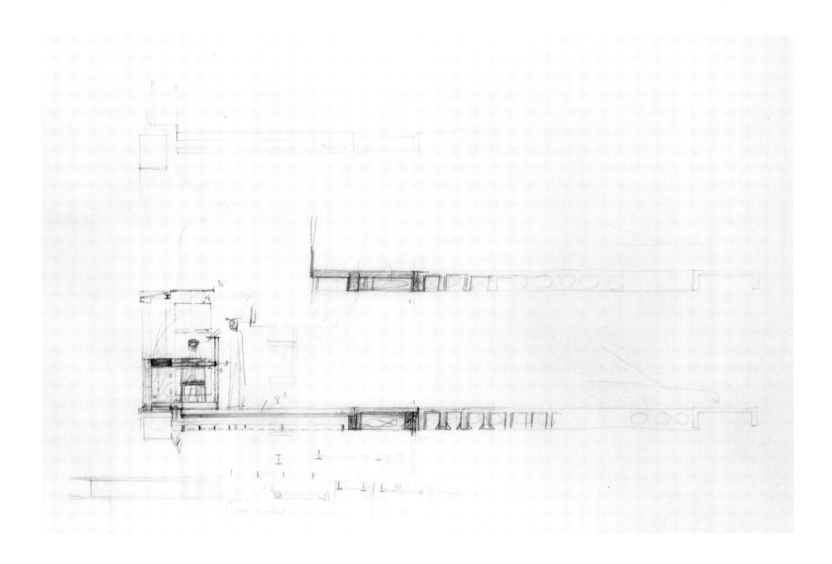

monuments through the use of modern constructional techniques. At Exeter, past and present are mediated by employing a traditional masonry structure to "harbor" the intimate spaces necessary for reading while also distinctly revealing the connection between the inner brick piers and the reinforced concrete floor slabs of the book stacks. Although this joint has a minor structural function (the masonry doughnut is merely stabilized), it visually conveys the dependence of brick on concrete. Masonry sheds its purely load-bearing, and therefore traditional, character by participating in a modern constructional system:

Sometimes you ask concrete to help brick and brick is very happy . . . because it becomes modern.[52]

Kahn's conception of the reading zone grew out of ideas raised during the design of the Washington University Library. In his essay, he noted the way traditional brick construction, through its bays and alcoves, could create an ambience conducive to concentration and private study. At Exeter, the masonry structure delineates individual bays, which interact with natural light to provide the intimacy necessary for the isolated and passive act of reading.[53] Moving away from the relative darkness of the stacks, the student would discover this welcoming double-height space, located within the folds of the construction and in the light.[54]

The reading area defines a zone of quiet and privacy away from the central hall, the books in the stacks providing a visual and acoustic barrier. By blocking the view in this way, Kahn probably also acted on the conviction that staff supervision from the hall must not intrude into the student study space. The inner doughnut was thus used to thwart the potential panopticon of the concentric plan. For Kahn the library as a traditional institution was valued, yet the institutionalized empowerment of authority by privileged vision, a normative library requirement, was evidently singled out and subjected to a critical assessment.[55]

Within the reading area, one is offered a diversity of settings for study. Large tables, around which several students could work in the light falling from the high windows, are placed within the frame of each structural bay. For a greater degree of privacy and isolation, readers may occupy one of the wooden carrels placed along the perimeter within the system of major and minor piers. A sketch of a single

carrel (Fig. 23) describes a controlled, self-contained realm:

The carrel is the room within a room . . . I made the carrel associated with light. It has its own little window so you can regulate privacy and the amount of light you want.[56]

Various influential historical examples can offer some guidance to further understand Kahn's insight into the nature of space appropriate to reading. As demonstrated in his essay on the Washington University Library, a primary source of inspiration was the placement of the carrels in light at the medieval library. For an explicit and evocative visualization of the qualities Kahn admired in the library at Durham which was described by Sturgis, he could have turned to P. M. Letarouilly's *Édifices de Rome moderne; ou, recueil des palais, maisons, eglises, couvents et autres monuments . . . de Rome.*[57] Kahn related to Vincent Scully that as a student he had been influenced by this work, carefully tracing its plates.[58] One engraving shows a monk reading in the cloister of S.

24. *P. M. Letarouilly, "Santa Maria della Pace, Rome," from* Edifices de Rome Moderne *(1840).*

52
Quoted in L. Huxtable, "New Exeter Library: Stunning Paean to Books," *New York Times*, October 23, 1972, 33. It should also be noted that the external piers are not solid brick but contain a concrete block core.

53
Such an emphasis on privacy is related to Kahn's view that "Knowing cannot be imparted to the next man. Knowing is private." See Kahn, "Room, Window, and Sun," 55.

54
W. Marlin, "Within the Folds of Construction," *Architectural Forum* 139 (October 1975):26–35. The decision to use piers and flat arches was made at the relatively late date of August 1967. Semicircular arches had initially been chosen as best suited to the required intimacy of space. See Working Drawings, especially the section of November 10, 1966.

25. *Antonello da Messina,* St. Jerome in his Study, c. 1460.

55
On panopticism see Michel Foucault, *Discipline and Punish: The Birth of the Prison* (New York: Vintage, 1979). Supervision at Exeter is mentioned in LeCuyer, "Kahn's Powerful Presence at Exeter," 77. It was a major problem at the Graduate Theological Union Library and led to the rejection of Exeter's spatial-structural formulation. See the important sketch plan, L.I.K. 865.36, Fig. 37, discussed below.

56
Quoted in Wurman, *What Will Be*, 179.

Maria della Pace (Fig. 24). Although the light for reading here comes from the garden court, the way in which the seat is connected to the cloister walk and the light falls on the reader's book are close in spirit to Kahn's conception of the carrel at the periphery.

It is even possible that Kahn knew some of the more specific details of medieval and Renaissance monastic libraries. As the architectural historian James O'Gorman has shown, monastic libraries stored their books in dark alcoves.[59] After making a selection, readers would peruse their books whilst traversing the cloister walk. Seats were provided for the monks to halt and read in the light. The Exeter Library seems organized on remarkably similar

lines, so that a twentieth century student taking a book from the dark stacks to a carrel traverses a path identical in spirit to that of medieval and Renaissance readers. History thus assisted Kahn in his attempt to construct an atemporal order to architecture: the movement through past libraries would have an immediate relevance to the idea, or "form," of a modern library.

The foregoing analysis, examining the nature of each space, cannot reveal their meaningful interconnections. Profound psychological and social insights underlie relationships between the components (central hall, stacks, larger reading space, and carrels) and between the library and the school as a whole. As has been seen, Kahn carefully orchestrated the visitor's movements through a series of linked spaces: from the campus to the plaza, through the arcade to the foyer, up the stairs to the central space, to the stacks and the carrels beyond. In one sense, the Exeter Library reverts to a static organization of separated functions, which had been rejected in 1956 with the Washington University project. However, drawing on a decade of experience, Kahn acquired a more profound insight into patterns of human movement than mechanistic functionalism. His organization of spaces at Exeter was predicated upon what he believed would be a normative passage through the building, shaped by common human impulses such as the desire to meet and the urge to move forward to the peripheral light.

A major theme is the individual's place within a wider community. Thus the movement from plaza and central hall to carrels is also a passage from public to private realms. Two famous Renaissance paintings parallel and perhaps even inspired Kahn's articulation of the necessary interdependance of these two dimensions of human experience.

Antonello da Messina's well-known painting of *St. Jerome in His Study*, in the National Gallery of London, shows St. Jerome seated at a wooden carrel (Fig. 25). The surrounding circulation space, the views beyond into the landscape, and the light entering from the window above the carrel can also be found at Exeter. Significantly, the single carrel stacked with books encloses St. Jerome within his personal library. Similarly, Kahn surely conceived his carrel as a miniature library, a microcosm of the library as a whole, where the community of readers gathered in the central space are surrounded by the full collection of books in the

26. *The Master of Flémalle (Robert Campin),* Merode Altarpiece, *c. 1425–28. Detail: right panel, "Joseph in his Workshop."*

stacks. A hierarchical relationship between private and communal realms was thus created.

A second painting is particularly suggestive of Kahn's desire to locate the reader within the broader institution of the campus. The Mérode Altarpiece, by the Master of Flémalle, shows Joseph working in the varied light of his contained space (Fig. 26). Following medieval custom, he practices his craft, carpentry, in a workshop open to the street, so that one glimpses the busy thoroughfares of Bruges through the open shutters. In the same way, the reading spaces at Exeter are situated close to the periphery, offering the student views of the campus. Kahn stated that "the carrel belongs to the outside world. Occasional distraction is as important in reading as concentration."[60] Both painting and building insist upon the connection of the individual worker to the social realm of which he or she forms a part.

These different relationships were maintained within the overall architectonic organization. The concentric scheme, which appeared as the initial representation of "form," remained constant throughout the design process, and ultimately was translated without major disruptions into actual sizes and materials. The soaring hall, the stacks with their mezzanines, and the double-height reading spaces were forcefully brought together by the emphatic concentric zoning and the pervasive three-dimensional grid (see Fig. 1). Natural light filling the central volume is different in kind from that entering the reading spaces through windows; between, in relative darkness, is the ring of book stacks. Within the geometric frame, and rooted in different human activities, a drama of space, light, and materials is enacted.

As in Roman architecture, the building's full impact is only revealed upon gaining the interior. The use of brick was a response to the nature of private reading spaces and the surrounding campus buildings. A relatively austere cube, the exterior is also the frame for a reasoned and highly expressive design. The fenestration is composed of timber infill carrells with personalized windows and large windows above lighting the reading space behind (see Figs. 27 and 28). The exterior thereby represents the varieties of reading spaces within. A further articulation of the presence of readers was achieved by cutting the corners of the building to expose the depth of the reading zone. Consequently, both the sur-

57
P. Letarouilly, *Édifices de Rome moderne; ou, recueil des palais, maisons, eglises, couvents et autres monuments . . . de Rome* (Paris, 1840; reprint ed., London: Tiranti, 1929–30), vol. 5, plate 250.

58
Scully, *Louis I. Kahn,* 12,13. I would like to thank Peter Reed for drawing my attention to Scully's comments.

59
James O'Gorman, *The architecture of the monastic library in Italy, 1300–1600* (New York: University Press for the College Art Association of America, 1972), 3. Discussing a typical Cistercian layout, as exemplified by the monastery at Fossanova, a late twelfth century abbey near Rome, O'Gorman notes: "As a monk moved into the church, he passed an ambry set into the cloister wall just to the right of the entrance. This ambry . . . served as the library. Here the monks picked up the book they would need during the divine office in the church." Of especial relevance is the subsequent comment that "any other reading . . . was done in the seclusion of the monk's cell or while he walked the cloister arcades. Books for this purpose were distributed from a storage vault, or book room, often placed next to the sacristy. The book room at Fossanova is a windowless space 10 by 14 feet." I am indebted to Robert Baron for referring me to O'Gorman's book.

60
Quoted in William Jordy, "Criticism," *Architectural Review* 155 (June 1974):333–334.

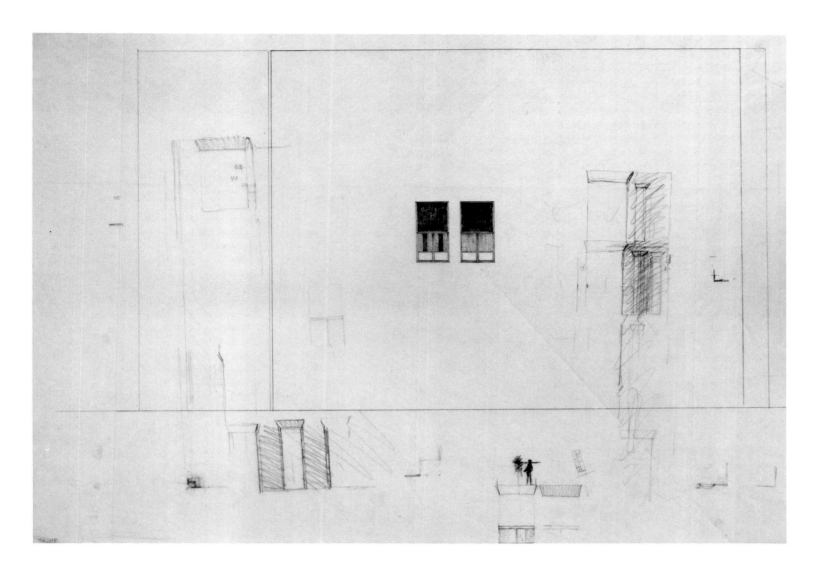

27. *Phillips Exeter Academy Library. Fenestration studies; L.I.K. 710.87.*

face and the depth of the brick doughnut directly state the activity of reading and the desire to learn.

Unlike the interior hall, where the communal meeting realm is represented through the monumentally overscaled circles, the exterior reveals the community of readers as a succession of discrete, humanly scaled elements. The genesis of the design is evident in a sketch at the bottom of one sheet (Fig. 27), where a human figure is used to fix the size and proportion of each fenestration unit. Such a body-centered approach to design determines the reader's experience. Whether seated in a carrel, at a large desk, in an armchair with a view of the campus through windows, or moving to a destination, the reader will always be sheltered within an architectural environment that is given intimacy and human warmth by

proportional concordance with his own body.

In Kahn's design for the exterior, the integration of body and building through proportion is complemented by a connection based upon a structural analogy. Each side of the building presents a self-contained brick unit (Fig. 28). This begins as a heavy arcade, rises to enclose the reading levels, and culminates in an open roof terrace, formed by now-slender piers. The brick pillars and arches visually convey a struggle of forces passing through the building. The external pillars become wider as they descend, and the profile of the arches flattens as the span narrows and loads diminish. Although these adjustments of form serve no real structural function, they convey a powerful illusion of structural stability. The user's response to the building proceeds through analogy with the structural workings of one's body. Both building and human being are resisting gravity, so that the user experiences the building empathetically: in Kahn's words, "the weight of the brick makes it dance like a fairy above and groan below." [61] The diminution of the pillars toward the top of the building symbolically respects the "order of nature" in structural terms; makes a connection with the monuments of the past, especially Greek temples, which tend toward pyramidal configurations; and suggests a feeling of ascension that was surely relevant to Kahn's idea of the library as a place where readers strove to attain higher realms of knowledge.

At the uppermost level of the brick doughnut, a roof loggia surrounds the rare book room and classrooms (Figs. 28, 29). Like the courtyard and central hall, it is a place to meet. Here social activity takes place in the open air, in the presence of trees and vegetation. No doubt Kahn felt that contact with nature would refresh the readers and prepare them for reading and meditation.

While the Exeter library retains the majestic simplicity of the Washington University scheme, major changes founded on a reconsideration of activities and relationships have occurred. These are revealed in the "form" sketch. The desire to learn, to meet, and to experience a sense of well-being—those constituents of the realm of Silence—were here ordered into a cogent statement of what the library "wants to be." Ensuing design sketches show Kahn striving to translate these insights into architecture. By exploring the interaction of light and material, appropriate spaces were grown. The animating power of human desires is nowhere more evident than in the sketches for private and public spaces. While the desire to learn specifically generated the intimate reading spaces, it coexisted with the desire to meet in guiding the design of the grand hall. For Kahn, learning and a sense of well-being involved a balance between reading and oral communication, that is, between introspection in a quiet, intimate space and interaction in a public place. This harmony was subtly represented through the multiplicity of relationships set up between the private and communal realms. Kahn's sketches, as well as the building at Exeter, unfold around human capacities and desires. A lived reality, of which we all partake, was thus the grounds for architectural meaning.

* * * *

28. *Phillips Exeter Academy Library. View of exterior.*

29. *Phillips Exeter Academy Library. Perspective of roof loggia; L.I.K. 710.139.*

61

Quoted in Huxtable, "New Exeter Library," 33. See also Wurman, *What Will Be*, 178. Kahn believed that architecture could be invested with life which would be experienced empathetically by the viewer. He had debated this and its implications with Scully while they viewed the Kremlin walls in Moscow. See Vincent Scully, "Works of Louis I. Kahn and His Method," in *Louis I. Kahn, Architecture and Urbanism*, (1975), 287–300. Interpretations of the architecture of Frank Furness by Scully drew attention to American nineteenth century sources of the idea of empathy, especially found in L. Eidlitz, *The Nature and Function of Art, More Especially of Architecture* (New York: Armstrong and Sons, 1881); and Henry Van Brunt, "Greek Lines and Their Influence on Modern Architecture," in *Greek Lines and Other Architectural Essays* (Boston: Houghton Mifflin Co., 1893). The latter, which focused on the mouldings and curves, the "lines of life," of the Greek temple may have been discussed in the 1950s and 1960s, serving as a distant, yet potent, source for Exeter's tapering pillars.

62

Documents relating to this project, including the design brief, are in the Louis I. Kahn Archive, L.I.K. Box 113, and at the Graduate Theological Union Library. Kahn was extremely sympathetic to the ideals of the commission, commenting: "I am building a library which is an all-religious library for various sects. I can't speak about religious sects. I just know the Catholics, the Jews, and the Moslems—I have a vague idea of the various sects. But I don't have a vague idea about religion itself. I feel conversed with religion as a very sacred part of the intimate." Quoted in Wurman, *What Will Be*, 231.

63

As is confirmed by a brief sketch of carrels directly in front of the fenestration of one phase of the design (a small window beneath a larger one seen in drawing 865.42 in the L. I. Kahn Archive), Kahn intended the outer concentric zone at G.T.U. to contain the realm of private reading. That the Exeter library was in Kahn's mind when he

The Exeter commission represents the culmination of a search for the "form" of the library that had begun in the 1950s. Based on the same "form," the Graduate Theological Union Library of 1972–74 adds little to Kahn's central theoretical development. Nevertheless, it is a significant design which draws on many themes conceived throughout his career and, unlike the two earlier libraries, draws inspiration from its natural setting.

In 1972, the G.T.U. commissioned Kahn to design a library that would bring together the collections of seven disparate theological schools: three Roman Catholic theologates, six Protestant schools, and a center for Judaic studies.[62] Kahn's building would represent the ecumenical intentions behind the decision to combine divergent religious traditions. The "form" diagrams at the top of an early drawing (Fig. 30) denote the beginning of the project. A concentric plan was chosen, the servant spaces shown as circles within or without the central volume. Below and to the left in Fig. 30 is a "design" sketch, a section, where the servant spaces appear as dynamic spiralling lines, suggesting vertical movement of stairs and services within the shafts, which Kahn would liken to hollow columns. Expressing the essential meaning of a library, the "form" sketches also reflect the more direct experience of the conception, the design, and ultimately the occupation of the Exeter library.[63]

The earliest scheme broadly investigated the building's relation to the site (Fig. 31). A diamond plan cut across the existing thoroughfare, Ridge Road. A "Pedestrian Mall or Plaza" was created in front of the entrance. All the later proposals located the building parallel to Ridge Road, but continued to close it with a static plaza.

Subsequently, two distinct schemes were developed, and perspectives and a model presented to the client.[64] An early design of the first, seen in Figure 32, illustrates a major as-

30. *Graduate Theological Union Library, Berkeley, California, 1971–1974; completed in 1987 by Esherick, Homsey, Dodge & Davis and Peters, Clayberg & Caulfield. Plans, section, form sketch; L.I.K. 865.40.*

pect of Kahn's approach, the use of a geometric modular grid to generate the plan. The plan is square; six bays on each side, with a central well of two bays and servant spaces in the surrounding area. Crosses within each bay introduce the diagonal into the grid and determine a central point to locate the rectangular half-module. These then define the servant spaces, whose size conforms to the major module, but are shifted inward one-half bay from the perimeter.

The influence of the Exeter Library could be discerned in the concentric zoning of this scheme, the stacks and the perimeter realm for reading surrounding the central space. Yet a major change had occurred: the extraordinary doughnut organization of brick and concrete zones had been rejected in favor of a uniformly expressed concrete frame structure. This was motivated by the client's anticipation of future changes to the collection and its use. Any future reorganization could not have been accommodated by such a distinct juxtaposition of zones differentiated by materials.[65] The modular grid and zoning could remain but the design had to be opened up through the concrete frame. With this change, the four servant spaces near the corners no longer precisely framed and stabilized the zone of the stacks, as at Exeter. Instead, they were located purely through reference to the grid and its half-bay module.

This greater reliance on a pervasive structural grid can be related to other late works, such as the Yale Center for British Art and British Studies, New Haven, at that time his most important commission. In the plan for the G.T.U. Library, the different functions found their place within a predetermined system of order. Without contradicting the principle of growing discrete spaces from specific human activities, this approach reconsidered the formative impulses underlying design decisions. Particularized realms animated the given framework. In sum, this plan shows Kahn at a stage of synthesis, able to combine the doughnut zoning of Exeter with the more generalized open grid of the Yale Center.

Ensuing designs built upon the statement of the grid, zoning, and servant spaces which had been articulated by the first plan. At issue on the entrance level was the client's concern for adequate control over access and egress. An axial placement was chosen (Fig. 33).

Once such decisions had been made, the

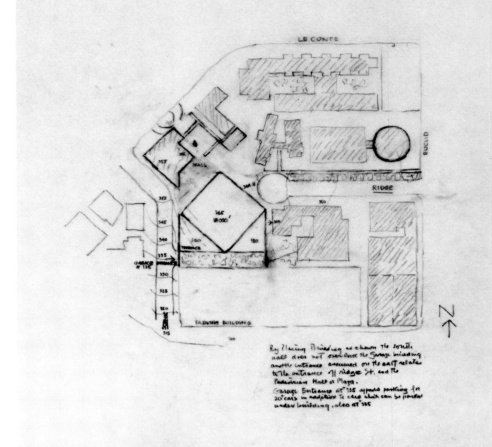

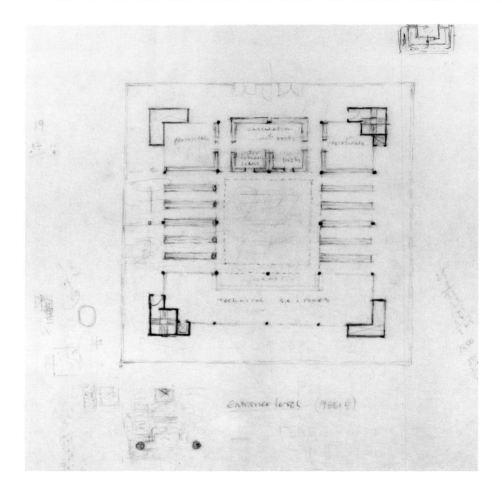

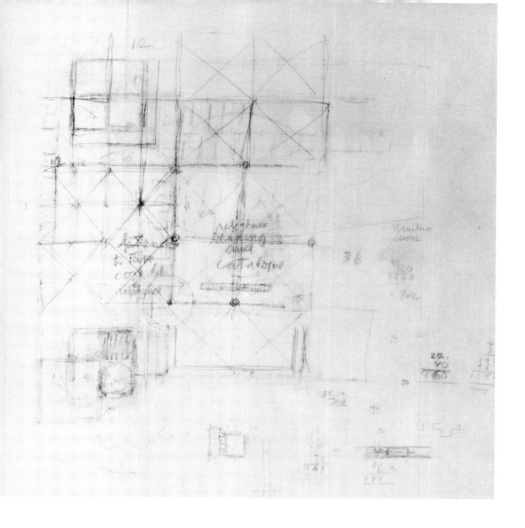

office documented the scheme in drawings and a model (Fig. 34), and Kahn prepared two perspectives, viewing the building from the front and rear respectively (Figs. 35, 36). The entrance level serves as a podium for two upper floors. Trees are shown on the podium and lower level, leaving the uppermost story to show, stark and massive, and open to the full impact of the sun. The perspectives, especially the rear view, emphasize the monumentality and pristine clarity of the forms set in a dramatically composed landscape.

Ultimately, however, this scheme was rejected. The building's imposing form elicited complaints from surrounding residents, who envisioned it overpowering the area.[66] In addition, the internal organization was criticized by the librarian, who felt that it did not adequately resolve the problems of security and supervision.[67] Evidently this was not merely a question of the entrance itself, but stemmed from the seclusion of the stairs in the servant spaces, away from the center of the interior. No doubt some discussion also focused on the top floor and the problem of glare from its unshaded windows.

Kahn had to rethink fundamental aspects of his design. The beginnings of a final scheme are present in a plan of the entrance level (Fig. 37), where, most significantly, the four large servant spaces in the corners have been removed. Supervision is clearly a primary consideration: Kahn has drawn an eye with its range of sight from the service desk. This eye is able to oversee the entrance, placed on axis, and the stairs, now prominently sited in the central hall itself.

In condensed form, the servant spaces reappear as the columns framing the central space. These are hollow, conforming to Kahn's theory on the capacity of modern materials to open up what was once solid, stated in his essay, "Monumentality." This was also explored in his 1959 sketches of Albi Cathedral (Fig. 38).[68] In these drawings, dynamically spiraling lines course through the buttresses. Matter is dissolved, leaving the space free to pass light into the interior (as in the Mikveh Israel Synagogue project for Philadelphia, of 1961–72) or to contain stairs and other services. This travel sketch can be profitably compared to the spiral of the early section for G.T.U. (Fig. 30). The small hollow columns of the later scheme functioned both in a structural capacity and to distribute air, electricity and other services throughout the building.

was involved with the new project is further demonstrated by a more mundane office drawing in the L. I. Kahn Archive, portraying the basic area requirements of the client's brief, which includes the Exeter plan for comparative purposes.

64
The client and Kahn first discussed the project on July 30, 1971, and the contract date was October 23, 1972. The first model and office drawings were shown to the client and rejected in April 1973. The second model and preliminary office drawings were presented for approval on October 30, 1973.

65
See "G.T.U. Brief," 3,25, L. I. Kahn Archive Box 113.

66
Ibid., 34. The zoning problem is discussed in a letter of August 30, 1973, Kahn Archive Box 113.

67
See letter from G.T.U. to Kahn, September 5, 1973, Kahn Archive Box 113.

31. *Opposite above: Graduate Theological Union Library. Preliminary site plan; L.I.K. 865.1.*

32. *Above: Graduate Theological Union Library. Plan; L.I.K. 865.34.*

33. *Opposite below: Graduate Theological Union Library. Plan; L.I.K. 865.26.*

34. *Below: Graduate Theological Union Library. Model, preliminary scheme.*

The large servant spaces of the first scheme for G.T.U. were reworkings, in a new structural context, of those at Exeter. This was no longer so in the final scheme for the G.T.U. Library, where the hollow columns contributed to the structural and spatial order of the building in a different, yet fundamentally analogous way. In the resolved plans and section (Figs. 39–42) and in the forceful articulation of the exterior walls of the model (barely perceptible in Fig. 43), the hollow columns generate the more complicated structural grid, of ABCBA rhythm, which has replaced the even, open grid of the previous scheme. The spatial ramifications of this can be considered on the upper level (Fig. 42), where the servant areas, such as vestibules and bathrooms, as well as external porches, coincide with the narrow bays of the structural grid. As with the related served spaces which are accommodated within the large bays, Kahn has reiterated his principle of conceiving activity and structure together.

In moving away from the grid of the Yale Center for British Art, Kahn returned in part to a much earlier project, the Trenton Bath House of 1954–59. In that building, the hollow columns, which he had acknowledged as marking the beginning of his realization of served and servant spaces, also determined the organization and rhythms of the plan.[69] In the earlier G.T.U. Library scheme, the large servant spaces containing the stairs were essential to the definition of the even grid. However, the supervision problem and relocation of the stairs led to a radical transformation: the servant spaces, now truly hollow columns, become integral with an entirely different organism, inspired by the Trenton Bath House.

The pervasive order of this final scheme derived from the grid set up by the hollow columns and from the supports necessary for the terracing of the three floors (see the plan of the lower level, Fig. 39, and the model, Fig. 43). In this terse structural system the rhythms existed within the rigorous biaxial symmetry. The terracing acted as a buttressing agent, while a grand cross (Fig. 44) appears to bind the whole together. The ideal perfection of this solution was a cogent statement of Kahn's theoretical demand that a building must respect "the order of nature."

Within the structural system, each floor accommodated a variety of functions. The design was thus more open than Exeter, where

68
See Kahn, "Monumentality;" and E. Johnson, "A Drawing of the Cathedral of Albi by Louis I. Kahn," *Gesta* 25 (1986):159–165.

69
See Tyng, *Beginnings*, 35.

35. *Graduate Theological Union Library. Perspective of front, preliminary scheme; L.I.K. 865.51.*

brick and concrete imposed vertical continuity of zones. Located around the circular opening of the upper level were four square rooms for offices and specialized library functions, with their subordinate servant spaces. The lower level contained a vast area of book stacks, carrels, and a student meeting room. On the main level Kahn devised an entrance sequence which led the readers past the circulation desk, with its staff area behind, into the central space. Ringed with card catalogues, this rose up through the circle cut out of the floor above to culminate in the cross beams of the roof. The stacks formed the section of the inner doughnut not occupied by the staff area, and beyond were carrels.

The early plan of the entrance level (Fig. 37) indicates that Kahn had yet to realize a method of bringing natural light to the large expanse of floor below. His eventual solution, triangular clerestories, allowed light to filter down through triangular voids cut out of the entrance floor (Fig. 40). The use of two kinds of light wells created a variety of spatial ambiences, each characterized by different textures and intensities of light, responding to external conditions. His thoughts on light can be explored in a sketch merging different levels (Fig. 45). Cut corners identify the main clerestory level, while to either side are the two lower, triangular-shaped clerestories. Kahn's notation "lightwell" suggests that he was

36. *Graduate Theological Union Library. Perspective of rear, preliminary scheme; L.I.K. 865.52.*

imagining the light pervading the interior from three sources, the two clerestory levels and the windows along the perimeter. The dark lines represent the relative absence of natural light, while the untouched paper signifies the ample light flooding in through the clerestories. One might apply Kahn's own evaluation of a nineteenth century engraving by George Cruikshank: "Each stroke of the pen is where light is not!"[70] While Kahn's brief charcoal sketch conveys a sense of the light, it is also charged with his deepest theoretical meditations on the meanings of darkness, light and shadows. Rapidly drawn sketches, such as this study or the early form sketches for Exeter, are more illuminating than precise drawings since they were made not only when Kahn was deeply immersed in the realm of silence but at the very moment when ideas attained a state of resolution.

The interior, although more open than that at Exeter, employs similar cross beams to catch light entering from the upper clerestory. A visitor moving through the interior experiences a constant expansion and contraction of light-filled space, a quality Kahn admired in antique architecture and in the drawings of Piranesi. Furthermore, the light entering from above has a symbolic meaning in a library, especially one dedicated to theological studies, as it suggests the efforts of the readers to attain a higher order of knowledge.

The integration of the building with its natural setting was a major departure from the earlier library designs. As Kahn himself observed:

The plan does not begin nor end with the space he [the architect] has enveloped, but from the adjoining delicate ground sculpture it stretches beyond to the rolling contours and vegetation of the surrounding land and continues farther out to the distant hills.[71]

At G.T.U., the site is a treed area above the Berkeley campus surrounded by low-scale buildings. From the front of the library, the land slopes down to the northeast, and panoramic views of San Francisco Bay open out to the west and east.

For an understanding of Kahn's response to the site, one can turn to an early sketch (Fig. 46) as well as to the perspective (Fig. 47) and model (Fig. 43) shown to the client shortly before Kahn's death in 1974. The design sketch reveals a succession of ideas for the plaza and connecting paths. At the top of the drawing is

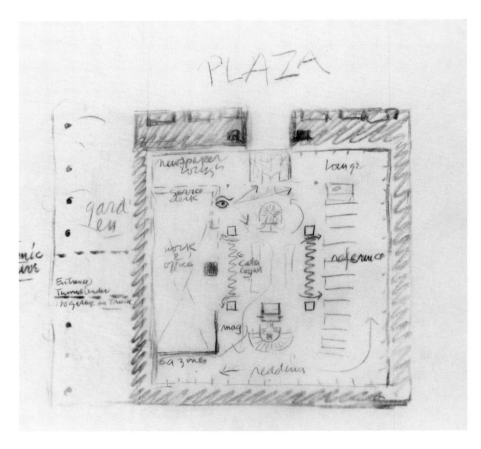

37. *Graduate Theological Union Library. Plan; L.I.K. 865.36.*

a bridge, which passes over a moat (suggesting the presence of water) to bring the visitor to the entrance. A processional pathway leading diagonally to the building is complemented by an alternative route involving a sequence of steps with a right-angled change in direction. By contrast, the plaza in front of the building is more static in character, as a place to pause and meet. The diagonal entranceway is a recurring theme in Kahn's work, often employed to provide a dynamic experience of a building which is itself stable and symmetrical.

In the minds of both client and architect, the plaza was a major space in its own right, serving a vital function as the realm where members from the various religious schools at Berkeley would come together.[72] Kahn saw this social activity to be as essential to the institution of a library as that of reading. Exeter's intended plaza, with its linking paths, was here elaborated in response to the site to form a carefully controlled spatial sequence, what Kahn had earlier defined as "an architecture of connection." In his terms, the large plaza is the

70
Quoted in Marshall Meyers, "Louis Kahn and the Act of Drawing: Some Recollections," in *Louis I. Kahn: Sketches for the Kimbell Art Museum* (Fort Worth: Kimbell Art Museum, 1978). Also see Kahn, "Architecture: Silence and Light," 32.

71
Kahn, "Monumentality," 585.

72
"G.T.U. Brief," 22–23.

73
Kahn's conviction that the paths, the plaza with its surrounding trees, and the bridge are all vital to the meaning of the library seems to draw inspiration from the classical tradition, especially as exemplified by Henri Labrouste's plans for the Bibliothèque Ste. Geneviève of 1838–1850. Labrouste, who had wanted to include a garden in front of his library, commented that the

38. *Sketch of Cathedral of St. Cecile, Albi, France, 1959.*

presence of such a forecourt "planted with big trees and decorated with statues laid out in front of the building would serve to shield it from the noise of the street and prepare those who came there for contemplation." Faced with the restricted urban site, Labrouste transformed the vestibule of his library into an illusionary garden with painted trees and sky. Such concerns seemed to be mirrored at G.T.U.

See N. Levine, "The Romantic Idea of Architectural Legibility: Henri Labrouste and the Neo Grec," in *The Architecture of the École des Beaux-Arts*, ed. A. Drexler (Cambridge: M.I.T. Press, 1977), 334–338, and P. Loud, "The Kimbell Art Museum, 1966–1972, by Louis Kahn," (1980), unpublished manuscript in the L. I. Kahn Archive, 108–109.

74
See Loud, "The Kimbell Art Museum, 1966–1972."

first "place of invitation," preceeding, as at Exeter, the second "invitation" of the central hall. The transition from external to internal communal space was, for Kahn, a ceremonial event. At Exeter it is marked by one's movement up the monumental stairs. At G.T.U., where the two spaces are at the same level, one bridges the moat. Both libraries enhance such statements of entrance through the complex routes the visitor must follow.[73]

Kahn's desire to shape an entrance sequence with trees and water at G.T.U. can be seen as well in other schemes designed in the last decade of his life. At the Kimbell Art Museum of 1966–72, the visitor approaches the building along a "sacred way" bordering quiet pools, moving through raised forecourts and a ceremonial avenue of holly trees.[74] Contemporary with G.T.U. was the competition for the Roosevelt Memorial in 1973–74. In response to the site, the narrow tip of Roosevelt Island in New York, Kahn created a corridor of space defined by converging avenues of trees. These urged the visitor forward to the monument on

its raised podium at the far end. In these schemes, as at G.T.U., the approach through nature was intended to place the visitor in a suitably contemplative frame of mind. The serenity assists meditation, whether on works of art or books, or related to a specific commemorative act.

Even more than in these other projects, the final G.T.U. design was conceived as a symbiosis of built form and natural environment. One can see this beginning in the perspective of the building from the vantage point of the plaza (Fig. 47). Perhaps with the earlier protests from residents in mind, the chosen view diminishes the building's bulk. It now nestles into the surrounding landscape. Sunk within the moat, the lower level acts as a base for the entrance floor with its deeply recessed portico. The moat serves to set off the library from its setting, thus stating the separateness of the unique architectural event, while the bridge defines the linking passage between the two.

The upper level is almost entirely concealed by its trees. Above, the top clerestory can be seen, yet its solidity is eroded by the cut-away corners. In a sense, the pyramid form, terracing, and trees transform the building into a hill. Architecture has become one with nature. Earlier theorists, for Kahn most notably Boullée, had speculated that pyramids were erected in imitation of mountains. Kahn's landscape sketches, such as that of the peak at Arachova in Greece (Fig. 48), evince a classicist's intent to reveal the geometric order underlying the apparent irregularities of individual landscapes. As demonstrated by the model for an early project for the Levy Memorial Playground of 1961–66, the pure form of the pyramid was important for Kahn. At G.T.U., the pyramidal shape is a concrete manifestation of nature's order. At the same time, one's vision of the pure geometric form is deliberately obscured by the trees on each level, so that architecture and setting are blended. It is tempting to think that Kahn was influenced by eighteenth and nineteenth century picturesque theories of visual perception. Yet the presence of nature in architecture had a much deeper meaning. In a discussion of cities, he explored the role of trees and water:[75]

Deep down in our experience we lived off such foliage. There must have been something which we deeply venerated and is still part of us . . . trees must be made part of our living pattern because they are part of our life. You can extend it to water as being something which makes a fountain a necessity, and not just a decoration in the city . . .[76]

In functional terms, the trees in "terracotta planters"[77] shade the library from direct sun. This particular quality of sunlight, filtered through leaves, was an important element in Kahn's conception of the interior space, just as it had been at Kimbell, of which he wrote:

I cut across the vaults, at a right angle, a counterpoint of courts, open to the sky, of calculated dimensions and character, marking them Green Court, Yellow Court, Blue Court, named for the kind of light that I anticipate their proportions, their foliation or their sky reflections of surfaces or on water will give.[78]

At G.T.U., Kahn envisaged an interior reverberating with green light, reflected from the movement of sunlight on the leaves. Library users would be refreshed by the colored light and the view; here, as elsewhere, the experience of nature would strike a deep chord within us and enhance meditation.

The screen of trees at the G.T.U. Library is also related to Kahn's layer of "ruins" wrapped

75
Water had an important symbolic function in many of Kahn's buildings, especially at the national capitol for Bangladesh at Dhaka.

76
From L. I. Kahn article in *Canadian Art*, January-February 1962, quoted in Tyng, *Beginnings*, 111.

77
This is denoted on certain office drawings.

78
Quoted Rohner et. al., 349.

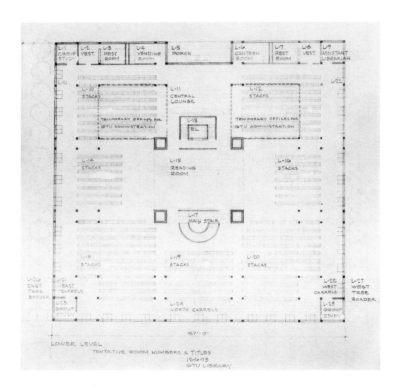

39. *Graduate Theological Union Library. Plan of lower level, sepia print.*

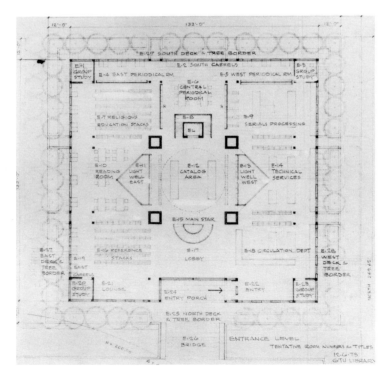

40. *Graduate Theological Union Library. Plan of entrance level, sepia print.*

79
See Kahn's studies of a "wall for glare" in Rowan, "Wanting to Be," 141.

80
In creating such contrasting representations, Kahn may well have been influenced by the late eighteenth century concept of classicism, which encompassed opposing interpretations of the one building. As demonstrated by Stuart and Revett's well-known *Antiquities of Athens*, individual buildings were depicted both in their original pristine glory, as if existing on an ideal plane outside of history, and as architectural fabrics intermeshed with their setting, subject to the vicissitudes of time and place. J. M. Gandy's famous depictions of Soane's Bank of England, showing the once pure neo-classical forms crumbling in a sprawling ruin, expresses this same fascination with the entropic passage of time. For J. Stuart and N. Revett's *Antiquities of Athens*, see D. Wiebenson, *Sources of Greek Revival Architecture* (London: Zwemmer, 1969), chapter 1, plates 7,9. For John Soane, see *John Soane*, Architectural Monographs (London: Academy Editions, 1983), 64–5.

around such earlier buildings as the United States Consular Office at Luanda, the Meeting House of the Salk Institute in La Jolla, California, and the National Assembly Building at Dhaka, Bangladesh.[79] In these designs, the "ruins" enclose the major structures in a second skin, filtering sunlight and creating a sense of the passage of time alien to the modern movement. In the case of the Library, the trees become the doubled periphery, layering space and baffling light. The building seems a grandiose ruin gradually being reclaimed by nature. The perspectives for the two G.T.U. Library schemes are relevant here. In the earlier drawing (Fig. 36), Kahn stressed the severity of the forms in a primitive landscape. The image is of a timeless order. Later, the form is dissolved, transforming a vision of classical purity into one of Romantic decay (Fig. 47).[80]

Kahn's understanding of history and geometry pervaded all dimensions of his architecture. His respect for historical buildings and projects was most fruitful when it contributed to the difficult search for "form." The Romanesque library, for instance, was crucial to the initial conception of the Washington University project and to the more comprehensively-worked-out social and psychological relationships of the Exeter and G.T.U. commissions. In his view, the past was not ordered according to the classicist's belief in the primacy of the

Graeco-Roman tradition, nor the historicist's theory of the uniqueness of each age and style, including the present. Instead, he regarded history as an array of monuments resonant with meaning, all potential sources of inspiration. In accessing this unlimited reservoir of examples, the determining factor was his insights regarding the nature of an institution. Whether his ideas and questions led him to historical examples or were themselves inspired by specific instances is neither knowable nor relevant, since both reinforced each other. In the case of the Washington University Library, the point is only to realize that there is a reciprocal relationship between the Romanesque building and Kahn's intuition regarding the appropriate spaces for his new library. Both were finally located in "form."

Geometry, often inseparable from history, also belongs to "form." Again, it is possible to suggest that in the search for order and meaning, Kahn's intuitions led to geometric order, and the truth of the insight was confirmed by historical buildings. He was profoundly moved by the simple geometries of ancient architecture, and saw them as a direct emanation of the psyche, free from the interference of accumulated conventions. The austere masses of such buildings were still capable of conveying a powerful meaning to Kahn. Preclassical and non-Western monuments were therefore just as

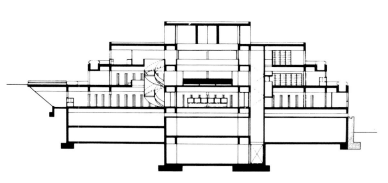

41. *Graduate Theological Union Library. Section.*

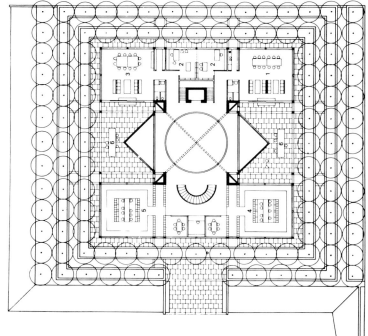

42. *Graduate Theological Union Library. Plan of upper level.*

valuable as reflections of human motivations and beliefs as the traditionally privileged heritage of Greece and Rome. Kahn's knowledge of such buildings was substantial. He followed the progress and documentation of archaeological discoveries, much of it carried out in the Near East by the University Museum of Archaeology and Anthropology, at the University of Pennsylvania, as they appeared in exhibitions and archaeological journals.[81] Geometry and history reinforced each other in articulating a timeless architecture.

The convergence of these three aspects of "form" (geometry, history, and the nature of the institution) in Kahn's design process can be studied at G.T.U. through those historical examples that were surely embedded in his memory. Boullée's projects were particularly inspirational. Kahn was impressed by the monumental character of Boullée's designs: his use of light, his search for origins, and his stimulating insights into the meaning of different institutions. Of particular relevance to the G.T.U. Library, because of the incorporation of trees into the monument, are the Cenotaph for Newton and the Conical Cenotaph.[82]

Similarly, Kahn would have known reconstructions of the mausolea of Hadrian and Augustus, such as those in J. N. L. Durand's *Précis des leçons d'architecture données a l'École royale polytechnique* and Bannister Fletcher's *A History of Architecture on the Comparative Method*, which stress the buildings' terracing and pure geometries.[83] Non-Western architectural sources that he may have been influenced by include ancient stepped pyramids such as those of the Near East and of Mexico, and reconstructions of the famed Hanging Gardens of Babylon. Awareness of modern buildings which drew on similar historical sources, such as the Oakland Museum by Roche Dinkeloo, then under construction nearby, may also have played a part, as well as the memory of Frank Lloyd Wright's Mayan works of the 1920s and the East Coast art-deco skyscrapers of the 1930s.[84]

In 1951, while at the American Academy in Rome, Kahn visited the pyramids of Egypt, which were to have a major influence on the formulation of his mature theory.[85] Significantly, a pyramid provides the motif in the "Silence and Light" sketch drawn almost twenty years later (Fig. 2). As Joseph Burton has shown, Kahn's understanding of the pyramids was assisted by a book on Egyptian architecture which he received at about this time.[86] In this

study, the author, I.E.S. Edwards, investigated the symbolism of the pyramids by considering the meaning of hieroglyphs. He pointed out that the hieroglyph in the shape of a stepped pyramid denoted the idea of ascension. The stepped pyramid, functioning as a stairway by which the dead pharaoh passed from earth to heaven, was the monumental expression of this idea. Such an interpretation was a poetic source of inspiration. The stepped pyramid of the

81
Several architects who had worked with Kahn have noted his interest in archaeological studies.

82
Boullée's Cenotaph for Newton and Conical Cenotaph are illustrated in Kaufmann, *Three Revolutionary Architects.*

43. *Graduate Theological Union Library. Model, final scheme.*

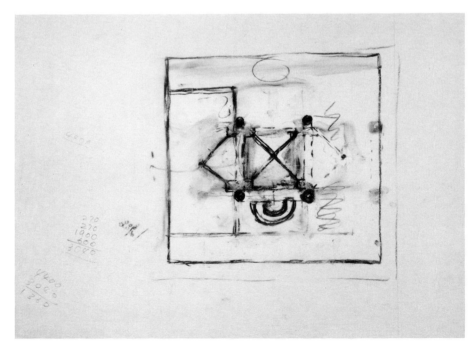

44. *Graduate Theological Union Library. Plan showing cross beams and clerestory; L.I.K. 865.49.*

Washington University and G.T.U. projects
was intended to be a direct expression of the
meaning of the institution of a library, that is,
ascension to knowledge.[87]

The two stepped pyramids, however, are
the outer frames of two very different buildings. At G.T.U., the experience of Exeter and
the response to the Berkeley site underlie major
transformations in the interior and exterior design. The most important inheritance from

Exeter is the tripartite organization of a grand,
top-lit public space surrounded by stacks in
relative darkness, with carrels at the periphery.
Accommodated within the stepped pyramid,
the clerestory of the public space has become
the upper level of the building. Consequently,
a student approaching the Berkeley library can
acknowledge the grand room wherein books
offer the invitation to read. Concealment of
such an important space behind Exeter's brick
doughnut for quiet reading denies an external representation of the public sphere. The
G.T.U.'s stepped pyramid remedies this by
revealing the balance of public and private activities that in both buildings is experienced
while moving through the interior. Expression
of the interior at G.T.U. is enhanced by the
external statement of the pervasive structural
system founded on the hollow columns. At the
clerestory level this occurs, paradoxically, by
cutting away these columns, which no longer
distribute services to the floors nor carry a
heavy load. The corners suggest the role of the
hollow columns, passing through the building
and framing the central space. The structural
frame radiating from the columns is evident as
the concrete members frame infill metal panels
and apertures that respond to the variety of
internal occupations, of which the most significant is the readers in their carrels.[88]

In its surfaces, the G.T.U. Library differs
radically both from the simple concrete-and-
glass bays of the Washington University project and the warmly textured brick lintels and
rising piers of Exeter. At G.T.U., particular
natural lighting conditions could create both
the transparency of Washington University and
the opacity of Exeter. Like the Yale Center, at
times scintillating and shimmering surface
effects dematerialize the exterior. Such external
dynamism surely complements the flux of light
Kahn created within the interior communal
space; both reflect his philosophy of Silence and
Light.

In this final library project, Kahn locates
the spatial zoning of Exeter within the stepped
pyramid, now clad with metal panels. This
pyramid stood proudly aloof in the Washington University site. In the final G.T.U. design,
however, it has been subordinted to the Berkeley setting. Absorption within nature—both
in terms of the undulating landscape and the
changing seasons—is almost complete.

* * * *

45. *Graduate Theological Union Library. Plan; L.I.K. 865.48.*

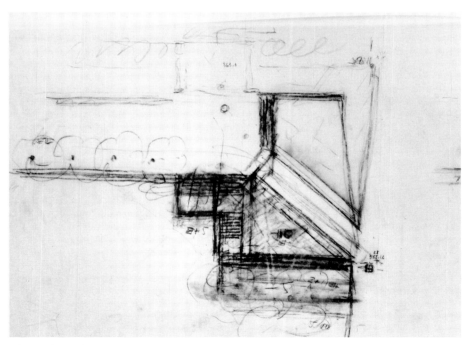

46. *Graduate Theological Union Library. Plan of plaza; L.I.K. 865.7.*

47. *Graduate Theological Union Library. Perspective, final scheme; L.I.K. 865.53.*

In the last twenty years of his life, Kahn was fortunate to obtain commissions that allowed him to develop his understanding of human nature and society. His theory was defined by the twin poles of feeling and thought.[89] For Kahn, all building types contributed to the wholeness of life and well-being of society. In these terms, the presence of a vigorous literary culture was also essential; the knowledge contained in books accumulated in a library provided sustenance for modern life.

Kahn's library commissions were particularly challenging. Their quality was surely related to his love of books and his affinity for oral expression.[90] His buildings accommodate a variety of potentially enriching learning experiences. The private activity of reading and writing was valued as it enhanced introspection, therefore enriching the individual's interior life. Equally important, however, was face-to-face interaction between students where ideas discovered through reading were voiced and debated in public.[91] To grasp the relevance of speaking in a public place, attention must be focused on Kahn's search for beginnings. Literacy, a relatively recent human invention, could not alone define the meaning of a building devoted to learning, since it developed within an existing oral culture. Kahn devoted the grandest space to this earlier form of communication. Orality, with its accompanying facial expressions, gestures, and vocal inflections[92] complements literacy, creating a connection between two activities necessary for a full realization of human capacities.

Furthermore, the libraries expose the reader to a societal continuum. Views from the reading spaces into the center and to the world outside suggest a reciprocal relationship between literature and society.

Kahn's conception of the "form" of a library was inspired by the discussion of the organization and use of medieval libraries in Sturgis's book. As an investigation of the origins of the post-antique library, it impressed Kahn by describing a spatial setting that grew out of the monks' desire to read and learn. These impulses had once shaped the institution, but recently they had been disregarded in favor of compositional techniques founded on the rational separation of functions. By reawakening these fundamental human desires and aspirations, Kahn was able to expose and ultimately reject the prevailing functional values. In overcoming such a myopic vision of the possibilities of architecture, he created a modern library that embodied a more complex and substantial understanding of individual and social experiences.

84
At the time that these earlier buildings were going up, although he was fascinated by the archaeological material that inspired Wright and the art-deco architects, Kahn's modernist stance precluded any such overt historical references. It was not until the 1950s that he rejected the values of the International Style and thus opened his design to just these ancient sources.

85
See Scully, *Louis I. Kahn*, 18; and Vincent Scully, "Introduction," *The Travel Sketches of Louis I. Kahn* (Philadelphia: The Academy of the Fine Arts, 1978–790, 18–20.

86
Burton, "Notes from Volume Zero," 78. The book is I. E. S. Edwards, *The Pyramids of Egypt* (Harmondsworth: Penguin, 1947). See especially 288–289.

87
A less direct statement of ascension can be found in the tapered piers at Exeter and in the early schemes for that building, where a conical pyramid covers the central space (Fig. 13). Some sense of that pyramid is retained in the way the cross beams catch the light in the completed building.

88
The treatment of metal and glass was to be similar to that used at the Mellon Center for British Art.

89
Tyng, *Beginnings, passim*.

90
Several of Kahn's friends, including Richard Peters, mentioned this to me.

91
I am indebted to W. J. Ong's *Orality and Literacy: The Technology of the Word* (New York: Methuen, 1982); see especially 43, 44, 67–74, 82. These ideas were discussed with Professor Marco Frascari of the University of Pennsylvania.

92
Ibid., 47.

48. *Sketch of Peak of Arachova, Greece. Drawn in Philadelphia in 1955 from sketches made in 1951; L.I.K. 945.23.*

Acknowledgements
I would like to thank Peter Reed for helpful discussions on Kahn, and Dean G. Holmes Perkins, Professor David Leatherbarrow, and Professor George Hersey, who read and commented on an early stage of the essay. My studies on Kahn's libraries began with an exhibition I was invited to curate for the opening of the completed Graduate Theological Union Library, titled "Idea and Manifestation: Louis I. Kahn and the Library." This opened at the library in Berkeley on April 8, 1987. This text accompanied a second and larger travelling exhibition, which opened at the Kroiz Gallery, Louis I. Kahn Archive, in September 1987. I would like to thank the curator of the Architectural Archives at the University of Pennsylvania, Julia Moore Converse, for her continued assistance in organizing these exhibitions.

Peter Kohane is an architect in Melbourne, Australia. He received his B. Arch and M. Arch from the University of Melbourne, and is currently a Ph.D. candidate at the University of Pennsylvania. He curated the travelling exhibition "Transformations: Louis I. Kahn's Library Projects," which formed the basis for this article.

D. S. Friedman

PENNSYLVANIA STATION

. . . In the rotunda, where people appeared as small and intent as ants, the smell and sense of snow still lingered, though high now among the steel girders, spent and vitiated too and filled with a weary and ceaseless murmuring, like the voices of pilgrims upon the infinite plain, like the voices of all travellers who had ever passed through it quiring and ceaseless as lost children.
—William Faulkner, "Pennsylvania Station"

The demolition of New York's Pennsylvania Station left its underground structure and functions intact, lest the trains stop running. There was neither final, photogenic plume nor explosive catharsis. Demolition was carefully staged to take away only the most public-looking part of a complex that urban historian Carl Condit rightly called America's "greatest single work of building art."[1] This praise aims past architecture. Big as Pennsylvania Station was (it overran two city blocks), the head house served only to signify a larger construction, an expanse of technology and engineering that brought the Pennsylvania Railroad system under the Hudson and East Rivers into Manhattan. The enabling detail of this complex was electric traction—steamless, electric locomotives—which in the end provided the joint for Pennsylvania Station's undoing.

Penn Station lasted about fifty years, from its opening in 1910 until its demise in the early Sixties. Over unavailing protest, the last work of Charles Follen McKim was sacrificed for a taller building. The wrecking twined along the critical path for the construction of the new Madison Square Garden.[2] The original track beds and platforms were safely disposed fifty feet beneath the site of this unseemly transformation. Neither the primary technical operations of the station nor its name were altered, though all other evidence of the original architecture was removed or remodelled in the design of the usurper, a 22,000-seat sports arena and office tower complex. Today the station is indistinguishable from the underground commercial labyrinth that surrounds it.

Though civic in spirit and classical in countenance, Manhattan's first Pennsylvania Station was not, strictly speaking, a public thing. In an editorial published on the day the station opened, *The New York Times* noted that neither law, public mandate, nor popular clamor compelled the owner to build it; the station was "a purely voluntary addition . . . , the idea of which . . . ripened to adoption through . . . the modern conception of business self-interest of the men who direct the Pennsylvania Railroad."[3] As a new century approached, after a long period of economic

1
Carl. W. Condit, *The Port of New York: A History of the Rail and Terminal System from the Beginnings to Pennsylvania Station* (Chicago: University of Chicago Press, 1980), 259.

stagnation, the Pennsylvania regarded the extension of its direct rail operations from New Jersey to Manhattan as paramount to the company's growth and longevity, no less its supremacy along the Atlantic corridor; a new station in Manhattan constituted the means with which to secure the company's share of a burgeoning New York market. This paper aims to question the site and forms of appearance embodied in the architecture of Pennsylvania Station, which as compactly as any urban building of its era expresses the conflicting vectors of public and private intentionality.

Pennsylvania Station was the biggest commission in the prolific and influential practice of McKim, an Ecole *élève* and founding partner of the New York firm of McKim, Mead & White. At work, McKim was portrayed by close associates as an expert "citationist."[4] The terms of McKim's classicism had little to do with the classical tradition; his work was driven by matters of style, propriety, and exemplary taste, rather than any theoretical interest in the deeper structures of architectural expression (such as analogies to the body or the primitive hut).[5] Consistent with McKim's mentality, it seems, the architectural intentions of Pennsylvania Station are best described as formal and historicist—following not from any *première idée,* but from grids, symmetry, economical geometries, and historical references. Pennsylvania Station embodied a representational structure that was not symbolic (an imitation of first principles), but rather instrumental (a copy of imitations).

I

Pennsylvania Station belonged to a tradition of making which recast distinctions between industry, engineering, and architecture. At the heart of this tradition was the steam locomotive, or more precisely its liberating rail, a "magician's rod" that coursed across the ground of the nineteenth century, binding up its horizons.[6] Walter Benjamin noted that iron rail was the precursor of the I-beam girder, the decisive impetus in the evolution of prefabricated iron construction; new commercial applications using iron girders influenced the design of what he called "constructions with a transitory aim"—arcades, passageways, and exhibition halls.[7] Train sheds were the largest of these. They preceded the great iron-and-glass pavilions, which answered similar demands for span and natural light through a

technology derived from train shed engineering. The giant iron-frame sheds clad in glass combined "astounding dimensions" and new interior luminescence, producing a "secular, non-symbolic and non-iconological brightness and almost limitless adaptability to ever new purposes."[8]

Ends and points between ends of inter-urban rail lines constituted a new *topos* for the architecture of the city, giving rise to terminals and stations. But mere monuments could not civilize the locomotive. As iron rail penetrated urban centers, the navigable corridors of industrial cities fell prey to what Lewis Mumford described as the "wanton immolation of the puffing Juggernaut." This was true enough in Chicago, where by the turn of the century railway operations consumed thirty-five percent of the land in the central city.[9] In Manhattan, railroads were equally intrusive. The New York Common Council outlawed the operation of steam locomotives below Forty-second Street in 1856, confining their use to the city's periphery. Sanctions against steam locomotives were further compounded in January 1902, after condensing vapors and smoke obscured signals in a tunnel under Fourth Avenue, causing two trains to collide, killing seventeen. Soon thereafter the state enacted legislation that prohibited the use of steam-powered locomotives for passenger service in tunnels.[10]

Smoke and steam figured so arrestingly in the experience and imagery of the nineteenth century railroad as to constitute a kind of "locomotive weather." The representation of locomotive smoke in cities and in the landscape, though often suggesting an ominous and even transgressive discordance, embodied a conceit for mechanical parity with nature commensurate with the nineteenth century's exaltation of technology, in particular mechanized transportation. Painting and poetry reflected copiously on views of the locomotive complex—on iron rail, engines, passengers, station and terminal buildings, bridges, and trailing plumes—drawn to its new marks, its new temporal and territorial rhythms, its social fabric. All of industry could be compressed into the closed, perspective institution of rail's two vanishing points, one ahead and one behind, past and future. In the space between, the locomotive subjugated time by girding distance over endless iron reticula.

2
The original Madison Square Garden, designed by Stanford White, occupied the block along Madison Avenue between East Twenty-sixth and East Twenty-seventh Streets, at the northeast corner of Madison Square. It was constructed on the site of the original New York and Harlem Railroad terminal, owned by Cornelius Vanderbilt. Vanderbilt vacated the site in 1871 after he consolidated the Harlem, New Haven, New York Central, and Hudson River Railroads, for which he had constructed the giant Grand Central Depot at Forty-second Street, now Grand Central Terminal. Between 1871 and 1884, the old terminal building at Madison Square was modified to house popular entertainment spectacles. Threatened with loss of this divertissement, a consortium of powerful investors (including J. P. Morgan, Andrew Carnegie, W. W. Astor, and Stanford White) purchased the property and built White's immense entertainment complex, completed in 1888. On June 25, 1906, White was shot to death on its roof garden by the jealous husband of a former mistress. The complex eventually floundered and closed in May 1925, and was shortly thereafter demolished. Madison Square Garden's new owners, retaining its original name, moved their operation to Eighth Avenue and Forty-ninth Street. In 1968, developers constructed the third Madison Square Garden and office building on the site of Pennsylvania Station, bringing about the demolition of McKim, Mead & White's arguably greatest accomplishment. See Leland M. Roth, *McKim, Mead & White: Architects* (New York: Harper & Row, 1983), 158–165, 326–327.

3
"The Pennsylvania Terminal," *The New York Times,* 27 November 1910, 12.

4
H. Van Buren Magonigle testified:

I heard another architect of less eminence characterized recently as "practicing architecture at the top of his voice" and the description would apply measurably to McKim; he liked to sit down at a draftsman's table . . . and design out loud . . . ; the room reverberated with architectural terms that sounded most recondite: Cyma Recta; Cyma Reversa; Fillet above; Fillet below; Dentils; Modillions; and so on. . . . [H]e anxiously consulted the books, and had his assistants spend hours and hours looking up data for him, particularly in Letarouilly, *which was a kind of office bible—if you saw it in* Letarouilly *it was so! And if he could not find, somewhere, authority for a certain combination of mouldings or other elements he desired to make, he would give up and use something else for which he could find a precedent. He was the most convinced authoritarian I have ever encountered.*

H. Van Buren Magonigle, "A Half Century of Architecture, 3," in *Pencil Points* (March 1934): 116.

5
See Joseph Rykwert, "The Ecole des Beaux Arts and the Classical Tradition," in *The Beaux Arts and Nineteenth Century Architecture*, edited by Robin Middleton (Cambridge: M.I.T. Press, 1982), 17.

6
C. Hamilton Ellis, *Railway Art* (Boston: New York Graphic Society, 1977), 12.

7
Maria Louisa Mareca, "Reservoir, Circulation, Residue: J. C. A. Alphland, Technological Beauty, and the Green City," *Lotus International* 30, notes 27, 60; also see Michel Ragon, *L'architecture des gares: Naissance, apogée et declin des gares de chemin de fer* (Paris: Éditions Denoël, 1984), 9.

8
Ulrich Krings, "Large Spaces: Design and Meaning," *Daidalos* 15 (September 1986): 35.

9
M. Christine Boyer, *Dreaming the Rational City: The Myth of American City Planning* (Cambridge: M.I.T. Press, Inc., 1983), 85.

10
Roth, *McKim, Mead & White*, 316.

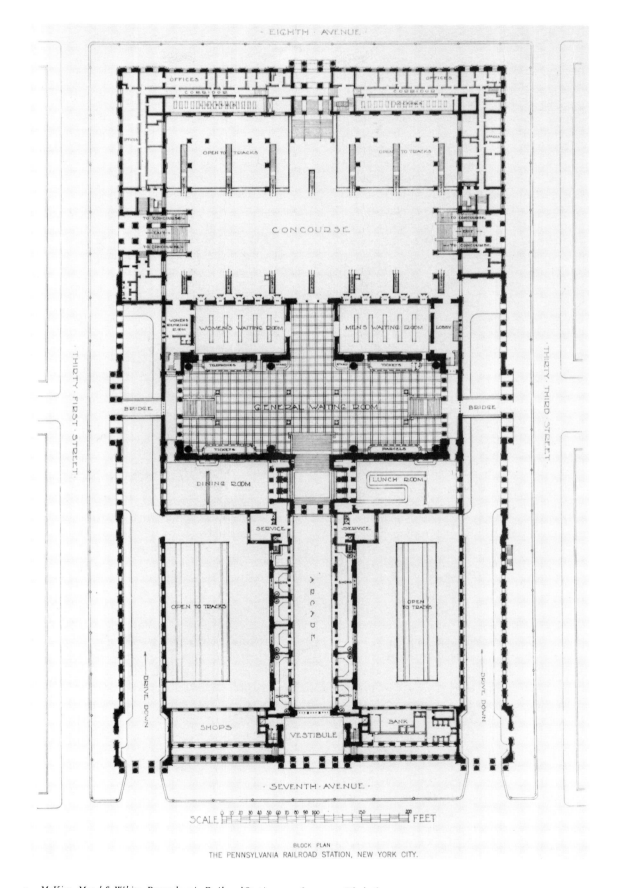

BLOCK PLAN
THE PENNSYLVANIA RAILROAD STATION, NEW YORK CITY.

2. McKim, Mead & White, Pennsylvania Railroad Station, 1906–1910. Block plan.

Tall sheds with long spans and large skylights were built to house crowds, locomotives, and grounded clouds in a single space.[11] Unencumbered by columns, these buildings provided necessary area and light for unstructured assembly and movement amidst the safe dissipation of vapors, smoke, and particulate waste expelled by arriving and departing engines. Early railway terminals required spatial cooperation between two structurally distinct components which together mediated a jump in scale from the technological and social forms of railway transportation to the existing circulatory patterns of the city. Existing types offered no single, unifying form with which to resolve this junction; architects were pressed to rectify a conflict between the functional and representational obligations of the shed and head house.[12]

The bifurcation of utility and grace was not reconciled in the design of the new Forty-second Street Grand Central Depot, built between 1868 and 1871 and New York's largest station. Its shed boasted thirty-two semicircular trusses and rose nearly a hundred feet, spanning twice that measure and covering three acres of track. It was wrapped on two sides by a narrow, three-story L-shaped head house, designed after French models and dressed in a somewhat overeager marriage of Renaissance and Second Empire themes. Cornelius Vanderbilt, its owner (and owner of the New York Central, which it housed) wanted light and space without smoke. He so thoroughly disliked the foul exhaust of locomotives that he painted the interior ironwork of the shed white, to advertise its cleanliness and purity, and then forbade locomotives to enter it. Vanderbilt instituted a "lunatic mode" of track-switching called "flying in": the locomotives of moving trains were manually uncoupled and diverted to side tracks before reaching the throat of the terminal, such that passenger cars coasted into the depot on their own momentum, engineless.[13]

Vanderbilt's chief competitor, the Pennsylvania Railroad, faced a more daunting obstacle than smoke. It was isolated on the New Jersey side of the Hudson, unable to cross the water, forced to ferry its passengers across the river to Manhattan. Alexander Cassatt, who became the railroad's seventh president in 1899, was no less determined to eliminate this impediment than his fellow executive officers, who for many years had vacillated between bridging the Hudson and tunnelling under it. The company pursued costly but unfruitful studies aimed at solving the problem, including circuitous routes and bridges. In 1887, the Pennsylvania Railroad sent a delegation to London to study newly-deployed electric subway cars. Though the London visit triggered new interest in tunneling, the directors remained cautious. Tunnel construction, especially under the Hudson, was precarious. The prospect of accident and loss of life encouraged the directors to wait for the development of safer construction technology.[14]

On the recommendation of his officers, Cassatt sailed to Paris in 1900 to see a new railway station that used electric locomotives. The Gare d'Orsay, built to serve as one of the urban *foyers* to the Paris Exposition, utilized "sophisticated innovations that had no parallel in American practice."[15] Among these were electric locomotives that brought passenger trains into the center of Paris through tunnels and trenches which connected the station to the edge of the city. The elimination of steam in the Gare d'Orsay permitted its architect, Victor Laloux, to integrate the shed and the waiting areas: head house functions (administrative offices, ticket counters, restaurant, hotel, baggage claim areas, and so on) were arranged along the perimeter of the building, parallel to the vast, sky-lit train shed, which had been called "the most dramatic public space in Paris" at the time.[16] Here Cassatt found a demonstration that would resolve any doubts about his railroad's path to Manhattan.

Tunnel construction engineering and the steamless electric locomotive constituted a technological unity on which the entire Pennsylvania Station complex was based: with it Cassatt had found the means to gather both banks of the Hudson over Pennsylvania rail. Not long after Cassatt returned from Paris he had at his disposal a safer tunneling tool called the Jacobs-Greathead shield, a jack-driven, circular, cast iron diaphragm that acted like a movable retaining wall to hold back the alluvium as excavation and construction advanced.[17]

11
Steam has been called the "modern hero" of Edouard Manet's *The Gare Saint-Lazare* (1872–74). Harry Rand suggests that Manet, like his confrere Stéphane Mallarmé, was drawn to its "peculiarity" in the landscape, its weightlessness and unreliable contour. Fog and steam are recurrent themes in Mallarmé. These lines from *L'Azur*, written in 1864, grasp at the locomotive's signature:

*Brouillards, montez! Versez vos
    cendres monotones
Avec de longs haillons de brume
    dans les cieux
Qui noiera la marais livide des
    automnes
Et batissez un grand plafond
    silencieux!*

[Fogs arise! pour your
    monotonous cinders
With long tatters of haze in the
    sky
That will drown the livid bogs of
    autumn
And erect a great silent ceiling!]

In Manet's *The Gare Saint-Lazare*, steam is presented as a white and pewter cumulus adrift in the painting's middle ground. Rand notes that one-third of Manet's canvas is given over to it. Smoke colonizes the atmosphere outside the station, marking a corridor of historical movement: it is the opposite of the locomotive—evanescent, diffusive, silent—and yet it points to it, uncoiled by it, set by it into the air of the painting like a "grounded cloud"; see Harry Rand, *Manet's Contemplation at Gare Saint-Lazare* (Berkeley: University of California Press, 1987), 62–63.

12
This bifurcation was described by Léonce Reynaud, designer of the 1847 Gare du Nord, in the 1878 edition of his *Traité d'architecture*:

. . . these new forms, characteristic of our time . . . present themselves naturally here: arrangements without precedent, materials not utilized until now on a grand scale. . . . Art does not have the rapid progress and the sudden developments of industry, with the result that the majority of the buildings of today for the service of the railroads

leave more or less to be desired, be it in relation to the form or to the arrangement. Some stations appear to be appropriately arranged but having the character of industrial or temporary construction rather than that of a building for public use. Others have been . . . too stamped with reminiscences of the past

F. Leonce Reynaud, "Treatise on Architecture," in *From the Classicists to the Impressionists: Documentary History of Art and Architecture in the Nineteenth Century*, ed. and tr. Elizabeth Gilmore Holt (New York: New York University Press, 1966), 296–300. Kenneth Frampton also notes part of this passage in *Modern Architecture: A Critical History* (London: Thames and Hudson, 1980), 33–34.

13
Condit, *Port of New York*, 95.

14
Ibid., 256.

15
Ibid., 217.

16
Arthur Drexler, "Beaux-Arts Buildings in France and America," in *The Architecture of the Ecole des Beaux-Arts* (New York: The Museum of Modern Art, 1977), 459–461. The reconstituted architecture of the Gare d'Orsay now houses the widely-acclaimed Musée d'Orsay.

17
Condit, *Port of New York*, 296.

18
Jon A. Peterson, "The City Beautiful Movement: Forgotten Origins and Lost Meanings," *Journal of Urban History* 2 (August 1974): 418.

19
Roth, *McKim, Mead & White*, 179.

20
Henry Adams, *The Education of Henry Adams*, ed. Ernest Samuels (Boston: Houghton Mifflin Co., 1974), 343; also Roth, *McKim, Mead & White*, 179.

II

Two years after his visit to the Paris Exposition, Cassatt chose Charles McKim to design the New York Pennsylvania Station. The assignment came on the heels of the final report of the McMillan Commission, a formidable triumvirate comprised of McKim, Daniel Burnham, and Frederick Law Olmsted, Jr. These three experts had been retained under the aegis of Senator James McMillan of Michigan, Chairman of the Senate Committee on the District of Columbia, to evaluate the park system and plan of the capital city. Their final report, which recommended an embellished restoration of Charles L'Enfant's original scheme for the mall, has been called one of the "first usable examples of comprehensive city planning."[18]

McKim's commission for Penn Station can be linked to earlier work with Burnham, who ten years earlier had recruited McKim for the architectural committee of the 1893 Chicago World's Columbian Exposition. Weighted with East Coast offices, Burnham's convocation of establishment architects typified the historical moment of Chicago's *fin-de-siècle* expositionship and its particular economic warrants. At Chicago, architectural form and urban character emerged from a single, unified intention. Taking position against Victorian eclecticism, the White City unfurled a classical rhetoric befitting the French *concours*: palatial fronts, monumental posture, persuasive axiality, common cornice heights, exuberant waterworks and promenades, and what Montgomery Schuyler called "thoroughness of illusion."[19] "Chicago," mused Henry Adams, "asked in 1893 for the first time the question whether the American people knew where they were driving . . . Chicago was the first expression of thought as a unity; one must start there."[20] Apologists and promoters arrogated to the White City's architecture and planning not only artistic but moral authority. The fair set the agenda for American public space: disciplined, Europeanized, perspectivival, uniform. Its architecture and urbanism argued that social reform required an adjustment of style. As an ideological vision, it looked over its shoulder for signs of the oncoming century.

Reform-mindedness needed no ignition in McKim. He was raised by dedicated Pennsylvania Quaker abolitionists admired for their intelligence, reserve, humility, and steadfast ethics. In the McKim household, moral sensibilities found expression in a fully engaged political life. The young McKim chose not to follow his father's path into journalism, religion, or politics; instead, he entered the engineering program at Harvard in 1866. After a year in Cambridge and three months of drafting in the New York office of Russell Sturgis, a fervent Ruskinian ideologue, McKim set out for Paris and the Ecole des Beaux-Arts. He returned from Europe in 1870, took a job in the New York office of H. H. Richardson, and within two years launched his own practice. For McKim, aesthetic perfection was a form of right conduct. He thrived among the genteel and the plutocratic; his ethics perfectly suited the projects of those in whose world view material wealth was taken to be "a form of moral capital."[21]

McKim had helped the World's Columbian Exposition give moral capital a persuasive urban image, though the reprise of its themes in the tumult of New York in 1900 seemed beyond the means of government or industry. Nowhere was resistance to the ordering power of public planning and architecture greater than the island of Manhattan, almost all of whose features were subjugated by its peremptory street grid. The city's densely-packed rectangularization would hardly admit Baroque radii. Notwithstanding the intentions of the City Improvement Commission, which were to foster a civic identity on par with the great cities of Europe, its plan of 1907 skirted Manhattan's larger problems, focusing instead on superficial programs largely concerned with aesthetic improvements to the street, with parks, and with appearances.[22] When asked by Mayor Seth Low in 1903 to serve on a commission to study New York's parks, McKim declined, noting that the difficulties to be overcome in the city were "insuperable."[23]

McKim did not, however, decline the opportunity to supply another model: Pennsylvania Station, smaller certainly than Manhattan but larger than any permanent structure built there before that time. It was decorum, not mere appearance, that motivated McKim to persuade Cassatt and the directors to abandon the idea of building an office tower over the station.[24] On the Court of Honor at the Exposition, McKim had given voice to a rationality "that challenged the forest of skyscrapers" in Chicago.[25] He saw in the program of Pennsylvania Station a conflation of capitalist necessity and civic virtue. The city had grown menacingly vertical; Pennsylvania Station would hold to the ground against this irreligious skyscraping, restore the horizon, and establish an exemplar for urban order amidst the unruly accretions of west Manhattan. McKim intended to design a gate for memorable passage, no less from one epoch as from one destination to another.

III

The sheer physical magnitude of Pennsylvania Station was a much-paraded feature. "Doubtless we are dealing with a big thing," reported *Architectural Record* in 1910; "no . . . costlier building than the station has been under construction concurrent with it [and certainly] no larger." [26] One hundred million dollars (in 1910 currency) was spent on the station complex, including tunnels and yards; another $59 million was spent to improve and integrate existing systems. This whole array—subaqueous and subterranean tunnels, new and renovated trackage, embankments, signaling and switching equipment, train yards, the twelve-mile extension from Harrison, New Jersey, to Queens—was ennobled in the design of the head house. [27] Its exterior appearance was ruled by a highly disciplined, archaeological classicism. It aimed to be imperial, but not at the expense of solemnity.

The major spaces in Pennsylvania Station were disposed along its primary longitudinal and transverse axes, which bisected each other at the building's center. The distribution of space in the station was ordered by an ensemble of three primary rooms anchored at this crossing. Directly over the intersection of the building's two central axes rose the Great Room, the station's general waiting area. To the west of it, parallel and of roughly equal area, stood the Concourse. A long, narrow arcade connected the central spaces to Seventh Avenue. The Great Room was encased by smaller, symmetrically arranged secondary spaces. On the west, twin waiting rooms for men and women flanked the foyer between the Great Room and the Concourse. On the east, dining rooms—a lunch counter and formal restaurant—flanked the foyer at the top of the grand stair that led down from the arcade to the floor of the Great Room. The perimeter of the building was defined by a fifty-foot-wide enclosure that housed administrative, commercial, and service spaces. A U-shaped section to the west contained offices for the station and the Pennsylvania Railroad, which over-

looked the broad, glass-inlaid floor of the Concourse as well as the area open to the platforms below.

In Lewis Mumford's view, the station's plan endowed its circulation with "the effortless inevitability of . . . gravity." [28] Major entrances, archways, and stairs insisted on axial progressions. The front entrance on Seventh Avenue was set into the middle of the large central portico, centered on the longitudinal axis; the portico opened into a spacious vestibule at the top of the arcade, exactly opposite the Eighth Avenue entrance to the Concourse, situated on the same axis 800 feet away. Between these two points everything obeyed symmetry. Station traffic moved in and out of the Great Room through an impressive succession of formal volumes and layered planes ordered about the transverse axis—along stairs, past columns, across porches and foyers, under archways, onto bridges, into the city's air but not yet onto its streets. In the adjacent Concourse, additional exits were provided at either end of a secondary transverse axis that roughly bisected the west half of the plan. These exits augmented the four centrally located entrances and helped to discharge the flow of local commuters.

At the time of its construction the architects of Pennsylvania Station declared that the Great Room, the heart of the building, was the largest of its kind in existence. [29] It covered nearly 25,000 square feet—a space 147 feet high, 103 feet wide, and 277 feet long. Comparisons with the nave of St. Peter's and the Baths of Caracalla (which it exceeded in dimension by twenty percent) were liberally repeated in commentaries of the day. The authority and centrality of the cella-like Great Room was signified in plan by the dominating mass of its enclosing elements: eight giant Corinthian columns, seven feet in diameter and sixty feet high, set just inside the room's thick perimeter walls. The columns 'supported' each corner of the ceiling's three groin vaults, though the structural loads were borne by steel hidden beneath veneer. The corners of each vault were gathered in by huge entablatures, so big that Schuyler was inspired to note that it would have been more to the point if the columns beneath them were turned upside down. [30]

In the Great Room McKim aimed to reconstruct the frigidarium of the baths of Caracalla (A.D. 212–216): "The conditions of modern American life," reasoned project architect W. Symmes Richardson, "are more nearly akin to the life of the Roman Empire than . . .

21
Richard Sennett, *The Fall of Public Man* (New York: Vintage Books, 1974), 12.

22
Condit, *Port of New York*, 262–263; also Robert A. M. Stern, Gregory Gilmartin, and John Montague Massengale, *New York 1900: Metropolitan Architecture and Urbanism 1890–1915* (New York: Rizzoli, 1983), 29–30.

23
Richard Guy Wilson, *McKim, Mead & White Architects* (New York: Rizzoli, 1983), 34.

24
Roth, *McKim, Mead & White*, 327.

25
Manfredo Tafuri and Francesco Dal Co, *Modern Architecture* (New York: Rizzoli/Electra, 1986), 1:39.

If McKim felt some disdain toward tall buildings, it was not a expression of the policy of the firm. At the same moment McKim was working up the early iterations of Pennsylvania Station, McKim, Mead & White was invited to submit a scheme for the redevelopment of Grand Central Terminal, to be commissioned in concert with the New York Central's program for the electrification of their terminal operation. Stanford White submitted a design for the world's tallest building—a sixty-story office tower that rested on a giant, square fourteen-story high office block set above the tracks (Roth, *McKim, Mead & White*, 316–317).

26
"The Pennsylvania's New York Station," *Architectural Record* (27 June 1910): 519.

27
For a thorough quantitative description of the Pennsylvania Station complex, see "Completion of the Pennsylvania Railroad Tunnels and Terminal Station," *Scientific American* (May 14, 1910): 398–399; and Condit, *Port of New York*, 263–310 and notes 30 and 36 (p. 388) and note 58 (p. 392).

28
Lewis Mumford, *The Highway and the City* (New York: The New American Library, 1953), 154.

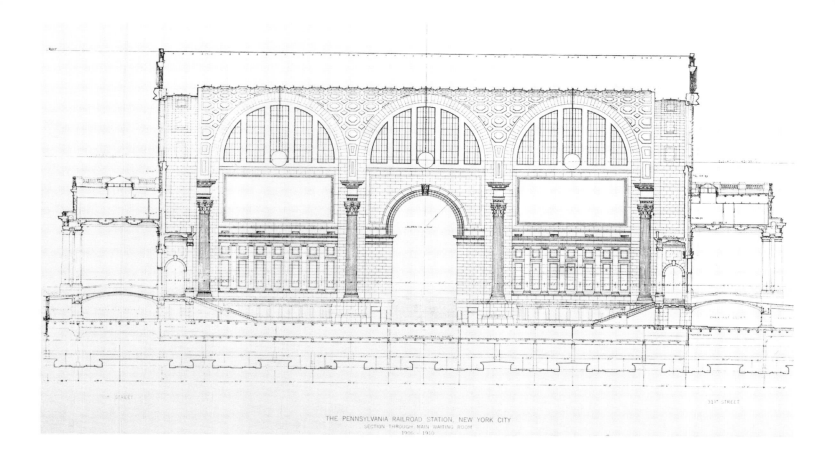

THE PENNSYLVANIA RAILROAD STATION, NEW YORK CITY
SECTION THROUGH MAIN WAITING ROOM
1906 - 1910

3. *McKim, Mead & White, Pennsylvania Railroad Station, 1906–1910. Section through main waiting room.*

29
W. Symmes Richardson, "The Terminal—The Gate of the City," *Scribners* 52 (October 1912): 402, 415; also Condit, *Port of New York*, 280.

30
Montgomery Schuyler, "The New Pennsylvania Station in New York," *The International Studio* 41 (October 1910): xciv.

31
Richardson, "The Terminal," 414.

any other known civilization."[31] Penn Station enfolded the whole of American railroad enterprise into its Roman aggrandizement of the Pennsylvania's New York extension. Six murals by Jules Guerin broadcast these claims in atmospheric pastels. They were painted inside large, rectangular panels high on the side walls and above the entablatures of the Great Room's exit porticos, illuminated by the daylight which entered through the eight giant lunettes located just above them. Some murals depicted blue and buff-colored maps of the world, others maps of company routes.

Leading pedestrians into the space of the Great Room from the east was the arcade of the station, its primary retail appendage. The position of the arcade, which supplanted a section of Thirty-second Street, was preordained by the unusual depth of the central waiting room and the need to route passengers across a considerable distance from the Seventh Avenue entrance to the station proper. Forty-five feet wide and 225 feet from end to end, this long, vaulted, and slightly inclined interior avenue was lined on both sides with uniform storefronts and office entrances. McKim's arcade bore little resemblance to the narrow, irregular passages of its nineteenth-century Parisian antecedents. It was less an arcade than a rational axis decorated with the simulation of urban commercial life—straight, uniform, more like

a wide chute than a boulevard (certainly no place for the turtle-paced *flâneur*).

The problem of vehicular traffic was resolved with partially-colonnaded, enclosed carriage drives that ran parallel to the arcade, extending along the eastern two-thirds of the Thirty-first and Thirty-third Street frontage. These ramps provided access to large service courts located in hollows on either side of the arcade, and to carriage courts one story below grade, where baggage and passengers were deposited and picked up at the level of the Great Room. The arcade and service drives grafted the circulatory systems of the city onto the network of the railroad. McKim's preference for these forms over open urban space suggests an adjustment of terms for the social space of the city; movement subordinated rest, which when accommodated at all was largely predicated on the flow of money.

The Concourse, which occupied a third of the building's plan, worked as a reflex of the Great Room. It was rendered in the industrial idiom of its predecessors, the great iron-and-glass train sheds and exposition halls in Europe and America, though by its lyricism and sheer athletic complexity McKim's design surpassed the best of them. Unlike the great sheds, span was neither the problem nor the achievement of the Concourse structure, since columns footed between the tracks and on the concrete platforms supported the room's intricate network of primary and secondary vaults. The exposed structure of the Concourse belied rather than revealed its load. Set beside the compression and solemnity of the other room's Roman syntax, its latticed ironwork seemed agile and acrobatic. It was by analogy rather than replication that the Concourse transposed the classical contours, modulation, and typological references of the adjacent waiting room; though it was not all akin to the Roman bath, it participated in the 'purifying rites' of urban socialization.

The luminescence of the skylight is the central theme of the Concourse. It both transmits and re-presents the light of the weather-vault, which is the domain of the locomotive. Only under open sky—underway, with its throttle open, when it is a pure line of force—is the locomotive most at home. In the Concourse, McKim ignored the architectural advantages of electric power, as Laloux had seemed to do in the Gare d'Orsay (though there light and height were a function of span); instead, he chose to fuse the image of the luminescent shed with the "memory" of the steam locomotive in its milieu. The vaulted skylight imitated and gathered the virtual space of the locomotive over the space of its momentary loadings and emptyings, where the urge for velocity was latent in its standing.

To encase the functional heart of the Pennsylvania Station complex, McKim fashioned vivid architecture in the coupling of unlike projects—the city and the locomotive, steam and electricity, history and technology. Everything about the setting McKim made for the Pennsylvania's New York station suggests that he looked beyond its technological practicality toward something else—civility, urban reform, order—toward the moral equilibrium he found in classical architecture. In the detail of the Concourse, however, McKim built a structure that was less a functional than a typological requirement of the brief, much more as Quatremère would have had it than Durand.

IV

Pennsylvania Station was designed as a gate. McKim had this image foremost in his mind when he was presented with the commission.[32] According to Richardson, the composition and order of the great Seventh Avenue colonnade was indebted to the Brandenburg gate in Berlin (1789–1793), designed by C. G. Langhans.[33] Langhans made a portico without a building; he set a large, free-standing hexastyle colonnade, cast in the Doric order, between pedimented tetrastyle end pavilions, patterned after the Propylaea of the Acropolis in Athens. The Seventh Avenue facade, divided into five parts, was similarly composed, with a projecting hexastyle portico at the center and projecting tetrastyle porticos at each end; each had enlarged central intercolumniations like the Brandenburg, and all three elements were held together by the colonnade. The front elevation's greater debt, however (by way of Letarouilly), was to Bernini. Bernini's gate to St. Peter's offered the designers an appropriately scaled Doric model with the added bonus of equally spiritual and secular urban significations, though in this case the colonnade was straightened out and pressed flat along the station's Seventh Avenue side. Here, the spatial consequence of Bernini's oval was jettisoned on the way to scenic effect.

Richardson is forthright in his insistence on the central importance of the gate metaphor: "Not only did the architects desire to give an adequate expression to the exterior, but they recognized the equal importance of giving the building the appearance of a monumental gateway and entrance to one of the great metropolitan cities of the world. This idea, in their opinion, has not always received the recognition which it deserves in the solution of problems of this character."[34] In its most fundamental manifestation, the function of a gate was to permit a crossing in space between between two discrete territorial domains.[35] In the precarious depth of a gate's threshold, one is neither in-here nor out-there, but suspended in the condition of passage. Moreover, the value and meaning of a city gate is a function of the physical and cosmological integrity of bounding elements; the decay of the latter surely reduces the efficacy of the former. In the case of Pennsylvania Station, decay was ensured by the "fluid limit" of the railway, which "nullifies the differences between inside and outside," turning cities into "points" of arrival and departure.[36]

32
Charles Moore, *The Life and Times of Charles Follen McKim* (originally published in 1929; reprint, New York: De Capo Press, 1970), 274.

33
Though McKim retains credit for its design, W. Symmes Richardson became the project architect and contemporaneous voice of Pennsylvania Station during McKim's illness and after his death in 1909. Educated at the University of California-Berkeley and M.I.T., Richardson spent a year and a half at the Ecole des Beaux Arts, joining McKim Mead & White on his return. He became a successor partner of the firm (Roth, *McKim, Mead & White,* 318, 336).

34
W. S. Richardson, "The Architectural Motif of the Pennsylvania Railroad Station," in *The History of the Engineering, Construction and Equipment of the Pennsylvania Railroad Company's New York Terminal and Approaches*, William Couper, ed., quoted at length in Condit, 280.

35
Joseph Rykwert explains that the walls into which a gate was set constituted a much more fundamental and inviolable union, that between heaven and earth; in ancient times, he tells us, gates were complex bridges over a forbidden tract of ground "charged with menacing power"; Joseph Rykwert, *The Idea of a Town* (Cambridge: M.I.T. Press, 1988), 137.

36
Beatriz Colomina, "On Adolf Loos and Josef Hoffmann: Architecture in the Age of Mechanical Reproduction," in *Raumplan Versus Plan Libre*, ed. Max Risselada (New York: Rizzoli, 1988), 69–70.

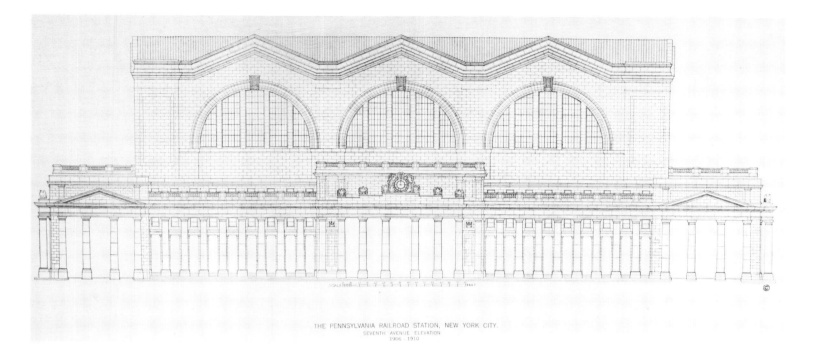

THE PENNSYLVANIA RAILROAD STATION, NEW YORK CITY.
SEVENTH AVENUE ELEVATION
1906 - 1910

4. *McKim, Mead & White, Pennsylvania Railroad Station, 1906–1910. Seventh Avenue elevation.*

37
Richard Sennett, speaking in a doctoral seminar, University of Pennsylvania, October 25–26, 1988.

38
Mark Harrison, *Crowds and History: Mass Phenomena in English Towns 1790–1835* (Cambridge: Cambridge University Press, 1988), 105.

39
Alexander Tzonis and Liane Lefaivre, *Classical Architecture: The Poetics of Order* (Cambridge: M.I.T. Press, 1986), 277–278.

40
Peter Hall, *Cities of Tomorrow: An Intellectual History of Urban Planning and Design in the Twentieth Century* (Oxford: Basil Blackwell, 1988), 183.

On Manhattan's homogenizing grid, components of center and boundary that constitute an ideal or coherent urban composition are obscured; in such a schema there is no urban wall or clear bounding surface, nothing in which to fix a gate. The economic instrumentality of the grid precludes effective geometrical hierarchies. In this setting, the perception of Pennsylvania Station as an urban "gate" was thoroughly corrupted by a positional uncertainty that distorted the conventional sensation of entry and exit, a disorientation amplified by subterranean arrival and departure and by platforms situated four stories below the city surface. Uncertainty about location was carried into the order of the station walls: "inside" caromed off "outside" in a confusion of elevational codes, in its interior storefronts, porticos, and fenestration. One can argue that Pennsylvania Station had no sustainable centrality. In absorbing a block-long segment of Thirty-second Street, the plan of the station literally incorporated Manhattan's grid.

Situated over the center columnation of the station's four entrance porticos were giant, wreath-encircled clocks, each supported by two twelve-foot maidens, one for Day and one for Night. In addition to these gate-guarding, allegorical sentinels, at least ten clocks of heroic dimension were positioned above both sides of all the primary entrances and above every major passageway. Richard Sennett has argued that the clock imposed a mechanical grid over time comparable in operation to the grid imposed by planning over modern urban space.[37] The face of the city clock, he suggests, made time visible, transformed it into a secular periodicity suitable to the regular spacings of labor in modern commercial production. In this sense, clocks were a fundamental component of urban ordering. Insofar as the city was the crucible for industrialization, the processes that furthered its aims were "simultaneously a sustained attack upon irregular work routines."[38] Thus, as an economic instrument, the whole station was predicated on time (the time of the railroad); fittingly, mechanical time presided over all its thresholds.

McKim's assiduity in matters of classical composition had little to do with the archaic operations of the classical canon, with *temenos*-making, or with "pricking the conscience."[39] The building as a whole constituted an understandable deformation of canonical meanings in the service of the powerful ideologies propelling industrial expansion and private enterprise, and to these its designers exhibited uncompromising fealty. As an ideological instrument, the first intention of the design of Pennsylvania Station was to propagandize the terms and representations of modern American urban life. And insofar as this view fused the projects of capitalism with the ideals of democracy and the dominant social order of the city, the building was taken by its makers to be an authentically public good.

Like Burnham, McKim wanted to reconstitute the memory of "a city of the past that America never knew."[40] Ironically, McKim took a stand against the only architecture that could be said to constitute American urban memory, since early expressions of tallness (especially in Chicago) reflected an indigenous

American style. In the design of Pennsylvania Station, McKim's nostalgia took the form of surprising lowness. The building's horizontality was both constituted and relieved by monumental columns, immutable expressions of the body matrix which McKim deployed as the stewards of decorum. McKim wanted to sustain both what Royal Cortissoz called "the great pageant of our material progress" and also a higher order of value, a *spiritual* dimension.[41] The design of the station resisted horizontality without negating it, as though to preserve the play of horizontal and vertical axes that both defines and dignifies the compass of being. In Pennsylvania Station, McKim attempted to mediate between expressions of movement and equilibrium. But even in the arcuated soaring of the Great Room and Concourse, the column remained sovereign. For his last work McKim upheld the primacy of "standing" in its most fundamental aspect, which points to the physical and moral condition of "uprightness" (and, therein, to the deep connection between bodily and ethical postures).

In its borrowings, Pennsylvania Station made references to historic buildings as though aspects of the personality of each could be cast into the assembly of the station's image. Fragments of type and style were gathered into a precedence with the conviction that their reassembled details would accrete to authentic meanings. McKim had in mind publicness, but his gaze lingered in the materiality of the historical object. He could not look through it to the complex social geographies of city and site. The appropriation of publicness had more to do with the theatrical projection of private, corporate personality than it did with the provision of meaningful space for the appearance of social and political interaction, such as was present in the great public baths of antiquity. Pennsylvania Station was a building expressly made for *passing through*; it was thus by design that its great "public" spaces—arcade, waiting room, and concourse—were want for seating. Station architecture became an accessory to the technological mission of the project, what Richard Sennett has called the coalescence of architecture with the technology of transportation.[42] In the coupling of regional and urban transportation infrastructures, space was provided for the appearance of architecture, which in turn "appeared" to be public.

V

Fear, revulsion, and horror were the emotions which the big city crowd aroused in those who first observed it.
—Walter Benjamin, "On Some Motifs in Baudelaire"

McKim visited the Baths of Caracalla in Rome during his tour with the McMillan triumvirate in 1901. The team spent a June afternoon in the ruins of the *thermae* during which time McKim, sketching, hired workmen to mill about in the space of the frigidarium so that he could "observe the scale and see how the building adapted to the movement of crowds."[43] The positioning of the crowd helped McKim translate the ruins of the bath into a utopian conception of public urban space. His "crowd" is benign and unhurried, like the civilized stroll of fair-goers along the basin of the White City's Court of Honor: "in all his designing," wrote one biographer, McKim "had in his mind's eye the people, men and especially well-gowned women, who would sweep up and down his broad staircases."[44] This image of McKim—sketch pad in hand, directing workers to enact crowdedness amidst the ruins of the great Roman bath—suggests an essential dimension of the ethos of Pennsylvania Station.

"The crowd—" Walter Benjamin declared: "no subject was more entitled to the attention of the nineteenth century writer. It was getting ready to take shape as a public in broad strata . . . It became a customer . . . "[45] In the density of the nineteenth-century crowd and its velocities, in its press of mixed classes, Benjamin hoped to locate the shifting space of modern urban habitation. The syncopations of the crowd-borne body, which must brook the shocks of physical contact, revealed "the true connection between wildness and discipline"; pedestrians in the crowd "act as if they had adapted themselves to . . . machines and could only express themselves automatically."[46] Benjamin sensed the presence of crowd in the conditioned nerves of the modern worker and the numbing drills and rhythms of the factory. As it emerged in the fiction and poetry of the nineteenth century, the crowd laminated into one rhetorical image the disenfranchisement, alienation, compound sufferings, and compul-

41
Royal Cortissoz, "Some Critical Reflections on the Architectural Genius of Charles F. McKim," *The Brickbuilder* XIX (February 1910): 34.

42
Sennett, *The Fall of Public Man*, 14; see also Lewis Mumford, *The City in History* (New York: Harcourt, Brace & World, 1961), 461.

43
Moore, *Life and Times of Charles McKim*, 274–275; see also Roth, 321; and Lewis Mumford, "The Disappearance of Pennsylvania Station," *AIA Journal* 30 (October 1958): 40.

44
Moore, *Life and Times of Charles McKim*, 275.

45
Walter Benjamin, "On Some Motifs in Baudelaire," in *Illuminations*, ed. Hannah Arendt (New York: Schocken, 1969), 166–177; in parts V through IX of this essay, Benjamin interprets the presence of the crowd in the works of Baudelaire, Barbier, Poe, Engels and Marx, E. T. A. Hoffman, and Hugo; cf. Herman Broch, *The Sleepwalkers* (New York: Pantheon Press, Inc., 1947; reprint ed., San Francisco: North Point Press, 1985), 46–50.

46
Benjamin, "Motifs in Beaudelaire," 176.

47
Boyer, *Dreaming the Rational City*, 9.

48
Mark Girouard, *Cities & People: A Social and Architectural History* (New Haven: Yale University Press, 1985), 311–312.

49
Ibid., 312.

50
Jacob A. Riis, *How the Other Half Lives: Studies Among the Tenements of New York* (New York: Hill and Wang, 1957), 226.

51
Cortissoz, "Critical Reflections on the Genius of McKim," 33.

52
Stern et al., *New York 1990*, 41–42; also, Lorraine B. Diehl, *The Late Great Pennsylvania Station* (New York: American Heritage, 1985), 11, quoting Thomas Wolfe, *You Can't Go Home Again* (New York: Charles Scribner's Sons, 1940), 247–248.

sions that acquire political and economic force only in collectivity. By the century's end, especially in the social scientific literature of urban reform, the word "crowd" inhered the larval stage of insurrection.

The primary impetus for the statutory ordering of the late nineteenth-century American city, taken as a cooperation between physical and political-economic institutions, was crowd control.[47] Since ambient crowdedness (not yet the single-bodied crowd but ever on the verge of it) was most painfully exhibited in the tenements, the crowd and the slum became a coincident threat. Overcrowding in New York at the turn of the century was inflamed by the inadequacy of inter-borough transportation. Too few crossings to neighboring boroughs constricted circulation and resulted in the concentration of Manhattan's poor along two strips on the city's east and west sides.[48] By the end of the century, New York endured the most congested and unhealthy housing of any large city in the world. The density of the Tenth Ward in Manhattan at the turn of the century was more than four times the 1963 population density of Calcutta.[49]

In 1890, at the end of *How the Other Half Lives*, Jacob Riis warned that "the sea of a mighty population, held in galling fetters, heaves uneasily in the tenements."[50] Not uncommon in and around the twenty-eight-acre site secured for Pennsylvania Station was the kind of catastrophic poverty made famous by Riis's camera. With the city's support, the Pennsylvania Railroad cleared the ground of five hundred buildings and fifteen hundred people and erected in their place "a huge structure . . . fraught with ideas of tremendous and even ruthless power."[51] The building of Pennsylvania Station constituted a campaign aimed at urban antisepsis, waged through twin operations of cleansing and edification. It was heralded as a social remedy, as though the crowd it displaced was merely a heteromorphic episode in the history of the crowd it engendered.

Like Riis, Thomas Wolfe used the metaphor of the sea to describe the new crowd brought forth by the station. Wolfe wanted the sound of the crowd to transcend the cultural implications of the space that gives it its resonance:

Great, slant beams of moted light fell ponderously athwart the station's floor and the calm voice of time hovered along the walls and ceiling of that mighty room, distilled out of the voices and movements of people who swarmed beneath. It had the murmur of a distant sea, the languorous lapse and flow of waters on a beach. It was elemental, detached, indifferent to the lives of men. They contributed to it as drops of rain contribute to a river that draws its flood and movement majestically from great depths.[52]

Wolfe endowed the crowd with thalassic properties, with the mystery and formlessness of water, which (like time) is a "chaos" that cannot be dispelled by architecture. Crowd, ocean, and time operate here as transfusive elements. Linear distinctions of direction dissolve in their fluidity: channelings become transitory, motion overtakes movement. Within the station proper, distinctions between coming and going become synchronous and relative in the meandering currents and eddies of the crowd. This "sea" has no destination: in its ocean-likeness, it is ever arriving and on-the-way.

As a locus for the urban crowd the architecture of the railway station reveals a central feature of modern inhabitation. The monumentality of station architecture derives from the impulse to saturate the nodal transition between regional and local transportation systems with a stabilizing rhetoric, one that conveys a sense of occasion, of home-coming and home-leaving. But the genuineness of such sensations presupposes a sedentary community with deeply embedded social conventions—stable traditions of work, play, government, and home life—the idealization of which no doubt lay near the heart of McKim's nostalgia. Unfortunately, spatial constructions that supported the meaning of "home" and the sense of belonging to a particular place were steadily dislocated by the development of rail networks, which transformed the scale and perception of distance as well as difference. The World's Columbian Exposition in Chicago, which marked the closing of the American frontier, turned its focus (assisted in no small measure by McKim) to the city, to the points of collection and distribution; what had been *other* space was incorporated into *this* space, a domain of exchange and acquisition that is itself consumable.

Underlying the pervasive commoditization that helped destabilize modern urban space (and with it the space of urban public life, place-boundness, and belonging) is the inherent political structure of rail technology. Hardly yet obsolete, the locomotive was the apotheosis of movement in the mechanized world of the nineteenth century. But the mobility it afforded tends neither toward democracy (like the automobile) nor liberty (like the boat). Rather, the systemic railway complex—locomotives pulling human and material freight along track—tends toward an authoritarian configuration, insofar as any illusory image of freedom it presents is dependent upon the rigid distributive apparatus of a closed network with highly routinized, highly centralized controls and management.[53] The use of railroads under the German National Socialist bureaucracy between 1938 and 1945 illustrated this potential at its most infernal, wherein trains and "terminals" became the ultimate instruments of dispossession.

VI

. . . there is one particular quality that may greatly increase the convenience and even the life of a building. Who would not claim to dwell more comfortably between walls that are ornate, rather than neglected? What other human art might sufficiently protect a building to save it from human attack? Beauty may even influence an enemy, by restraining his anger and so preventing the work from being violated. Thus I might be so bold as to state: No other means is as effective in protecting a work from damage and human injury as is dignity and grace of form.
—Leon Battista Alberti, *On The Art of Building in Ten Books* (VI, 2)

Get hold of picks, axes, hammers and demolish, demolish without pity the venerated cities.
—Filippo Tommaso Marinetti

Demolition has long been a tool of urban reform. Since the rise of the city as a work of art, we have removed fabric in order to construct monument—the agora in Athens, Rome's fora, and the urban transformations of Bonaparte, Napoleon III, Mussolini, and Ceausescu's Bucharest bear this out.[54]

"What is logical is also beautiful," Burnham said. He pictured audacious excisions of old urban tissue and the construction of a new White City (this time it would be colorful and permanent). His plan for Chicago spoke French, extending an infinite diagonal grid of grand boulevards into the pastel hues of Chicago's western horizon. Burnham's intention was to purge the city of chaos by creating "the physical prerequisite for the emergence of a harmonious social order"; this his plan would do by "cutting new thoroughfares, removing slums, and extending parks."[55]

The Pennsylvania Railroad took to the blighted tissue of west Manhattan with similarly medicinal motives. Its demolition of buildings and displacement of the poor can arguably be gathered under the moral arc of *il piccone risanatore*, "the healing pick," which Haussmann (and Mussolini after him) swung to clear ground for traffic and glory.[56] But the traffic and glory of Pennsylvania Station was private, not public; space cleared by private corporations constitutes consumption, not public endowment. The technology of Pennsylvania Station, like the assets and governance of its owner, was opaque. Its largest elements, though heroic and circulatory, were concealed beneath the ground, not celebrated above it. The architecture seemed indifferent to the reality of the technological operations below. At the level of the city street, all newly cleared ground was given over to historical representations and "public" gestures, though in its generosity of scale it afforded no room for open urban space.

Nevertheless, McKim dissuaded his clients from building a tower because he sought to preserve at least the expression of publicness amidst a proliferation of buildings driven upward by elevators and rote area multiplication. Against greed, good nature is weak defense. In time, the value of the unoccupied envelope over the site superseded any other form of currency or signification. Realty liquidated history. Taller, cheaper extrusions of the property perimeter along its z-axis pressed speculation into the buildable limits of the owner's air rights. This time, the site was given over to spatial capacities of net rentable floor space and seating. The forces that erected Pennsylvania Station easily razed it.

53
See Ivan Illich, *Energy and Equity, Ideas in Progress* (New York: Harper & Row, 1974).

54
Daniel H. Burnham, "White City and Capital City," *Century* 63 (February 1902): 620.

55
Hall, *Cities of Tomorrow*, 179.

56
Spiro Kostoff, "His Majesty the Pick," *Design Quarterly* 118/119 (1982): 33–35.

57
Jacques Ellul, "The Technological Order," in *Philosophy and Technology*, ed. Carl Mitcham and Robert Mackey (New York: The Free Press, 1964), 90–91.

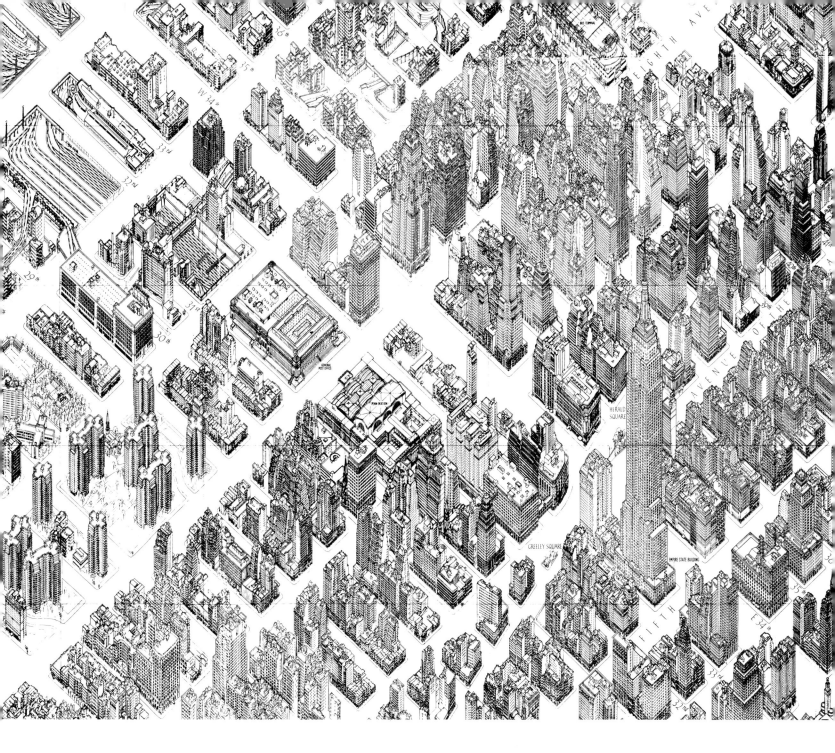

Acknowledgments

The author wishes to acknowledge the helpful criticism of Professor David Brownlee, University of Pennsylvania, in whose American City Beautiful seminar ground-work for this essay began. Gratitude is also owed to Kathleen James, to Professors David Leather-barrow, Marco Frascari, and Nadir Lahiji, and to Ann Marie Borys.
In memorium, Francis Lee Stieglitz, architect.

Fortune brought down Madison Square Garden on top of Pennsylvania Station, one form of crowd on top of another. Any vestige of ornament, or urban decorum and anchorage in public ground and the public good, was sub-sumed by clean and unambiguous commercial motives. Pennsylvania Station is now entirely invisible to the street and the architecture above it has not a square inch of public face about it. But the fate of the station was not merely a problem of site or air rights or prof-itability. As Jacques Ellul has argued, the technological society cannot be a genuinely hu-manist society; spiritual values cannot evolve as a function of material improvement.[57] McKim's monument lacked a pecuniary claim to existence. Whatever its genius, the architec-ture of the station was uncoupled from its essential machines with no less effort nor ethical introspection than the striking of a stage set.

Daniel Shay Friedman is an architect who lives and practices in Philadelphia.

1. Concentric farm: *Amish farm, Colerain Township, Lancaster County, Pa.*

Charles Bergengren

FORWARD SPRAWL: Amish Religious Community Expressed in "Frontless" Houses and Concentric Farmplans

1
Rev. Charles A. Place, "From Meetinghouse to Church in New England, I–IV," *Old Time New England* 13/2 (1922), 13/3, 13/4, 14/1 (1923); Peter Benes, *New England Meeting House and Church*, The Dublin Seminar for New England Folklife, Annual Proceedings 1979 (Boston: Boston University Press, 1979); Marion C. Donnelley, *The New England Meeting Houses of the Seventeenth Century* (Middletown, Conn.: Wesleyan University Press, 1968).

2
Clarence Kulp, "A Study of Dialect Terminology of the Plain Sects of Montgomery County, Pennsylvania," *Pennsylvania Folklife* 12/2 (Summer 1961). Note: this piece is really about plain meetinghouses and their use.

3
Paula Baymiller, "Mary Jackson: A Biology Honors Student Looks at Amish Agriculture," *Oberlin Alumni Magazine* (Winter 1986): 6–8. See also John Hostetler, "Agriculture and Subsistence," *Amish Society*, 3rd ed. (Baltimore: Johns Hopkins University Press, 1980), 117ff, particularly 123; and James T. Lemon, *The Best Poor Man's Country: A Geographical Study of Early Southeastern Pennsylvania* (New York: W. W. Norton, 1972), 91.

In contrast to the strikingly axial and emphatically hierarchical arrangements of Medieval church architecture—people at one end and the mysteries of the sacred both embellished and raised (not to mention sometimes hidden) at the other—the most radical of the Protestant groups have sought a more egalitarian arrangement. The Huguenot Temple of Charenton is usually cited as a major influence, with the altar itself reduced to near insignificance and the speaker's tower or pulpit bought out to the virtual center. Better that all alike could hear the word of the Lord expounded and explained in the clear light of day, than that a mystery be celebrated in a distant cloud of smoke.[1]

In Pennsylvania this impulse has resulted in many church buildings built on what is known as the "meetinghouse plan," that is, with the main door on the long side of the building rather than the short gable and the altar and, more importantly, the pulpit on the other long side. This enables seating in a U-shaped configuration, with everyone as close to each other as possible, and some actually facing each other across the center. The more radical Anabaptist groups have sometimes taken this egalitarianism a step further, not only in the seating arrangement but also, in the case of the Church of the Bretheren or Dunkards, providing a long bench for five preachers, lest one of them alone be off-base in

his interpretation of Scripture (Fig. 2).[2]

The Amish take the egalitarianism of the meetinghouse ideal to perhaps the ultimate step by literally meeting in each other's houses, in turn. In fact, so profound and pervasive is the Amish religious sensibility, in all that they try to live and make and do, that the entire farmstead and the landscape as a whole become the Amish work of religious art.

As a folklorist I must immediately ask whether there is anything which really distinguishes the landscapes of this community from that of another; whether there is really anything to set an Amish farm neighborhood apart from one of nearby Mennonite or Bretheren or Reformed or Lutheran neighbors. Although the manifest virtues of traditional farming techniques (i.e., without heavy machinery to compact the soil) do allow Amish farms to be somewhat smaller and closer to each other than their worldly modernized neighbors, at this level of neighborhood proxemics the differences might be admitted to be rather subtle.[3] If, however, we move in closer and look at the farmyard, and in particular at the farmhouse itself, I think a difference can indeed be detected. A fully developed Amish farmhouse is huge, rambling on with wings and appendages. There often does not seem to be any front or back to an Amish house, nor any clear or marked way in. But subtly and most fundamentally, the Amish house quite often refuses to face the road.

Like the distinctive clothing and horse-drawn transportation of the Amish, these architectural habits have evolved (albeit perhaps less consciously) in contrast to—and to set themselves apart from—the landscapes and communities of worldlier sorts.[4] The most conspicuous features of this more familiar early American landscape, the features which really unify Pennsylvanian and American farmsteads, are the clear separation of the house from the barns and the fact that the house (and often the barn as well) faces emphatically outward to the road and toward the world. This is true regardless of the particular ethnic origin of the builder, or whether the given house is of the earliest Germanic type (with asymmetric fenestration and central chimney (Figs. 3,4)), the later Germanic type (with symmetrical end chimneys but asymmetric fenestration) or canonically classical (whether English Georgian or German baroque (Fig. 5)).[5] In strongly English-settled areas, such as parts of Chester or Bucks Counties, the dwelling house itself usually stands well out in front of the other farm buildings and faces directly away from them, greeting the approaching visitor. In the German areas of Pennsylvania the farms are typically on a linear plan, with the house and the barn in a perfect line, each facing the road and on axis with each other. Henry Glassie, who first documented this pattern, noted that even where topography required a bend in this axis (to permit a southern exposure for the protective barn forebay while maintaining the frontality of the house), a strict and arbitrary right angle was chosen, whenever possible.[6] Even if the buildings form a continuous cluster the dwelling will be at one end, often facing south or east, and again out to the public way (Fig. 6). In all these cases, whether the house and barn are presented with equal importance, as with the Germans, or the house is given precedence over the barns, as with the English, there is a clear separation of animal areas from human areas, of work areas from dwelling areas, even of men's work (in the barns and fields) from women's work (in the yard and house). In both the older asymmetric houses and the newer rational and symmetrical ones, the front faces the outside world and greets it, making a clear approach and entrance. The arriving party is symbolically welcomed by a clearly visible door.

The houses within this cultural landscape, particularly those built between the middle of the eighteenth century and the end of the nineteenth, are of the regular and orderly five-bay, center-door type known as Georgian (whether of German or English inspiration (Fig. 8)). In Germanic areas there are also many of the four-bay, two-center-door type known as the Pennsylvania Farmhouse, or occasionally as German Georgian. Though not numerically dominant on the landscape, these two types, with their regular and symmetrical, well-proportioned facades, predominate our consciousness.[7] Sometimes these facades are elegantly and fashionably finished, projecting social prestige, and sometimes they are simple and plain, more morally reticent. But such a facade always projects its values in one direction: outward, frontally; toward the road, the outsiders, and the world.

The less-than-elegant, and less-than-symmetrical treatment of the sides and backs of Georgian houses also demonstrates that they are directionally conceived. At the Bricker house in Brickerville, for instance (Fig. 7), the two sides which face the road are quite dashing with alternating light and dark ashlar-cut sandstone. However, the other two sides rapidly give way to very vaguely coursed rubble stone, and unevenly spaced windows. Very commonly, the grace and perfect symmetry of the front of a Georgian house breaks down on the rear, because the rear door, tucked under the stair landing, must be off-center. Often, the entire rear of a house may be obscured by a

4
Though the differences to other groups are fundamentally in spiritual worldview, they are marked most visibly and consciously in clothing. For instance, within Amish groups the choice of buttons take on significance; between themselves and other plain groups (who also make their own clothing), the differences are in colors or patterns, or in the cut; in groups more removed from Amish ideology clothing is "store-bought" but consciously simple with some (Quakers, perhaps) or less so with others (Presbyterians, say). It should also be noted that whereas in the matter of clothing and transportation the Amish have increased their visible separation from the world by *maintaining* (rather than inventing anew) traditional styles and modes (originally common to most area farmers) in the face of worldly modernization and fashion, architecturally they have been both more inventive (the present housetype was not a commonplace to anyone in the past) and, I believe, less conscious of the process. Though they are quite conscious of why they dress differently (for community cohesion), they are often unaware of their architectural and proxemic distinctiveness. However, when this is pointed out to them, they do usually concur with the results of this study.

2. Egalitarian worship: *Franconia Meeting House (Brethren), Montgomery County, Pa., with Plain Folk scholar Clarence Kulp on the preacher's bench.*

5

The literature on American vernacular housetypes has been accumulating for some time. The best overview is still Henry Glassie, *Pattern in the Material Culture of the Eastern United States* (Philadelphia: University of Pennsylvania Press, 1968); a selection of the best articles and papers has been collected in Dell Upton and John Michael Vlach, eds., *Common Places: Readings in American Vernacular Architecture* (Athens, Ga.: University of Georgia Press, 1986), and the best new work comes out in the periodic *Perspectives in Vernacular Architecture* series by the Vernacular Architecture Forum. On Pennsylvania German housetypes in particular see G. Edwin Brumbaugh, "Colonial Architecture of the Pennsylvania Germans," in *Pennsylvania German Society Proceedings* 41 (Norristown, 1933); Robert C. Bucher, "The Continental Log House," *Pennsylvania Folklife*, 12 (Summer, 1962): 14–19; his "The Cultural Backgrounds of our Pennsylvania Homesteads," *The Bulletin of the Historical Society of Montgomery County* 15 (Fall 1966): 22–26; and his "The Swiss Bankhouse in Pennsylvania," *Pennsylvania Folklife* 28 (Winter 1968–69): 2–11; Henry Glassie, "A Central Chimney Continental Log House," *Pennsylvania Folklife* 18 (Winter 1968–69): 32–39; John Milner, "Germanic Architecture in the New World," *Journal of the Society of Architectural Historians* 34 (December 1975); and my own dissertation, *The Cycle of Transformations in the Houses of Schaefferstown, Pennsylvania* (Philadelphia: Department of Folklore and Folklife, University of Pennsylvania, 1988), Chapter 2.

6

Henry Glassie, "Eighteenth Century Cultural Process in the Delaware Valley," *Winterthur Portfolio* 7 (1972), reprinted in *Common Places*, 418ff.

7

A study of the entire corpus of the traditional housing stock of Schaefferstown, Lebanon County, Pennsylvania, reveals that symmetrical facades account for 45% of the houses, while traditional assymetric facades amount to 54% (Dissertation field data, Charles

3. Germanic house: *House near Gap, Lancaster County, Pa.*

telescoped wing of laundries and summer kitchens, relegating the work of women and servants to such embarrassed status that it must be done outside the body of the house proper.[8]

The Pennsylvania farmhouse, with its two front doors, has been interpreted to be a vernacular response to the high-style Georgian concept of frontality. It boasts a visibly and symbolically symmetrical facade, but fits this to a traditional way of life and the assymetric floorplan designed for it.[9] Indeed, a study of the entire corpus of traditional houses of Shaefferstown, Lebanon County, has shown that fully one quarter of the houses with such a symmetrical two-door exterior facade have the floorplan of the early German assymetric *flurküchenhaus* (see Fig. 4). The plan is altered only by moving the kitchen fireplace and its chimney to one gable, and by adding a second (stove) flue to the other gable, to maintain symmetry. Thus the traditional hospitality of rural economies could be maintained within the modernized exterior, which projected a fashion to the world but did not require a change in behavior.

The intention underlying the formal elegance in a Georgian house—in the house or extended to the entire landscape—was, of course, to impress the viewer, particularly one proceeding up the axial lane. The successive boundaries of the approach, such as terraces, steps, fences and gateways, carefully articulate welcome to some and undoubtably underscore the denial of welcome to others.[10] In the minds of some, but surely only the most erudite, the relationship of man and nature may have been

contemplated on a summer's eve in a garden gazebo at nether private end of the same axis, but the prime effect of such calculated harmonies was to impress one with the exulted station—and temporal power—of the owner. Indeed, some examples, such as Virginia's Mt. Airy or Philadelphia's Mt. Pleasant, with their terraces and ordered dependencies, nearly do achieve the courtly grandeur, the majestic heirarchical sweep, that the European Baroque was meant to impart.[11] An ancient allée of basswood, tulip, or even cedar trees overwhelms us not only with its processional and triumphal quality, but also with the arrogance of ordering an entire landscape, planting each bush and tree with the abstract regularity of Cartesian mathematics.[12]

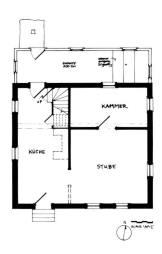

4. Germanic plan: *Brecht House, Schaefferstown, Lebanon County, Pa.*

5. English house: *House in Newcastle County, Del.*

It is by no means exaggeration to draw parallels between house, landscape and advanced mathematics, for all are part of the same shift in world view, part of a "crisis" in both science and cosmology which developed and spread northward in Europe beginning in the Renaissance, and of which the final intellectual component goes under the name of the Enlightenment.[13] Just at the time that Georgian houses were being built in numbers in America, Enlightenment luminaries were publishing their works. This subject is of course so enormous that a full dissection is not possible here; the few suggestive examples which follow will have to suffice. For instance, Denis Diderot edited his lifelong project, an Encyclopedia of many volumes, in which he compartmentalized knowledge into units so numerous that they had to be divorced from the organic and religious presentation schema of previous compendia, and were instead alphabetized.[14] Everything in Diderot's project could be measured: the latest scientific discoveries, the mechanical processes of industry and agriculture, even the beauty of the old masters (Fig. 9). The latter were even literally measured— the arms and legs of ancient statues were given numerical value, the better that proportions of the whole could be analyzed—and all was delineated, in hard black lines on cold copper plates. Joseph Priestley used the new experimental methods of science to discover oxygen, thereby splitting the very constituents of hitherto indivisible matter into chemical elements with new names and mathematical weights.[15]

6. Linear farm plan: *House south of Columbia, Lancaster, County, Pa.*

Bergengren, *Cycle of Transformations*). On the persistence of traditional open plans into the nineteenth century in Schaefferstown see p. 377ff.

8
On the gender and class implications of front/back distinctions in architecture see Roger L. Welsch, "Front Door, Back Door," *Natural History* 88 (June-July 1979): 76–83; and Dell Upton, "White and Black Landscapes in Eighteenth Century Virginia," in Robert St. George, ed., *Material Life in America*, 1600–1860 (Boston: Northeastern University Press, 1988), 357ff.

9
Glassie, "Eighteenth Century Cultural Process," 407. This house type—called here the "Pennsylvania Farmhouse" and the "Four-Over-Four"—is also discussed in Richard Pillsbury, "Patterns in the Folk and Vernacular House Forms of the Pennsylvania Culture Region," *Pioneer America* 9 (1977):12–31; and Bergengren, *Cycle of Transformations*, 74–78 and 381–387. I do not agree with the evolutionary scenario suggested in Henry Kauffman's "The Riddle of the Two Doors," *The Dutchman* 6 (Winter 1954–5).

10
Dell Upton, "White and Black Landscapes in Eighteenth Century Virginia," in St. George, *Material Life in America*, 362–366.

11
On the fundamental intention of the Baroque style to impress hapless viewers of lesser status with the exalted status of the owner, see Charles McCorquodale, "Chapter 4, The Age of the Baroque," *History of the Interior* (New York: The Vendome Press, 1983), 85–110; Germain Bazin, *Baroque and Rococo*, (New York: Oxford University Press, 1964) 1–7; Henry A. Millen, *Baroque and Rococo Architecture* (New York: Brazillier, 1967), 9, 27; and even William Hogarth, *The Analysis of Beauty, Written with a View of Fixing the Fluctuating Ideas of Taste* (London, 1753). (The edition I used was *The Analysis of Beauty, with the rejected passages from the manuscript drafts and auto-*

biographiacal notes, edited with an introduction by Joseph Burke [Oxford, Clarendon Press, 1955]). This text, written as a manifesto of the succeeding (rococo) aesthetic, nevertheless contains some choice insights into the preceding age, among them that the Baroque age impresses us chiefly by virtue of the dead mass of its objects—whether ecclesiastical altarpieces or the robes of State. For its influence on the vernacular decor in America, see my dissertation, *Cycle of Transformations*, 261ff.

12

On the impact of the Enlightenment on American material life and consciousness, see Henry Glassie, *Folk Housing in Middle Virginia: A Structural Analysis of Historical Artifacts* (Knoxville: University of Tennessee Press, 1975), Chapters 7 and 8: "Reason in Architecture," and "A Little History"; Rhys Isaac, *The Transformation of Virginia: 1740–1790*, (Chapel Hill: University of North Carolina Press, for the Institute of Early American History and Culture, Williamsburg, Virginia, 1982), Chapter 2, "Shapes in the Landscape: The Arrangement of Social Space"; and his "The Enlightenment and Everyday Life: Imagination and Practice on a Mid-century Plantation," a paper presented to the Philadelphia Center for Early American Studies, May 22, 1987; James Deetz, *In Small Things Forgotten: The Archeology of Early American Life* (Garden City, N.Y.: Anchor Press/Doubleday, 1977), 60, 125ff; James Deetz, Mark P. Leone, Barbara J. Little, and Ann M. Palkovitch, "The Archeology of the Georgian Worldview and the 18th Century Beginnings of Modernity," in Mark P. Leone and Parker B. Potter, eds., *The Recovery of Meaning: Historical Archeology in the Eastern United States* (Washington, D.C.: Smithsonian University Press, 1988); and Alan Gowans, *Images of American Living: Four Centuries of Architecture and Furniture as Cultural Expression*, (Philadelphia: J.B. Lippincott, 1964), 115ff. On England, try John Martin Robinson, *Georgian Model Farms: A Study of Decorative and Model Farm Buildings in the Age of Improvement, 1700–1843* (Oxford, Clarendon Press, 1983).

7. Georgian frontality: *Bricker House, Brickerville, Lancaster County, Pa.*

When these new chemical elements were mapped out in Diderot's tome (Fig. 10), the very diagrams took on the grid of the Cartesian integers, arbitrary and evenly spaced, quite unlike the pictorial emblemata of the spiritual alchemists who preceded him, or, even of the abstract but circular diagrams of the pre-Enlightenment (discussed in more detail below). It has even been pointed out that, due to the new technology of copper plate engraving, the pictorial illustrations themselves, which Diderot compiled in lavish, folio-sized volumes, contributed to this rationalizing trend. For however vivid and more "real" than woodcuts, they represent a reduction of the visible and physical world to a matrix of parallel lines, dots and points, delineated more in the spirit of the new mathematics (or the newly regular windows on a Georgian house) than the symbolic representations of old.[16] And we must not forget that ultimate product of rationalism, the *Mechanical View of the Faculties of the Soul,* an astonishing popular didactic print in which the inward and immaterial spirit itself is coldly dissected and again diagrammed as a grid-like flowchart. Lest we doubt the currency of such

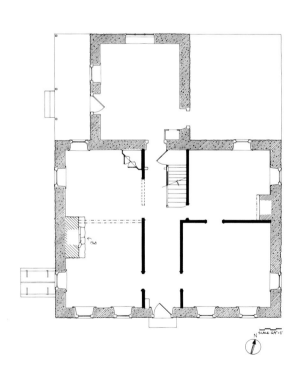

8. Georgian plan: *Tice House, Shaefferstown, Lebanon County, Pa.*

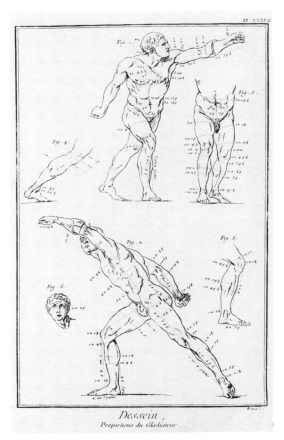

Dessein,
Proportions du Gladiateur

9. Enlightenment obsession with measuring: *Denis Diderot, analysis of* Discus Thrower. *From* Receuil de Planches, sur les Sciences, les arts libéraux et let arts méchaniques, avec leur explication (*1763 edition*).

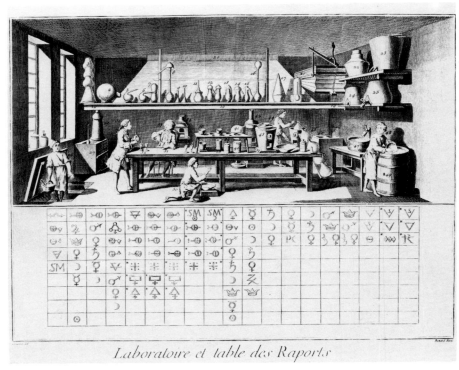

Laboratoire et table des Raports

10. Grid organization of knowledge: *Denis Diderot, "Laboratorie et table des reports," from* Receuil de Planches, sur les Sciences, les arts libéraux et let arts méchaniques, avec leur explication (*1763 edition*).

conceptions, the "Mechanical View" penetrated deeply enough that Betsy Clark, a schoolgirl in Litchfield, Connecticut, rendered a watercolor version by 1800 (Fig. 11).[17]

Such was the world of the Deists and the rationalists, publishers of penny-wise almanacs and supporters of the National Bank. The Amish, on the other hand, are oriented in quite a different direction, in their familial and social gatherings, their Sunday home religious meetings, their farmplans, and even in death. At first glance, for instance, an Amish cemetery such as the one on Gibble Lane outside of Schaefferstown, Lebanon County, does not seem to be so different from graveyards of other rural communities. The stones all face the same direction (toward the road) but they are clustered in extended family groups rather than evenly spaced, such as those of the Shakers or the military. However, the only entrance to this graveyard is from an enclosed grassy plot at the far end (itself a parking lot for horses), with none directly from the road. So it is with Amish community itself: tightly cohesive and supportive unto their own; equally disinterested in the outside, in the world, in its falterings of Spirit, in its silly foibles. The Amish simply *do not care* what the outside world thinks or understands of their ways and do neither proselytize nor address themselves to it.[18]

So it is with the houses in which they live. Like their builders, the houses of the Amish simply do not face or greet the world as do the houses of worldlier folk. In many Amish houses it is virtually impossible to tell where the front originally *was*, so completely has it been erased by the rerouting of traffic toward the barns, shops and farmyard. As with the graveyard, at first glimpse an Amish farm may not seem

13
See Alberto Perez-Gomez, *Architecture and the Crisis of Modern Science*, translated from the Italian by the author (Cambridge: M.I.T. Press, 1983).

14
Denis Diderot, *Encyclopedie, ou Dictionaire raisonné des sciences, des arts et des métiers* (Lausanne: Chez la Societé typographique, 1778–1781) and especially the separate folio of the illustration plates, *Recueil des Planches sur les Sciences, les arts libéraux et les arts méchaniques, avec leur explication* (Paris: Chez Briansson, David, Le Breton, et Durand, 1763).

11. Rationalist world view at the common level: Betsey Clark, Mechanical View of the Faculties of the Soul, *1800. Courtesy Litchfield, Ct., Historical Society.*

15
Joseph Priestley, *Experiments and Observations on Different Kinds of Air* (London: J. Johnson, No. 72 in St. Paul's churchyard, 1774).

16
Rhys Isaac, "The Enlightenment and Everyday Life: Imagination and Practice on a Mid-Century Plantation," paper presented to the Philadelphia Center for Early American Studies, May 22, 1987.

17
C. Kurt Dewhurst and Marsha McDowell, *Religious Folkart in America: Reflections on Faith* (New York: E. P. Dutton for the Museum of American Folk Art, 1983) 35, 42.

18
See Hostetler, *Amish Society,* 374ff and 383, on what he calls the "silent discourse" of the Amish, the only kind of persuasion they permit themselves in conflicts, especially with or toward outsiders.

19
Hostetler, *Amish Society,* 168–169.

noticeably different from its neighbors, for these houses were, after all, purchased from "the world" for the most part, as the Amish spread into new, but already settled, areas. In these cases we can still see the linear arrangement of the original farm, with the early center-chimney houses (for instance) nicely separated from and aligned with the forebay "Swisser" barns. However, the house has indeed been added to: not only has the door, like so many, been rerouted to the farmyard (as in fact non-Amish farmers often do), but, unlike most others, a porch has been enclosed across the front, as well as a wing projecting tangentially to the front. In other cases the separation of house and barn remains, but the barn overwhelms the house in size and projects significantly to the front of the house, substantially altering the linear farmplans of other Pennsylvania German farmyards.

However large or prominently positioned the barn might be, in most Amish houses the additions to the dwelling itself overwhelm the original house, in and of themselves. These are the so-called *Grossdaadi* or grandfather wings, built to house the elder generation as it retires to let the younger one take over the main operation.[19] Sometimes these additions engulf the original house from the rear, as do add-ons of others. Sometimes the wings swallow up the house from both sides. Many times the wing is tangent to the main block of the house (projecting to the front, but offset), apparently giving the elders a sense of autonomy in their own (new) section, being separate but not disconnected from the house they once ruled. And sometimes the wings and additions of Amish homesteads project directly to the front (Fig. 13). I have termed this tendency "forward sprawl," and it is something that

12. The occluded front: *Amish house near Brownsville, Lancaster County, Pa.*

worldlier types, who *present* themselves to the world, virtually *never* do. Such additions may incorporate dwelling spaces or meeting spaces or even work spaces; what they do not contain are show spaces. Gone too is the front door and every vestige of the triumphal approach. So strong are our own expectations of house designs that it is hard for non-Amish to believe, for example, that the house in Fig. 12 (from near Brownsville, Lancaster Co.) was photographed from the road. Other farmsteads project, or sprawl, even more extravagantly

into the former front yard. Clearly, such a house plan no longer faces the outside world, but looks inwardly to its own spiritual center: to the farmyard itself for physical sustenance, and to the community of believers for spirtual sustenance.

Looking at the farmstead as a whole, what we see is that sometimes—by no means always, but occasionally—this sprawling arrangement of the wings, these Amish additions to the farms acquired from others, result in a

13. Forward sprawl: *Amish house, Colerain Township, Lancaster County, Pa.*

20

"*Flur*" in German can be rendered as both "hall" and "lobby"; hence the chief feature of the *flurküch-enhaus* is that the "*küche*" (kitchen) is in the "lobby," or rather that it is open to the outside door. Unlike a Georgian house, for instance, in the *flurküchenhaus* no other barriers intercede between the hearth (and its hospitality) and all comers. For the literature of these houses see note no. 2.

21

Bergengren, *The Cycle of Transformations*, section entitled "Nowadays (Full Cycle)"; and a paper of the same name as the full dissertation, to appear in *Perspectives on Vernacular Architecture* IV in 1990.

22

Fascinatingly, when asked to diagram the Amish worldview, ranking other communities in terms of their spiritual affinities to Amish belief, one Amish scholar drew a diagram strikingly like those of Fludd. It consisted of a series of concentric circles on the page, with the center labeled Amish, like the Earth in Fludd's archaic system. Successive orbits were identified with other groups, first with other Amish groups more progressive than his own, then with Mennonites, Hutterites and other Plain Anabaptists, then with Brethren (whose beliefs are similar but who wear store-bought clothing), then with Quakers (plain, but non-German), then with Lutherans and Reformed and northern Protestants, and finally with Methodists, Baptists and other Revivalistic Protestants. Catholics were in the ethers beyond the outermost possible orbit, and all other religions were off the map altogether.

14. The giant kitchen: *Elmer and Florence Martin House (Mennonite), Buffalo Springs, Lebanon County, Pa.*

concentric farmplan. The house sits at the center, completely surrounded by work buildings, and the fields and meadows completely surround the whole. The convenience of proximity results in a mandala on the land.

Simultaneously, many Amish households have burrowed into the centers of their houses, creating the large open rooms in which the whole community can gather for religious services. At the center of these rooms is the kitchen, recapturing the social function, and sometimes even the literal position, of the kitchen in the houses of their earliest German ancestors. This plan (see Fig. 4) is often called the *flurküchenhaus* in the literature because of the openness of its plan, in both the social and literal senses.[20] To create these giant kitchens anew out of the houses of the worldly is usually a major project, sometimes requiring the removal of most of the interior walls of the house (Fig. 14).[21]

Though it may seem to be the result of haphazard additions and subtractions (or rather an organic growth), this concentric arrange-

ment of both buildings and rooms is no more fortuitous than the axial layouts of Georgian estates. Both are directly related to the worldviews that produced them. The Amish, with their extreme emphasis on mutual interdependence and community, are more in line with the pre-Enlightenment vision of the world than almost any people on the continent. The system of the Great Chain of Being, illustrated by Robert Fludd, the Rosicrucian cosmologist and holdout against the Enlightenment, is indeed more linked than linear (Fig. 15). It is an intricately interconnected and concentrically nested set of hierarchies and reciprocities between macrocosmos and microcosmos, between all forms of life and polity.[22] Even the charts of mathematical relations (such as are later represented on a rectangular grid) are laid out on a circular template in Fludd's diagrams. The various realms of intellectual knowledge, spiritual psychology, and physical properties of the elements all follow the same template. A particularly dramatic example (Fig. 16) depicts the workings of the mind, with Deus at the

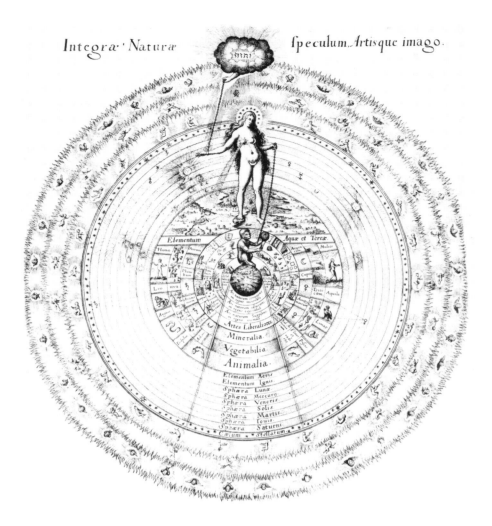

15. Concentric organization of knowledge: *Robert Fludd, frontispiece from* Utriusque cosmi historia: tomus secundus de supernaturali, naturali, preaternaturali, et contranaturali microcosmi historia, in tractatus tres de distributa *(1617).*

top, and sets of nested conceptions bursting out of the cranium like fireworks, quite unlike a Deist chart.[23]

So too the farmsteads of the Amish: some of them concentric, with every part dependent upon—and close to—the others, and the house nearly swallowed up, at the center of it all. And as God is at the center of Fludd's grand conception, so too is the large hearthroom or kitchen—a place for work, sustenance, prayer and socializing—again at the center of the house.

Seen in this light, the apparently "disorganized" qualities of Amish farmsteads take on perhaps a different meaning; their beauty radiates in a different direction. But to understand them fully we need to reach a deeper

level yet. If our concepts of "front and back" are no longer relevant to Amish houses, perhaps there are other aesthetic principles which, even more than the inward community focus of the Amish, explain the multidirectional, cumulative, radiating farmplans. Such principles are hard to approach, of course, and one must be sure that the principal applied is that of the community's creation (rather than our own, the analyzers). But perhaps an Amish concept of Beauty itself can help us understand these compositions in mud and wood and stone.

Having measured many farmers' houses for other studies, I have found that residents of these communites greet with befuddlement (if not consternation) the idea that one scrappy old piece of eighteenth-century chair-rail molding

23
On the pre-Enlightenment worldview see E. M. W. Tillyard, *The Elizabethan World Picture* (New York: Vintage Books, n.d.); Wayne Shumaker, *The Occult Sciences of the Renaissance: A Study in Intellectual Patterns* (Berkeley: University of California Press, 1972); and Titus Burckhardt, *Alchemy: Science of the Cosmos, Science of the Soul* (Baltimore, Md.: Penguin Books, 1967). On the Rosicrucians, see Frances A. Yates, *The Rosicrucian Enlightenment* (Boulder, Colo.: Shambhala, 1978). On Robert Fludd, see Jocelyn Godwin, *Robert Fludd: Hermetic Philosopher and Surveyor of Two Worlds* (Boulder, Colo.: Shambhala, 1979) and of course Fludd himself, *Utriusque Cosmi Maioris Scilicet et Minoris Metaphysica, Physica Atque Technica Historia* (Oppenheim: Johanne Theodore de Bry, 1617).

16. Pre-Cartesian worldview: *Robert Fludd, "The Spiritual Brain," from* Utriusque cosmi historia: tomus secundus de supernaturali, naturali, preaternaturali, et contranaturali microcosmi historia, in tractatus tres de distributa *(1617)*.

24
The photographs in the following section were taken on successive days from mid-July to October from the entrance of the Shady Oaks Campground in Stricklertown, Lebanon County, Pa., where I was resident during my dissertation fieldwork on Schaefferstown. Though the descriptions are clearly my own, resembling neither National Weather Service, much less Amish, diction, the data are derived from *Climatological Data* 29 (Asheville, N.C.: National Oceanic and Atmospheric Administration, National Climatic Data Center, 1987):7–11. Precipitation readings are from the Meyerstown station, about five miles from the campsite; the temperature readings are from Lebanon, about 13 miles away.

or another could be considered to be beautiful. Neither are the houses as a whole, dominant and enduring, appreciated as we appreciate them. But to these people there is no question about the landscape; it *is* beautiful: beautiful in a deep, brooding sort of way. The pastoral landscape is not just pretty for the Amish, as in the superficial postcard vision of sunny days and blue skies; it inhabits them, in all of its moods, as much as they inhabit it. I believe if we can get a glimmer of this landscape sensibility, this pastoral notion of Beauty, it can illuminate something more of the Amish sensibility as a whole. The Amish embrace the land so much more deeply than other rural people, that perhaps such a concept can help us understand in turn both the plainness and the

multidirectionality of their (religious) art, that is to say, their houses and their buildings and their farms.

The Amish sensibility can be conveyed, if at all, by changing gears completely, into perhaps a more poetic mode. I hope to provide the reader with something of an experience of the Amish context, less didactic and more allusive, that will show him something more of these Amish religious values—of an Amish sense of Beauty—than words alone ever could. Simply bear with me and let some of our art traditions illuminate some of theirs. Try also to grasp the shape of the whole of the following, as well as to the individual pieces, the details.[24]

July 12, 1987: Clear, crisp air and good visibility, a balmy 76°; scattered cumulous, but all the showers missed us.

July 13, 1987: Still relatively cool at 78°; good visibility and a good shower in the p.m. (.56″).

July 14, 1987: Sunny, temperature 87°; visibility moderate at 7 miles.

July 15, 1987: Warm front arrived, 90°; with low nimbus clouds almost grazing the ground and giving a slow, gentle rain (1.98″) all day.

July 16, 1987: Haze burning off enough for sun, 93°; visibility about 4 miles at the outside.

July 17, 1987: Overcast and marginally cooler, 89°; visibility up to 5 miles maybe, but no rain.

July 18, 1987: Still overcast, and thus less heat (86°); but no rain, not even a threat of it.

July 19, 1987: Increasingly muggy with the sun again breaking through, 94°; visibility fading in the glare.

July 20, 1987: Heat wave in full tilt, 96°; no rain in five days and getting hotter, blinding haze, visibility 2 miles, if that.

July 21, 1987: Another scorcher, 97°; getting insufferable, sticky humid, no air, white sky.

July 22, 1987: Stinking hot, hazy and humid, 98° in the shade; searing white sky, cornflowers wilt early.

July 23, 1987: Stinking hot, 98°; not a breath, visibility 3 miles, maybe.

July 24, 1987: Stinking again, 97°; dead still, blinding bright, visibility poor.

July 25, 1987: Just plain torrid, 96°; distant thunder, but no relief; visibility poor.

July 26, 1987: Muggy, hot, thunderstorms in late afternoon dropping a good .39″ of rain and the temperature to 87°.

July 27, 1987: Muggy, drizzle to rain in morning (.20″), 88°; white sky, visibility poor.

July 28, 1987: Balmy, light breezes, 90°; sunny with haze, oppressive again, visibility 8 miles.

July 29, 1987: Humid, but clearer, 88°; sky is very pale blue, visibility 10 miles.

July 30, 1987: Humid, clear, 87°; sky clear, glowing (about 8:38 p.m.) the color of a peach, a light mist, lavender, is rising; visibility 15 miles.

July 31, 1987: Humid, moderately hazy, 92°; white sky, visibility 4 miles, good thunderstorm in afternoon (.84″).

August 1, 1987: Hot, extremely hazy, 90°; deadly still, visibility zero (or it seems that way).

August 2, 1987: Hot, extremely hazy, 85°; sky slightly yellow, still not a breath of a breeze, visibility 1 mile.

August 3, 1987: Hot and humid and hazy, 85°; white sky, visibility up to 3 miles.

August 4, 1987: Humid, hazy and hot, 90°; visibility 3 miles, maybe, cornflowers withered before noon.

The point of all this is, of course,

August 5, 1987: Hazy and hot and humid, 95°; pale sky, visibility 3 miles, raspberry leaves beginning to droop.

August 6, 1987: A drenching rain, finally (1.21″), 80°; sky and air almost green, visibility zero.

August 7, 1987: Clear as a bell; cool, pleasant breezes from northwest, 80°; blue sky with just a few wispy cirrus late in afternoon; visibility 25 miles.

the weather.

August 8, 1987: humid, slight haze, 80°; alto-stratus, with pale sky; visibility 15 miles.

August 9, 1987: Humid, hazy, 90°; sky opaque white, visibility 6 miles.

The Amish, as farmers, as agrarians, are very close to the weather;

August 10, 1987: Cooler, 85°, with early shower, (.25″); clearing with visibility up to 15 miles.

August 11, 1987: Continuing warm, 84°; white sky, visibility 10 miles.

they take anxious note of it on a daily,

August 12, 1987: Continuing warm, 86°; same as above.

August 13, 1987: Continuing warm, 84°; visibility down to 4 miles; distant thunder.

if not hourly,

August 14, 1987: Humid, hazy, 83°; pale sky, dank stillness; a mist rose early over the corn; zillions of fireflies this year, but no mosquitoes!

August 15, 1987: Gradually clearing, humid, 83°; pale yellow sky, visibility to 5 miles.

basis.

August 16, 1987: Sunny, humid, warm, 88°; scattered stratus, visibility 10 miles.

August 17, 1987: Blaring heat, humidity; 92°; opaque muggy white sky, visibility 4 miles.

The rhythm of the days

August 18, 1987: Blaring heat, humidity; 94°; blinding sky, not a breath, sticky; visibility 2 miles.

August 19, 1987: Another scorcher; hazy and humid, 92°; bleary; visibility 1 mile.

marks the cycles of the work:

August 20, 1987: Continued hazy and hot but slightly lifted, 89°; sky opaque, visibility 4 miles. Raspberry leaves drooping again.

August 21, 1987: Hot and humid; getting insufferable again, except at dawn, when the air is clear, moving faintly. Visibility 3 miles by 10 a.m.

the cycles of rain and dry,

August 22, 1987: Hazy, hot and still, but a little cooler, 85°; opaque white sky, tending to the color of pear flesh. Corn beginning to wither.

August 23, 1987: Marginally cooler, 81°, but finally a good rain (.60″): sunny in morning, glowering skies by 2 p.m., violent thunderstorm at 2:27 (much lightning), but clear by evening. Glorious sunset!

Of blaring heat and drenching cool.

But more deeply,

August 24, 1987: Another storm in the night (another .60), then clear by dawn; bright, sunny, 75°; Blue Mountain (20 miles, receding down the valley to infinity) deep and crisp.

August 25, 1987: Balmy, scattered cumulus, breezy, a delightful 74°; visibility still good at 15 miles.

there is the evenness of the days, the regularity and even periodicity of them:

August 26, 1987: Continuing pleasant, a sunny 75°; high, wispy cirrus clouds arriving in early afternoon.

August 27, 1987: Warm front arrived: a slow rain, drizzle to hard, 76°; mists and miasmas all day, a pearly opalescent light.

for if either the rains or the sun come not on time, there is disaster.

August 28, 1987: Rains thinning in morning (.25″), with gradual clearing in afternoon, then another bank of clouds moved in; 72°.

August 29, 1987: Cloudy all day, 66°.

And deeper yet,

August 30, 1987: Gradually thinning clouds, warmer, 74°; visibility 5 miles or so under the slowly lifting sheet.

August 31, 1987: Humid and warm, 79°; visibility 8 miles.

ultimately,

September 1, 1987: Cold front passed, but we only got a brief shower (.21), then clearing, sunny, 72°.

September 2, 1987: Warmer, 78°; breezy and sunny, with scattered cumulus.

there is beauty in the sameness of them.

September 3, 1987: Balmy, a bright clear day, 76°; visibility 13+ miles.

September 4, 1987: Same as above, 76°; visibility 10 miles.

For Beauty is to be found either everywhere or nowhere,

September 5, 1987: Sunny in morning, with anvilheads visible in afternoon; two storms passed close by, but we got only a spritz, 71°. Much change of air.

September 6, 1987: Sunny and thunderstorms, we got hit with half an inch. Cooler at 67°.

on either all farms or none,

September 7, 1987: Warmer, 75°, thunderstorms still in area, some of them violent; we got .60″.

September 8, 1987: Continued warm and humid, 72°; very heavy rains (5.68″!), and flooding in Lancaster, but none here.

or on all days, rain or shine,

September 9, 1987: Continued warm and humid, the Deluge all around us (5.53″ at Honeybrook), but we are spared.

September 10, 1987: Sharply warmer with southern breezes, 82°; visibility hovering at 3 miles.

or none.

September 11, 1987: Continuing warm, 83°.

September 12, 1987: Cold front passed in the night, but no rain. Now a clear, pleasant 72°, visibility 13 miles.

The Amish do not believe that either Beauty,

September 13, 1987: Warmer, scattered clouds, 79°, visibility already down to 6 miles.

September 14, 1987: Clouds filling in by noon, good rain (.41″) by mid afternoon, 80°, visibility nil.

or Spirit,

September 15, 1987: Clearing slowly, 78°; visibility 7 miles; giant blue lobelia has come out near Fort Zeller.

September 16, 1987: A balmy 80°; sunny all day, with sweet zephyrs.

or Godliness,

September 17, 1987: Sunny in morning with cirrus coming in, 78°; clouds thickening all day, begins to drizzle at night (.04″).

September 18, 1987: Drizzle and light rain all day (. 94″), 77°, visibility 2 miles at best, but it's that yellowish-green light again.

is concentrated in one spot (such as a church) more than another (such as your house or mine):

September 19, 1987: Cold and wet, 57°, rain all day, sometimes hard, out of dark strato-nimbus, visibility poor, air steel gray.

September 20, 1987: Still raining, but lighter (.31″) and warmer at all of 63°, visibility still minimal.

therefore they worship in each member's house in turn.

September 21, 1987: Still a trace of drizzle in the early morning hours (.03″), clearing with haze burnt off by 11 a.m.; warming to 73°, visibility 7 miles.

September 22, 1987: Continued mild, hazy in morning, 71°; visibility 10 miles.

They do not believe that one person—you or me—is more qualified to speak the word of God:

September 23, 1987: sunny and humid, 69°; with a brief shower in mid morning (.23″).

September 24, 1987: Warmer, and continuing humid, 74°; but mostly sunny in afternoon.

therefore they draw lots from among their men to choose their ministers.

September 25, 1987: Cooler, 65°, with widely scattered showers, we got a small one with .12″, then clearing.

September 26, 1987: A little warmer to 70°; sunny all day, visibility good.

They do not believe that intense emotional highs (such as the Baptist and Holiness Churches strive for)

September 27, 1987: Much warmer at 77°, sunny all day, visibility 8 miles.

September 28, 1987: A balmy 80°, sunny and clear, visibility 8 miles.

are a proper goal. Rather,

September 29, 1987: Sunny and mild, 78°; scattered showers to the south, but none here, visibility 5 miles.

September 30, 1987: Cooler at 70°; a solid blanket of stratus clouds moving in all day, but we only got a sprinkle of .06″ by evening.

all days

October 1, 1987: Still cloudy and cooler, only 62°, but no rain, though it did rain elsewhere.

October 2, 1987: Warmer to 70°; clearing with some sun, visibility 6 miles; monkshood now in bloom.

October 3, 1987: Cold, only 55°; with scattered showers, visibility good under the leaden sheets: 10 miles.

October 4, 1987: Remains brisk, 57°; still cloudy.

all moments,
all people,

October 5, 1987: Finally it rains here in early morning: a good .35″; with clearing by morning and much warmer, to 67°.

October 6, 1987: Temperature the same, 68°; mostly sunny, strong breeze from the northwest.

all things,

October 7, 1987: Cold front passed, bringing temperature down to 61°, and a good shower (.45″), probably the last thunderstorm of the season.

October 8, 1987: Cool again and clear, a crisp fall day, 55°, sunny all day, visibility forever. Getting nippy at night, 36°.

should be imbued with the Grace and Joy of knowing God.

October 9, 1987: Clear and cool all day, high of 59°, air just makes the heart sing. First frost at night, 30°.

For as in Christ there is no East or West; therefore on an Amish farm there is no front or back,

October 10, 1987: Warming a bit to 66°, still sunny with high cirrus cutting across the moon.

October 11, 1987: Warm front in, clouds deepening all day, temperature only 56°, but only .16″ actually fell.

no work places hidden from show places,

no grand approaches.

October 12, 1987: Slightly colder, 53°; still drizzling early (only .13″), clearing gradually.

Therefore in an Amish farmhouse is again the kitchen a place to work in,

October 13, 1987: Sunny and clear, a fine fall day at 57°; froze last night, 28°; corn cut, shredded for silage.

a place to eat in,
a place to talk in,
and a place to pray in.

October 14, 1987: Same as above, 57°, but even clearer, visibility 13 miles; halo around the moon; froze again.

And therefore is again the kitchen at the center of the house, the house at the center of the farm,

and the farm at the center of the world.

Charles Bergengren was given a mainstream Protestant upbringing in the traditionally austere but intellectually liberal congregational Church of New England. He studied nature intensively as a child, took ballroom dancing with everybody else in junior high, art in high school and art history as an undergraduate at Oberlin. He moved to New York City where the music of John Cage and the theater of Richard Foreman (with whom he performed for five years) were major influences; nevertheless he finished his degree in art history and anthropology at CUNY. This led naturally to his graduate degrees in Folklore at the University of Pennsylvania in material culture and vernacular architecture. His dissertation (1988) is on the traditional architecture of the Pennsylvania Germans, of whom the Amish are a small but uniquely visible fraction.

POSTSCRIPT

This study of ethics has aimed to make us more conscious of the intentions that architects bring into design, and of the values that they edify with their projects. Like any artifact, a building communicates unintended meanings; architecture betrays an implicit agenda and provides the material for criticism of that agenda. Ethics is concerned with those questions that, although external to the discipline of architecture, shape the outcome of the architectural process.

Ethics is the study of moral problems and judgments which form the bases for conduct in society. A consistent set of moral judgments enables us to determine a purpose, and thus to act intentionally. Ethics questions what is appropriate and, more importantly, how we determine what is appropriate. Ethical knowledge, the understanding of these values, is gained by practice and action in culture.

One medium for such action is the discipline of architecture. While architecture depends on technical and aesthetic knowledge in order to take form, facts alone cannot make it useful, and beauty alone cannot give it meaning. Because architecture aims to be understood and used by its society, it cannot be autonomous and still maintain its relevance. Architecture, in this sense, can never be value-free.

We believe that the architect's understanding of the design task is preconditioned by a framework of values that are shared and defined by culture. Society's shared values become the "common knowledge" to which all else is referred, and the language through which concepts are first articulated. An individual has certain ideas of what to expect from society, and society holds expectations of the individual. Mediating between the two is responsibility, the covenant of obedience of one party to the expectations of another. Many intermediate cultures may stand between the individual and the society-at-large, creating an overlapping, and often conflicting, network of responsibilities. Thus the architect, for example, may feel responsibility to a personal agenda, to that of the client or user, to other criteria internal to the discipline itself, to the standards of the profession, and to moral and legal obligations bestowed by society in granting the title of "architect." In light of these competing responsibilities, we can discuss the political role inherent in the architectural process.

A work of architecture manifests the values of its designers and their clients in built form, providing a coherent document of a culture's underlying ethic. It is also an instructive laboratory for philosophical inquiry and cultural criticism, because it is a willful act whose product then takes on a life of its own. By giving ideas form and creating the setting for everyday life, architecture gives the values it embodies the semblance of inevitability. Architects, then, must be conscious of the responsibility inherent in this enormous cultural power, and conscious that only action can reveal their intentions.

ILLUSTRATION CREDITS

Cover
On permanent loan to The Art Institute of Chicago from the City of Chicago. Copyright 1989, The Art Institute of Chicago; all rights reserved.

Frontispiece
Courtesy Van Pelt Library, University of Pennsylvania.

Krukowski
1. Collection of Mr. and Mrs. Paul Mellon, National Gallery of Art, Washington.
2. Collection, The Museum of Modern Art, New York.
3. Collection, Wilhelm-Lehmbruck-Museum der Stad Duisberg. Copyright 1989 ARS N.Y./Cosmopress, Genf.

Bell
Photo by Giraudon, Paris.

Rockcastle
All photographs courtesy of the author. Sketches courtesy of Andrew Leicester.

Ventre
1. From the *McGraw-Hill Encyclopedia of Art*. Reproduced with permission.
2, 3. From Karl Fleig, ed., *Alvar Aalto* (Architectural Publishers Artemis, Zurich). Reproduced with permission.

Schwarting
Photographs and diagrams courtesy of the author except as indicated below.
2. Collection, Museo della Civilita Romana. Photo by E. Richter, Rome.
3. From W. H. Adams, *The French Garden 1500-1800* (New York: Brazillier, 1979).
4, 8. From J. C. Shepherd and G. A. Jellicoe, *Italian Gardens of the Renaissance* (London: Academy Editions). Reproduced by permission of Dr. Andreas C. Papadakis.
5. From the *Turgot Plan*.
6. From *Studies and Executed Buildings by Frank Lloyd Wright* (Berlin: Ernst Wasmuth, 1910). Reproduced courtesy of the Frank Lloyd Wright Foundation.
7, 13-17. From Le Corbusier and Pierre Jeanneret, *Ouvre Complet 1910-1929*. Copyright ARS N.Y./Spadem. As exclusive agent for SPADEM in the U.S., ARS represents the Foundation Le Corbusier. Reproduced with permission.
9. Copyright Centro Internazionale di Studi di Architettura "A. Palladio," Vicenza. Reproduced with permission.
10. From Leonardo Benevolo, *The Architecture of the Renaissance* (London: Routledge & Kegan Paul, Ltd., 1978).
11. From Anthony Blunt, *Art and Architecture in France 1500-1700* (Baltimore: Penguin Books, 1970).
12. From Colin Rowe, *The Mathematics of the Ideal Villa and Other Essays* (Cambridge: MIT Press, 1976). Reproduced with permission.

Kleihues
Photo courtesy of the author.

Fripp
1. Collection, Staatliche Museen Preussischer Kulturbesitz, Nationalgalerie, Berlin.
2. Collection, Herman and Margrit Rumpf Foundation, Museum of Fine Arts, Berne. Copyright 1989 ARS N.Y./Cosmopress, Genf.

Kohane
All illustrations copyright 1977 The Louis I. Kahn Collection, University of Pennsylvania and Pennsylvania Historical and Museum Commission, except as indicated below.
10. Courtesy of Mr. Jim Burger.
11. Courtesy of University of Pennsylvania Archives.
21. From Claude Leguany, *Visionary Architects: Boulée, Ledoux, Lequeu* (Houston: Gulf Printers, 1968).
24. From Paul Letarouilly, *Edifices de Rome Moderne* (New York: Princeton Architectural Press, 1984). Reproduced with permission.
25. Reproduced by courtesy of the Trustees, The National Gallery, London.
26. The Metropolitan Museum of Art, The Cloisters Collection, 1956 (56.70).
38. Collection, Williams College Museum of Art.

Friedman
1. Courtesy of New York Landmarks Preservation Commission.
2-4. From *Monograph of the Work of McKim, Mead & White*. Courtesy of the New York Historical Commission.
5. Reproduced with permission of Bollman-Bildkarten Verlag GmbH and Co. K.G.

Bergengren
Photographs by the author except as indicated below.
9, 10, 15. Courtesy Department of Special Collections, Van Pelt Library, University of Pennsylvania.
11. Courtesy of Litchfield, Ct., Historical Society.
16. Courtesy of The Historical Collections of the Library of the Philadelphia College of Physicians.

Endpiece
Courtesy Van Pelt Library, University of Pennsylvania.

Frontispiece: *Philibert De L'Orme, "The Bad Architect," from* Le Premier Tome De L'Architecture, *1567.*

Endpiece: *Philibert De L'Orme, "The Good Architect," from* Le Premier Tome De L'Architecture, *1567.*